AMERICA IN VIEW

LANDSCAPE PHOTOGRAPHY 1865 TO NOW

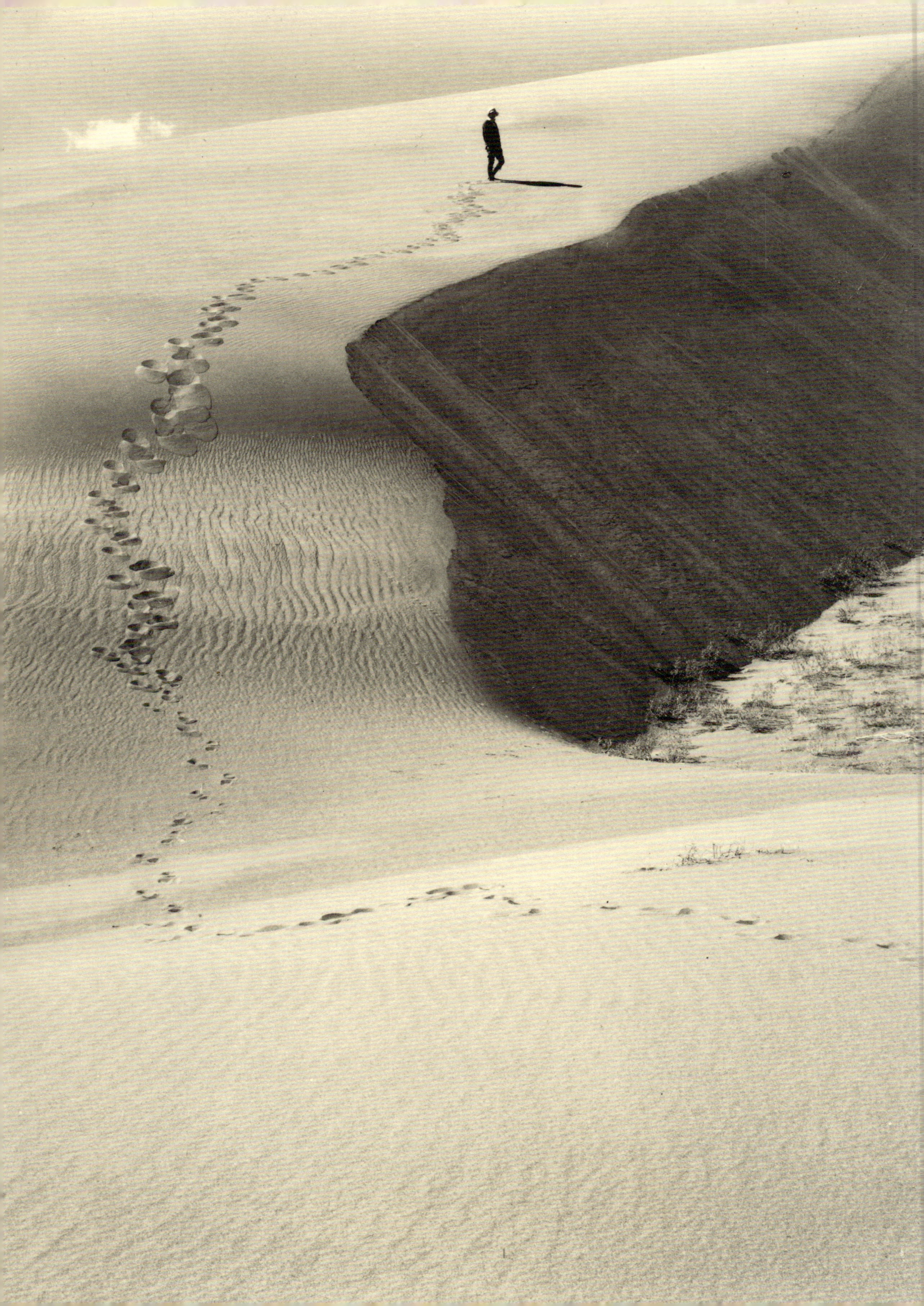

AMERICA IN VIEW

LANDSCAPE PHOTOGRAPHY 1865 TO NOW

essays by
DEBORAH BRIGHT
JAN HOWARD
DOUGLAS NICKEL

MUSEUM OF ART
RHODE ISLAND SCHOOL OF DESIGN

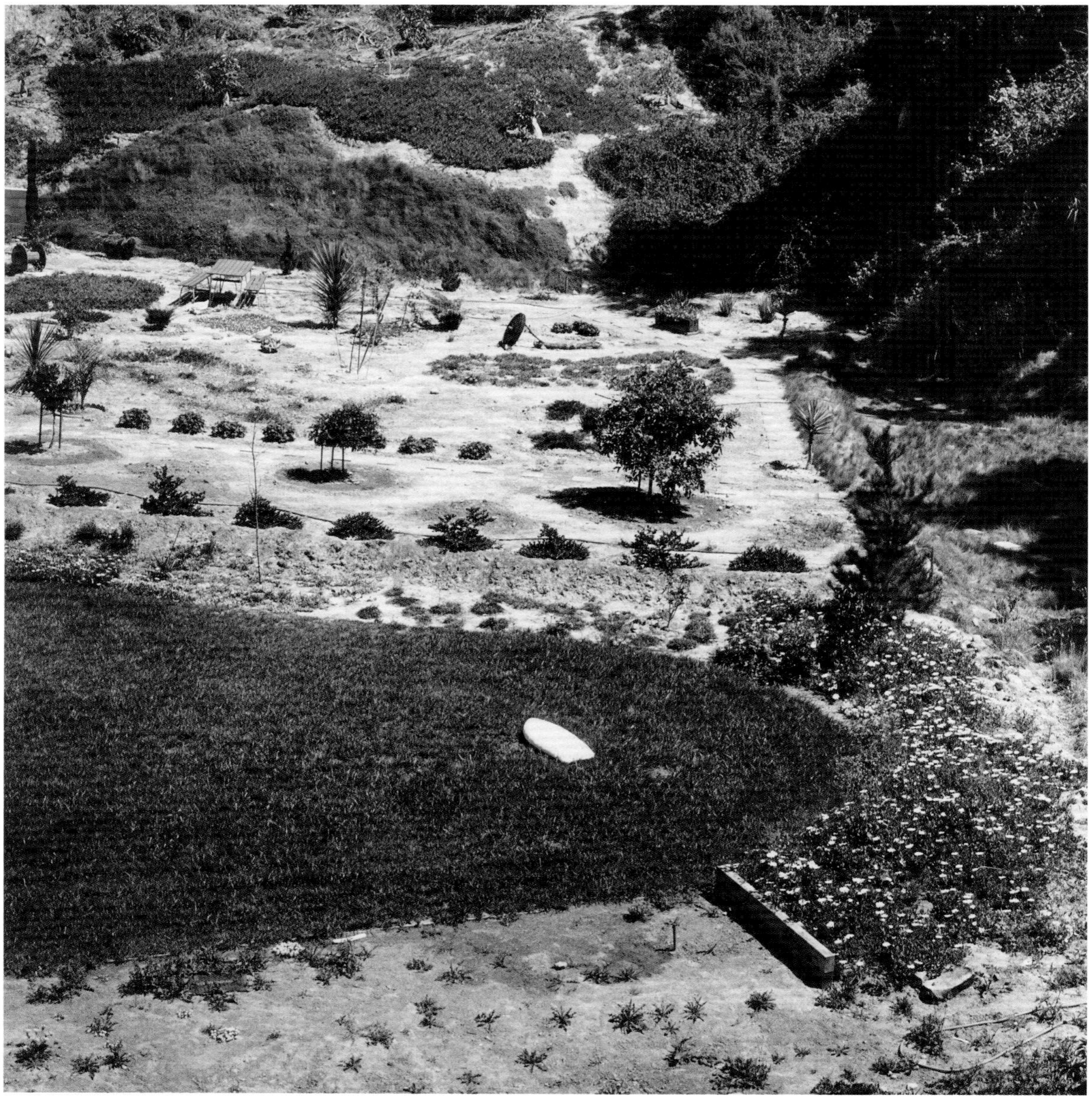

Joe Deal, *Santa Barbara, California*, 1978, from *The Fault Zone*

dedicated

to the memory of Joe Deal, who profoundly inspired the RISD community with his art, teaching, leadership, and generosity

CONTENTS

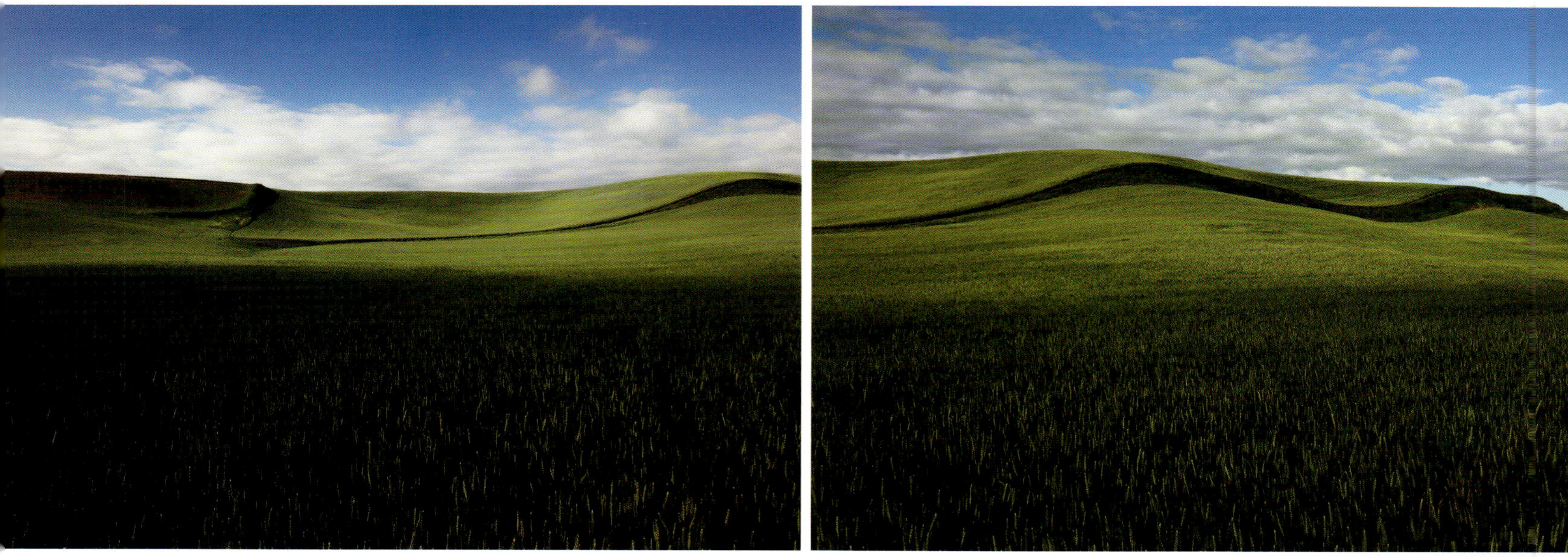

Neal Rantoul, *Near Pullman, Washington, Wheat*, 2009

FOREWORD AND ACKNOWLEDGMENTS

America in View: Landscape Photography 1865 to Now accompanies a major exhibition of that title tracing a history of photographs of the American landscape primarily through the collection of the RISD Museum. The show takes a broad look at the ever-evolving definition of American landscape photography—from seemingly pristine views of nature captured with 19th-century view cameras to images of the decaying contemporary urban streets composed from Google Street View. The RISD Museum's collection of American landscape photography begins at the end of the Civil War in 1865, when photographers traveled west with government survey teams and railroad companies to record the country's extraordinary natural features and resources. Ever since, the landscape has remained a compelling subject for photographers who have revealed through their images our nation's ambition and failings, beauty and degradation, politics and personal stories.

America in View was inspired by a generous gift of seventy-one photographs to the RISD Museum from the collection of the late Joe Deal (RISD Provost 1999–2005 and Photography Professor 2005–2009) and his wife, Betsy Ruppa, a selection of which is featured in the exhibition. Deal was one of the most influential landscape photographers of his generation. His work came to prominence through *New Topographics: Photographs of a Man-Altered Landscape*, a landmark exhibition presented at the George Eastman House Museum of Photography, Rochester, New York, in 1975. The show focused on Deal and nine other photographers' shift from a timeless view of nature toward one that acknowledged the impact of widespread industrial and residential development. Deal and Ruppa gifted many works by Deal's contemporaries, providing much-needed context for the rich collection of Deal's own work held by the Museum.

As Aaron Siskind enriched the RISD Museum's photography collection in the 1970s and '80s by giving his personal collection as well as encouraging others to give, Deal instinctively built on that tradition. In addition to their gift, Deal and Ruppa encouraged colleagues to be generous to the Museum, and more than twenty gave work in honor of Deal's retirement. We thank Ann Fessler and Josephine Sittenfeld for their assistance with this effort. While most of the gifts fit the exhibition's topic, not every piece did, and so we would like to acknowledge the generosity of Thomas Barrow, Deborah Bright, Jesse Burke, Fessler, Nancy Friese, Roger Palmer, Susan Rankaitis, and Thaddeus Russell, whose gifts will find their way to the Museum walls at a later date. The show also features a number of recent gifts outside of the Deal initiative, all of which are acknowledged in the checklist at the back of the book. We are grateful to all of these donors, who have given the Museum a new strength in landscape photography that we celebrate through the exhibition and its catalogue.

Deal understood museums and the importance of developing their collections. As a conscientious objector during the Vietnam War he was given a position as a museum guard and later an exhibition manager at the George Eastman House, the first museum devoted to photography, where he made substantial conceptual contributions to the *New Topographics* exhibition. After completing his MFA at the University of New Mexico, he took a faculty position at the University of California, Riverside, where he became the first (interim) director at the California Museum of Photography. Founded as a teaching museum, the institution benefited from Deal's belief in learning through the study of original works of art and in growing the collection for the benefit of the students and public alike. As Provost at RISD, Deal supported the first Faculty Fellow in the Museum's Department of Prints, Drawings, and Photographs, a position that gives a faculty member an opportunity to work one day a week in the department, encouraging other professors and students to study and teach from the collection.

This catalogue and its accompanying exhibition benefited from the considerable scholarly expertise of faculty at RISD and at Brown University. The exhibition and catalogue were organized by Jan Howard, the RISD Museum's Curator of Prints, Drawings, and Photographs, in association with Deborah Bright, Professor of Photography and History of Art + Visual Culture at RISD (1989–2012), and Douglas R. Nickel, Andrea V. Rosenthal Professor of Modern Art at Brown. Each has contributed insightful essays to the catalogue. Nickel examines the changing concept of landscape in art and, more specifically, in photography, over centuries; Bright chronicles landscape photography's role in shaping and responding to environmental issues; and Howard looks at the prevalent use of the figure in landscape photography today as a new way of examining the subject.

Many RISD and Brown students have been involved in conversations around the exhibition. Nickel taught a portion of his spring 2012 seminar "The Museum and the Photograph" at the Museum, bringing practical discussions related to the exhibition into the classroom. Emily Handlin and Kristen Oehrlich, Brown PhD students in History of Photography, and Scott Alario and Isaac Wingfield, RISD MFA students in Photography, each spent an academic year working diligently to bring the show to fruition. We are also grateful to Steven B. Smith, RISD Photography Department Head, who has worked closely with the Museum on the programming for the exhibition.

The catalogue would not have been possible without the contributions of many Museum friends. We are especially grateful for Dr. Joseph A. Chazan's initial challenge gift. We thank the Robert Lehman Foundation and Dr. and Mrs. William G. Tsiaras for their generous funding. We are grateful for the additional support of Mrs. Houghton P. Metcalf, Jr., Mary Kate Rittmann, Betsy Ruppa, and Mr. and Mrs. William A. Viall II. And we acknowledge Suzanne Fortier, Director of Museum Development, and Vernell Clouden, Museum Gift Officer, for coordinating this effort.

We thank Jessica May, Amon Carter Museum of American Art, and Susan Ehrens for their research assistance, and Andy Adams of FlakPhoto.com for his complementary selection of American landscape photography projected in conjunction with the exhibition. We further thank the following individuals and institutions for generous loans from their collections: Rachel Alexandra Lapkin and Holly Snyder at the John Hay Library, Brown University; Susan Ehrens; Putri Tan, Gagosian Gallery, New York; Jay Glasson and Tori Smith; Koichiro Kurita; Karen Marks, Howard Greenberg Gallery, New York; William Lamson; Mamie Tinkler, Mitchell, Inness & Nash, New York; Mr. and Mrs. J. Geddes Parsons; Carol Terry, Fleet Library at RISD; Laura Stanton and Craig Hopkins; Dr. and Mrs. William G. Tsiaras; Susan Swenson, Pierogi; and those who wish to remain anonymous.

The project would not have happened without the initial support of Ann Woolsey, who in her role as Interim Director embraced the project. The exhibition and its catalogue would not have been as beautiful without the enthusiastic support of the Museum's staff, associates at the College, and in the community. We are most grateful to Jennifer Liese, Director of RISD's Writing Center, for her excellent suggestions in shaping the essays and thoughtful

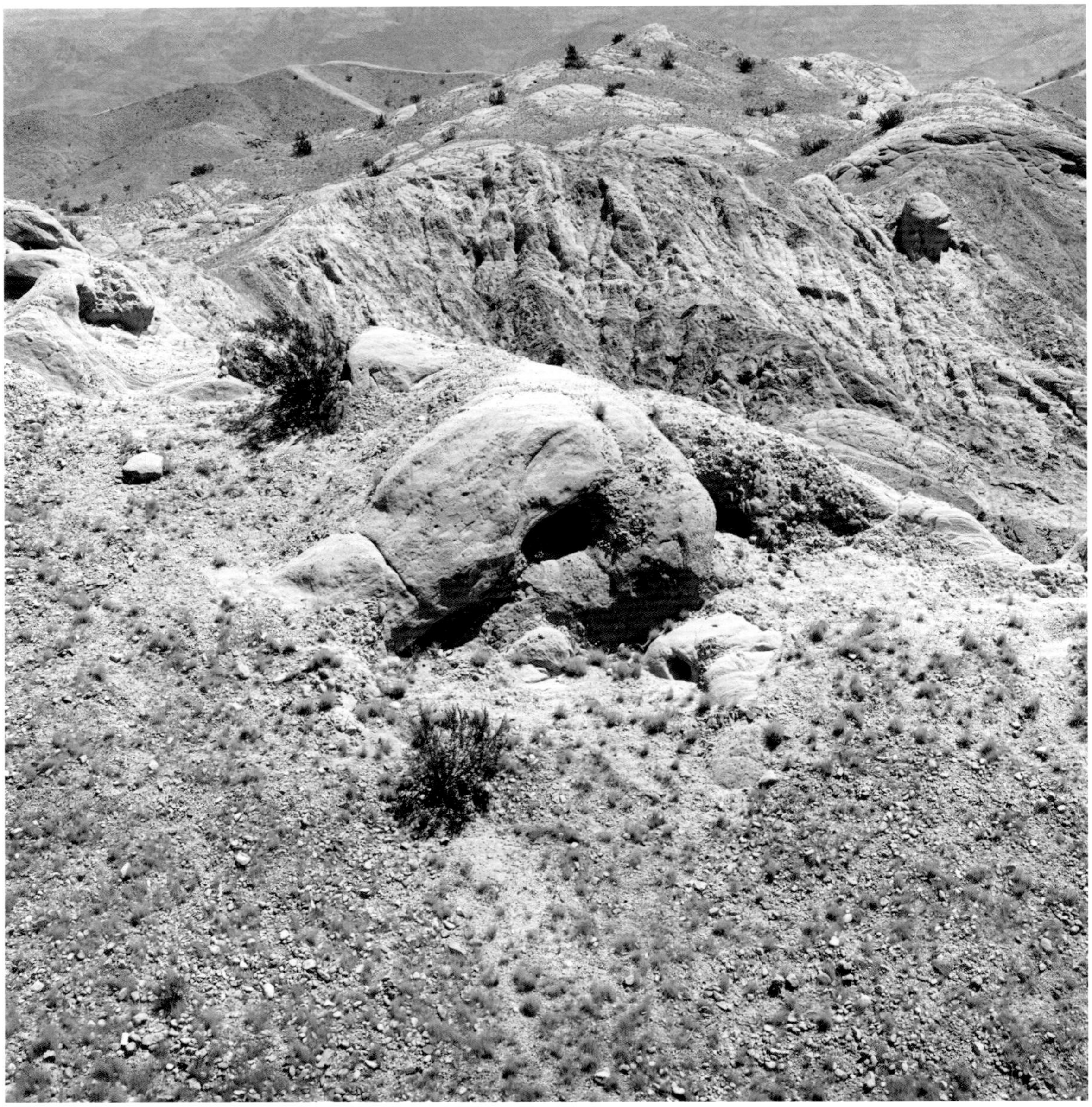

Joe Deal, *Indio, California*, 1978, from *The Fault Zone*

editing. Lucinda Hitchcock, Professor of Graphic Design, RISD, was the perfect designer for this book. Daniel Frank, Director of Fine Art Publications, Meridian Printing, and his crew offered exceptional support on press. Many Museum staff members deserve particular recognition: Emily J. Peters, Associate Curator, and Alison Chang, Andrew W. Mellon Curatorial Fellow in Prints, Drawings, and Photographs, for assistance with the departmental workload and with the exhibition's many details; Linda Catano, Paper Preservationist, Christin Fitzgerald, contract matter/framer, and Shu Min Lim, Jean Fain Memorial Intern, for their exceptional skill and sensitivity to the presentation of the photographs; Sarah Ganz Blythe, Director of Museum Education, and Deborah Clemons, Associate Educator, Public Programs, for their creativity with the exhibition's programming; Tara Emsley, Registrar for Exhibitions and Loans, for proficient management of the loans; Denise Bastien, Registrar for Documentation and Digital Resources, and Sionan Guenther, Assistant Registrar for Digital Resources, for ably managing the rights and photography schedule; Erik Gould, Photographer, for his beautiful reproduction of the work; Donna Desrochers, Director of Museum Marketing, and Lani Stack, Senior Marketing and Communications Associate, for attracting attention to the project; Stephen Wing, Manager of Installation and Preparation, and Derek Schusterbauer, Graphic Designer, for their attention to the exhibition's design; and Laura Ostrander, Michael Owen, and Kristin Samuelson for so ably installing the works.

While *America in View* surveys the nation's landscape photography as a whole, many of the extraordinarily distinguished photographers featured in the exhibition—among them Deal, Siskind, Bright, Harry Callahan, Emmet Gowin, Linda Connor, David Hanson, Sally Gall, Laura McPhee, Steven B. Smith, and Justin Kimball—have taught or studied at RISD. Callahan founded RISD's photography program within the Graphic Design Department in 1963, and ever since Providence has been a special place for photography. *America in View* is an exemplary opportunity to share the RISD Museum's rich collection with a wider audience and to celebrate the remarkable history, creative gifts, and collaborative spirit within our community.

John W. Smith
Director

PHOTOGRAPHY, PERCEPTION, AND THE LANDSCAPE

Douglas Nickel

In everyday speech, the word "landscape" denotes an area of open outdoor space regarded primarily for its visible aspects. It also refers to a type of picture that depicts such a locality. This seemingly ageless notion—that particular physical features of the land might be appreciated for their aesthetic appeal, independent of their usefulness—turns out to be a fairly modern one, however. For most of the history of literature and art in the West, landscapes, if they appear at all, have served chiefly as settings for stories about humans and their divinities, not as something worthy of attention themselves. It was only between the 17th and 19th centuries, when attitudes toward wilderness, the land, and the functions of art all changed, that the genre of landscape painting as we know it first appeared. Photography's arrival in the 1840s corresponded to just the moment when this change of attitudes was fully realized, a bit of timing that made the photograph's emulation of the Romantic landscape seem inexorable and our acceptance of the category seamless. But in fact there is nothing natural or inevitable about the photographic landscape, and if we scratch the surface of the history and aesthetics leading up to it, an abundance of complexities emerges.

There is of course a long history—dating back to before classical times—that proposed certain natural places as special or sacred. In the Judeo-Christian tradition, Paradise is configured as a setting where the first humans lived in full sympathy with nature. Here grew the Tree of Life (which promised immortality) and the Tree of Knowledge of Good and Evil (which, in Genesis, results in the forfeiture of eternal life); here humans and beasts could peacefully cohabitate in a state of innocence. But Eden is a garden—that is to say, a sanctuary, a protected place removed from the perils of wild nature. The concept of refuge

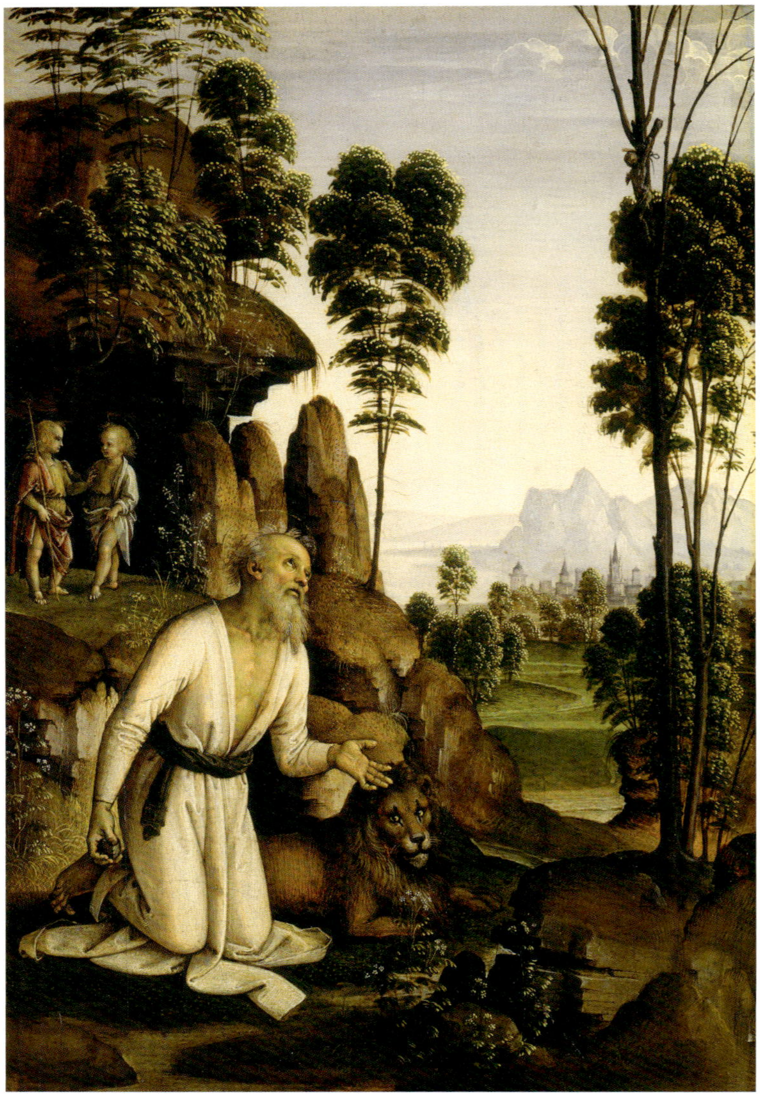

fig. 1 **Follower of Perugino** *Saint Jerome in the Wilderness,* ca. 1490/1500, tempera on panel, $23\frac{5}{8} \times 16\frac{1}{2}$ in., National Gallery of Art, Washington, DC, Samuel H. Kress Collection 1939.1.280

and removal is crucial to early attitudes toward the land. From their very antiquity in Mesopotamia, cities represented civilization; behind their walls city-dwellers sought security from enemies, dangerous wildlife, and the capriciousness of the elements. The garden was civilization's way of idealizing those parts of nature it found benign and agreeable into an essentially distorted, urban take on the rural. Classical writers exalted agriculture through poems about the untroubled rustic lives of shepherds and cowherds, placing such figures (as the Latin poet Virgil did) in the utterly civilized nature of a legendary Arcadia. The stylized landscape encountered in these poems became the mise-en-scène for the idyll, a utopian fantasy of a former "golden age" where nature (in the form of shady groves and pastures dotted with shrines to the gods) stood for a political condition far removed in time and space from contemporary urban fact. Depictions of these imaginary scenes made their way into Roman wall paintings as what appear to be populated mythological landscapes, and Virgil's *Georgics* became canonical—required reading for the literate.[1] A dream vision of the pastoral was installed in the Western imagination for the next millennium.

The reality of the countryside was quite different. Until the 18th century the unsettled intervals between cities and towns in Europe and America harbored all kinds of dangers: travelers might be thrown from horses, trapped by storms, frozen, attacked by predatory animals, or set upon by "highwaymen" ready to murder and steal. Swamps, deserted woods, and impassable rivers and mountains signified threat, not respite. The term "wilderness" was at this time equivalent to "wasteland": an inhospitable region outside the law, empty of comfort, and suitable only for the uncivilized, a zone to be avoided or traversed with great caution. It was also that terrible place the guilt-ridden went to do penance. Renaissance paintings of saints in the wilderness typically portray Jerome, John, or Anthony Abbott in or near a cave, living in isolation amongst beasts and barren trees, situated in a landscape where a distant city symbolized the society denied him (see fig. 1).

Given that nature-in-the-raw carried generally negative associations, it is no surprise that pure landscape subjects entered early Western art only rarely. In addition, there lay another obstacle: the legislation of artistic hierarchies mandated by Europe's official academies. The hierarchy of artistic genres—enforced by professional organizations like the Académie royal de peinture et de sculpture in Paris and the Royal Academy in London—first arose in the late 16th century, a time when most fine art was commissioned by monarchs, the Church, and the aristocracy. These cultured patrons valued erudition, moral allegory, and abstract ideas; they embraced a humanism that considered Man the pinnacle of creation, and found his highest achievement in virtuous thoughts and deeds. Thus, in

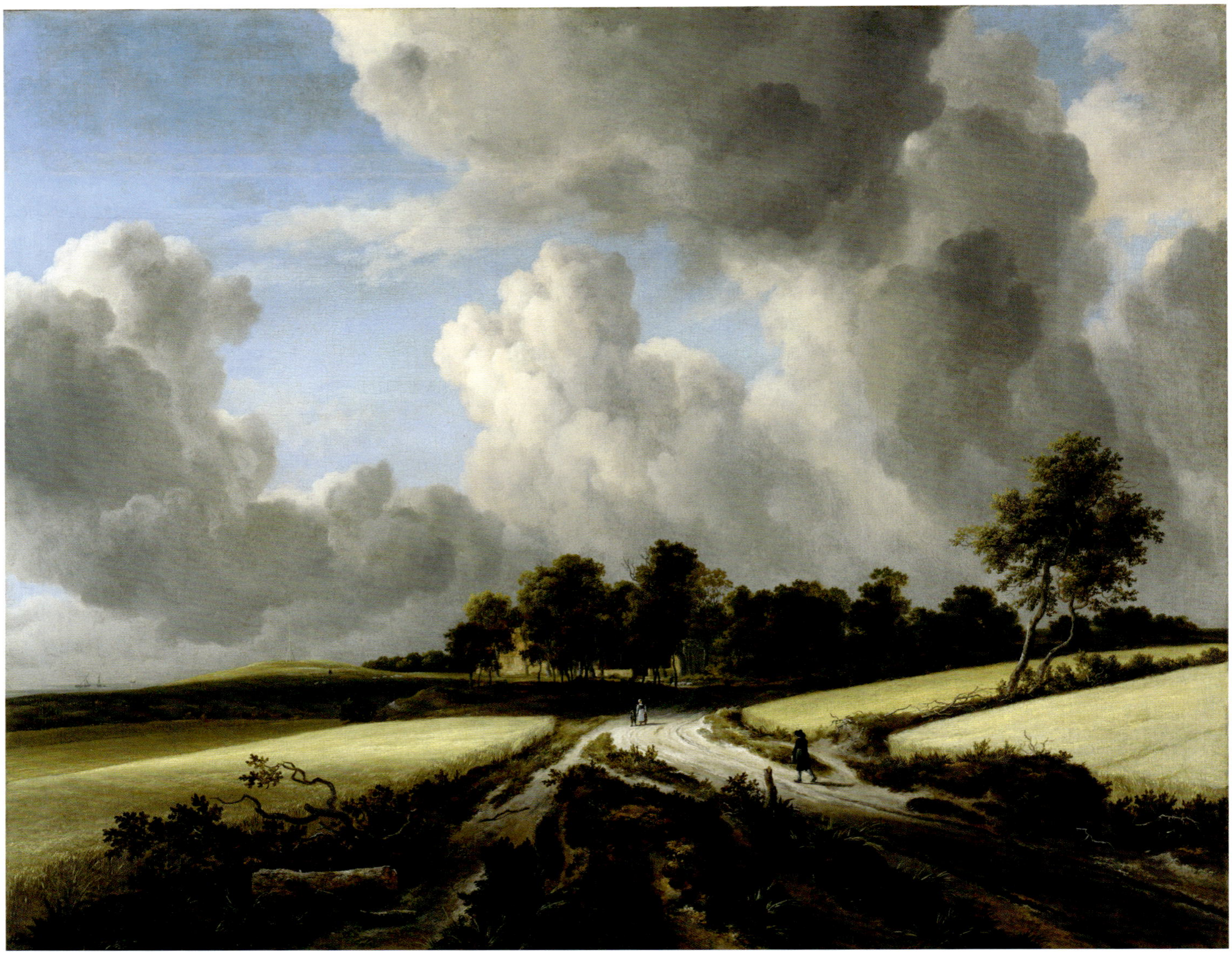

fig. 2 **Jacob van Ruisdael** *Wheat Fields*, ca. 1670, oil on canvas, 39 3/8 × 51 1/4 in., The Metropolitan Museum of Art, Bequest of Benjamin Altman, 1913 14.40.623

literature, the epic was ranked above the lyric, with drama and comic poetry falling below, and in painting, history (including religious themes, mythology, and great secular events) surmounted portraits, scenes of everyday life, and finally landscapes and still lifes, in descending order of edifying human content. History paintings were typically larger, more complex (featuring multiple figures interacting) and showed off the artist's talent for invention; they were often public works, destined for display in churches or civic buildings. The academies held that a talent for copying the exact appearance of things was less important than the ability to give life to a complex thought.

Yet in regions where a different class of patrons prevailed, the hierarchy could be ignored or even overturned. In the Protestant North, for instance, Calvinism essentially ended the market for religious painting by the 17th century. Successful Dutch burghers preferred the "lower" genres of painting because their smaller scale and less pretentious themes better suited their modest homes and because their practical nature inclined them to the real and familiar over the imaginary and ancient. Further, the Netherlands was a country nearly free of dangerous wilderness, but it waged a constant battle to keep the ocean from overwhelming the land. For this reason, the Dutch Republic looked upon its countryside as precious, a vital part of its economy and identity, and hence a good subject for a painting hung above the mantel. It was the Dutch who first coined the term "landscape" (*lantscap*) in the late 16th century to describe a type of picture that featured naturalistic-looking scenery (see fig. 2), and, with their Flemish neighbors, it was they who sponsored the first real flowering of what we today recognize as landscape art.

As other countries moved fitfully to more democratic forms of government, and patronage shifted, academic officialdom began to lose its grip on the hierarchy of figurative art. New wealth from industry in 18th-century England and France corresponded with an increasingly open market for paintings—now more often made on speculation than commission—and unprecedented accommodation to popular taste. The Englishman Thomas Gainsborough plied a trade painting fashionable portraits of the landed gentry and the smart set of London in the middle of the century, but more flexible genre conventions could abide a work like *Mr. and Mrs. Robert Andrews*, ca. 1750, a hybrid Grand Manner portrait where half of the composition is given over to scenery (fig. 3). The couple was married two years before the work was conceived, and their union brought together the two adjoining estates that figure as a background. Over time, Gainsborough gravitated to painting naturalistic rural subjects without any portrait alibi, though these scenes always derived as much from the artist's imagination as from observation. Such works helped

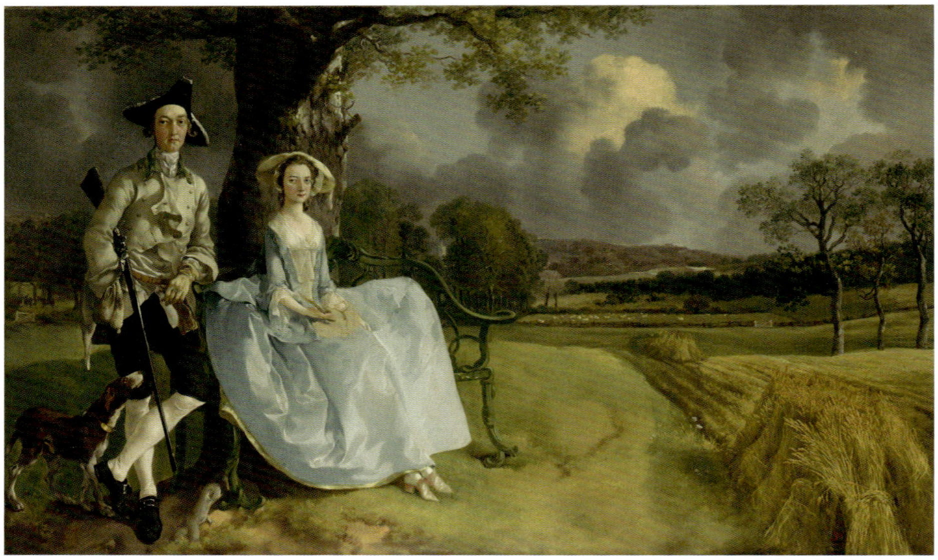

plant the Dutch idea on British soil. By the end of the century, landscape subjects had come to typify English painting, while in Germany a budding taste for Romantic themes allowed Casper David Friedrich to invent contemplative, allegorical landscapes distinctly inspired by real places and a close observation of nature.

The widespread embrace of landscape imagery at the beginning of the 19th century set the stage for the photographic landscape. But neither could have taken the form they did without specific circumstances in and outside of art. First, wilderness had to acquire its modern, transcendental associations. As the cities of Europe (and, soon enough, the United States) dilated in size in the 1800s, so too did their problems. Poor sanitation and overcrowding resulted in deadly epidemics of cholera and typhus; crime, worker riots, and pollution cast the countryside in an ever more favorable light, as a pleasurable and salubrious alternative to the metropolis. In the late Augustan period, innovative techniques for paving roads and amenities like inns and regular stagecoach service made tourist travel popular; in England, the Napoleonic Wars of the Continent encouraged more local exploration of places like Northern Wales and the Lake District. The physical domestication of nature was accompanied by an intellectual one, as science (then called "natural philosophy") sought to codify mechanical, observable laws for the way nature worked. If nature could be explained, it could be mastered and manipulated to human ends. Photography's invention was one proof of this mastery: the sun's rays and the properties of certain natural compounds could be forced to make optical pictures, letting "nature copy that which nature made," as it was put at the time.[2] The wilderness that was once seen as hostile now became a place of spiritual renewal and connection with God the Creator, author of the book of nature that science endeavored to interpret.

A new scientific strain is also found in art theory of the late 18th century. The Irish philosopher Edmund Burke inaugurated landscape theory with his 1757 essay "A Philosophical Enquiry into the Origins of Our Ideas of the Sublime and the Beautiful." Burke asserted that what we consider "the beautiful" is characterized by symmetry, smoothness, small size, and delicacy. By contrast, the sublime is that which is vast, irregular, obscure, or menacing. Burke was primarily interested in accounting for our emotional responses to phenomena—the beautiful, he argued, derived its appeal from its association with the feminine, which (for many males at least) originates in sexual attraction. The sublime was that which activates fear, flight, and survival responses. In the field, rolling hills, puffy clouds, and calm bodies of water will trigger the former response; large mountains, blasted trees,

fig. 3 **Thomas Gainsborough** *Mr. and Mrs. Andrews*, ca. 1750, oil on canvas, 27½×47 in., National Gallery of Art, London, bought with contributions from The Pilgrim Trust, The Art Fund, Associated Television Ltd, and Mr. and Mrs. W. W. Spooner, 1960 NG6301

precarious boulders, and wild storms tend toward the latter. The essay is noteworthy for stressing that our responses to subjects in pictures are not the same as our responses to those same subjects in the real world: a lightning storm or the black of night might well terrify us if confronted firsthand, but when represented in a painting or a poem, they produce a distinct kind of pleasure. By shifting the framework of landscape aesthetics from the rational to the psychological—and, specifically, to our most primitive emotions—Burke helped catalyze the Romantic view that was soon to follow.

Landscape theory provided a rationale for the centrality of the genre at what then turned out to be the dawn of photography. The Rev. William Gilpin, another British writer, extended Burke's analysis of aesthetic response to include a third category—the "picturesque." He characterized the picturesque as "expressive of that peculiar kind of beauty which is agreeable in a picture" (hence the name), noting how subjects that were rough, ruinous, and intricate in their variety and texture presented observers with this peculiar beauty without falling into either of Burke's two categories.[3] Gilpin was an avid tourist, and his theory was spelled out in the pages of the several travel guides to provincial England he published before 1810, illustrated with his own sketches. The purpose of "picturesque travel" was to seek out prospects in the country that were especially pleasing, spots where the elements came together to look like a landscape painting. To facilitate the best viewing experience, such travel guides recommended the use of a small, dark mirror, or "Claude glass," as an aid. Upon encountering a potentially picturesque vista, users would hold the mirror before them and, with their back turned to the desired scenery, discover in the mirror a reflected image of it, reduced, enframed, and softened in tonality by the tinted glass.[4] The picturesque thus amounted to a significant redefinition of landscape, for it prescribed mentally removing scenery from its surroundings and transforming it into an aesthetic object, into an image. Nature was not an array of objects so much as a visual field, there to be looked at, awaiting the proper visual appropriation and recording that would bring meaning to its chaos. But not all scenery was created equal. While in general the picturesque was something to be found, in those instances where the topography failed to present sufficient balance, variety, and texture, it could be physically rearranged with the removal of trees and other obstructions. Gilpin famously recommended in his *Observation on the River Wye* that the medieval ruins of Tintern Abbey might be made more picturesque with the application of a mallet.[5]

The picturesque took the ends of the classical, imaginary landscape—aesthetic delight —and found them in actual landscape, by proposing the mind be put into a particularly

fig. 4 **William Henry Fox Talbot** *Lock Katrine*, plate 12 from the book *Sun Pictures in Scotland*, 1845, salted paper print, plate: 6¾ × 8⅛ in., courtesy of George Eastman House, International Museum of Photography and Film

receptive condition for framing and seeing things, a condition of willful scrutiny that went looking for what it knew and wanted.[6] What was invented might be termed "landscape perception": the graphic reduction of empirical observation to a set of salient formal elements that make a picture. The compositions and subjects of landscape depiction at the end of the 18th century were highly conventionalized, formulaic even, based on recipes inherited from the previous century worked out by Claude Lorraine (after whose effects the Claude glass was named) and Salvatore Rosa. But as techniques like *plein air* sketching were increasingly deployed in their service, the creative potential of these more empirical, less conventional studies was recognized. The second half of the 19th century developed its landscape painting and photography upon a unitary principal—the simultaneity of landscape perception and representation.[7] One need only recall the sketch-like arrangements and shimmering light and color effects in Monet's poppy fields or Signac's harbors to see this simultaneity at work. It is not clouds, flowers, or water so much as the artist's immediate observation of these things that is the subject of the painting.

We might say, then, that photography was born into a pre-existing, albeit incipient, notion of the photographic, one based on conceiving of the world as already containing an infinite number of latent pictorial compositions awaiting discovery by the eye. After photography was introduced, some users did the obvious thing and searched the world for the very same compositions they knew from Western art. William Henry Fox Talbot, the English inventor, was well versed in picturesque theory, so it comes as no surprise that he would seek out picturesque scenes and subjects for his 1845 publication of original photographs titled *Sun Pictures in Scotland* (see fig. 4).[8] The first generation of French photographers likewise avidly pursued Romantic and picturesque motifs—ruins, the trees at Fountainebleau, rustic scenes around Sèvre—which happened to be the haunts of illustrators, printmakers, and the contemporary Barbizon School of landscape painters as well. The picturesque landscape photograph was to endure in perpetuity: Seneca Ray Stoddard, working in upstate New York in the 1880s, crafted landscapes as conventional and painterly as any of the local Hudson River School painters who preceded him in the territory (see fig. 5), and even today Barbara Bosworth can cleverly re-imagine Frederic Church's grandiose *Niagara* from 1857 (see fig. 6).

But much of the topographic photography that followed the first generation hardly qualifies as "landscape" in these conventional terms. The art historian Rosalind Krauss has argued that the Western exploration photographs of William Bell and Timothy O'Sullivan (see fig. 7), for instance, made on geological surveys in the 1870s, were never intended to

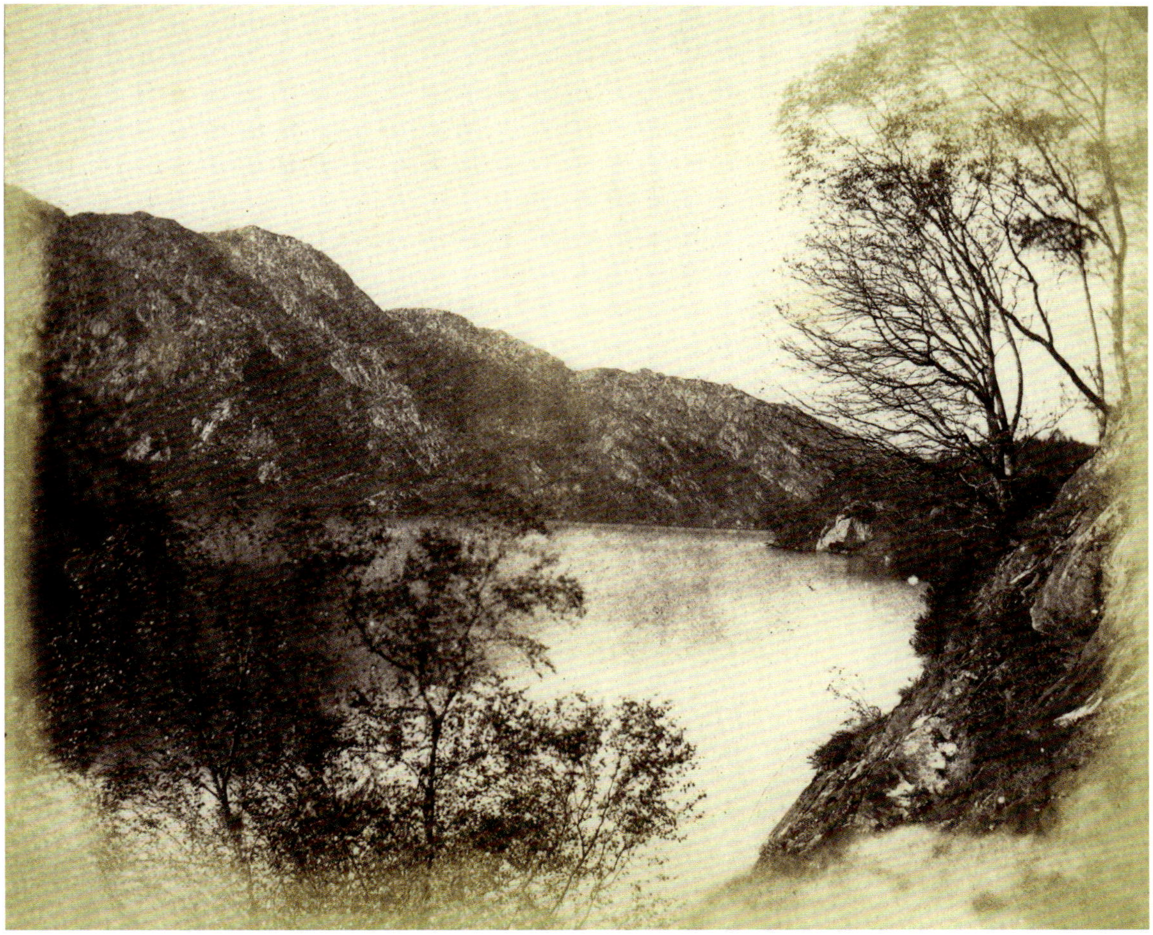

fig. 5 **Seneca Ray Stoddard** *The Adirondacks, Upper Au Sable Lake from Boreas Bay*, 1887, albumen print, 14 7/8 × 18 7/8 in., RISD Museum: Gift of Professor Barton St. Armand 1988.077

fig. 6 **Barbara Bosworth** *Niagara Falls*, 1986, gelatin silver print, 8 x 10 in., Private collection

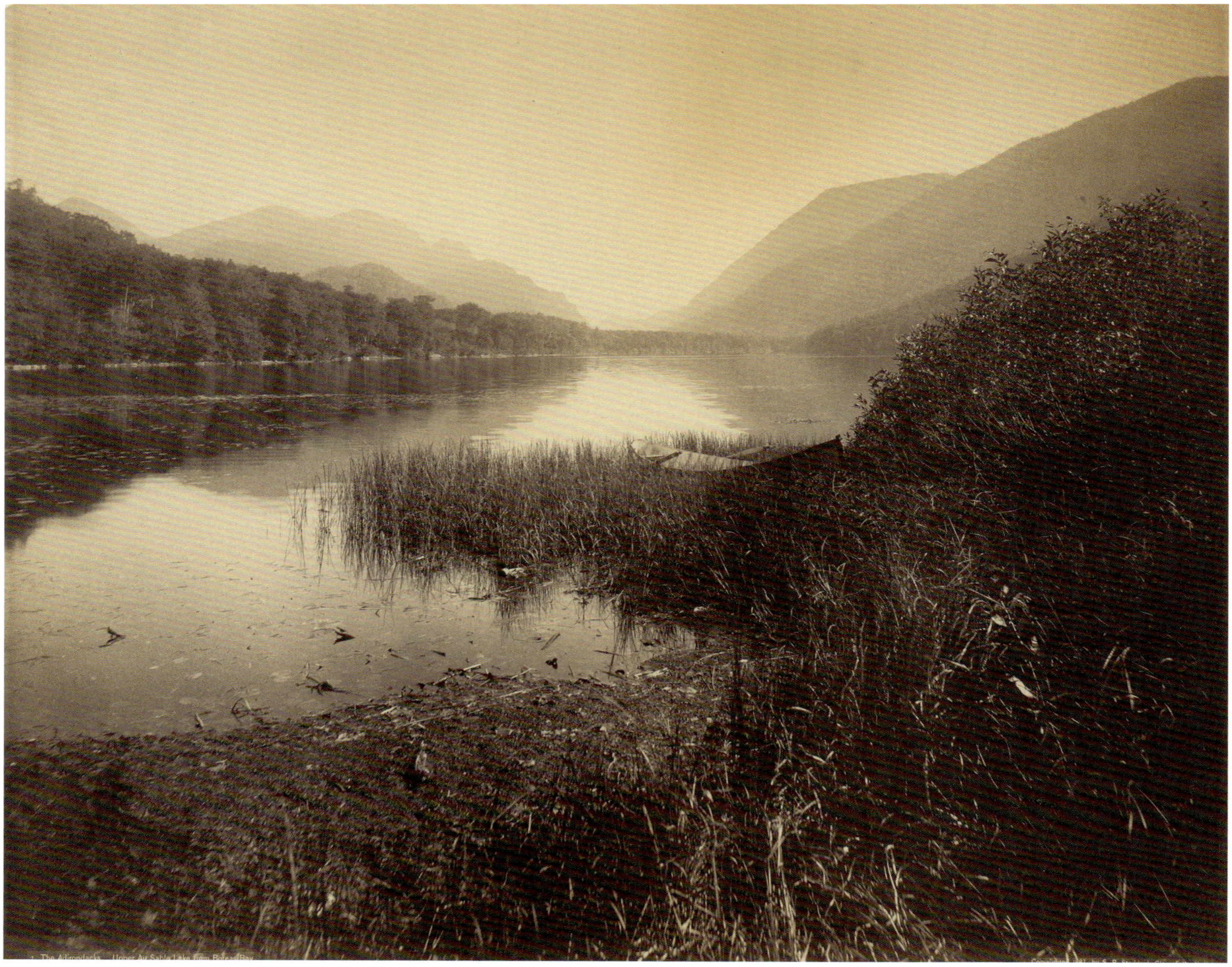

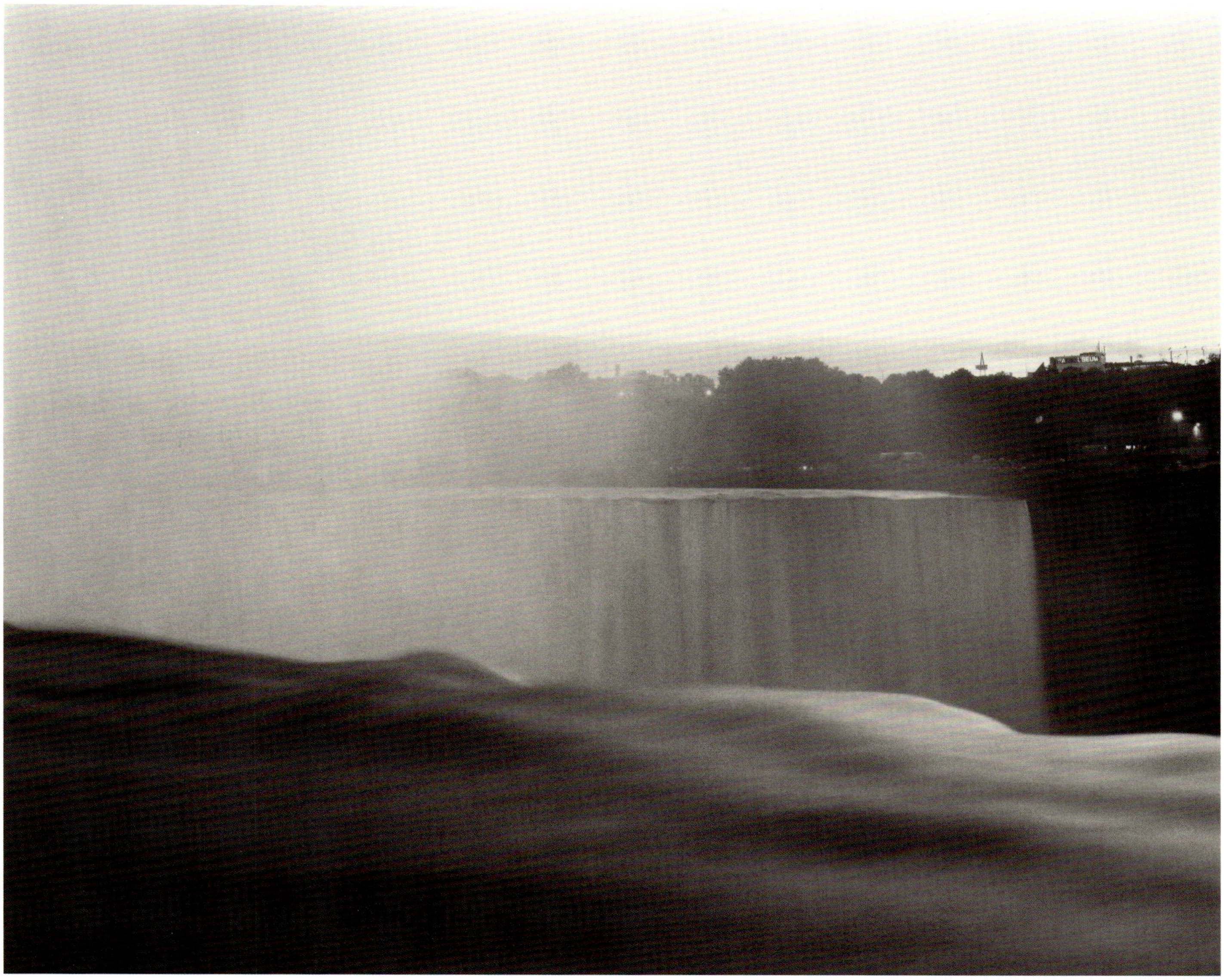

fig. 7 **Timothy O'Sullivan** *Ancient Ruins in the Cañon de Chelle*, 1873, from the album *Explorations and Surveys West of the 100th Meridian*, albumen prints, mount: 16×20 in., courtesy John Hay Library, Brown University

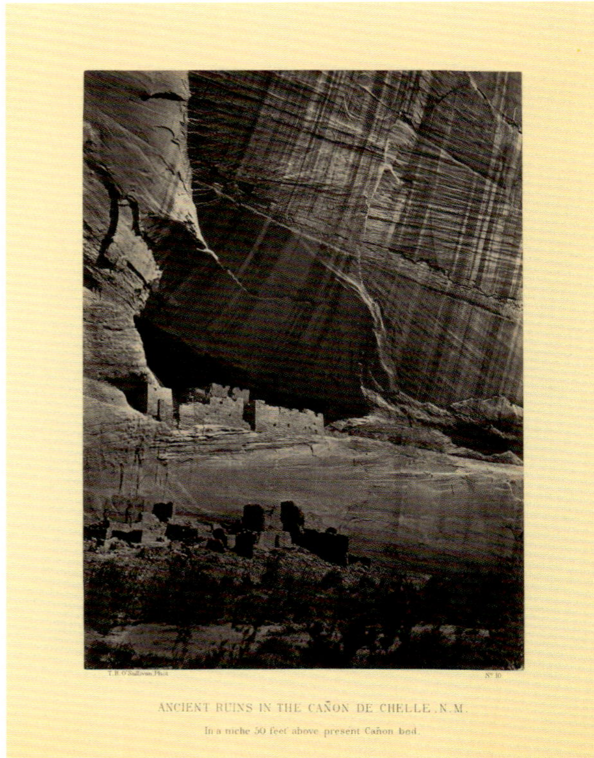

hang on walls, like art, but were instead conceived to go in albums and the filing cabinets of government archives. She contends that treating such photographs as an anticipation of the formal concerns of modern art represents a distortion of history, that as essentially scientific documents, topographical photographs like O'Sullivan's have no place in the art museum. They were, as the period identified them, "views," not "landscapes."[9] Other scholars, most notably Joel Snyder, have asked whether the practical imperatives of survey work necessarily mean that an O'Sullivan photograph cannot exhibit its own stylistic features and formal coherence. A documentary function should not presume the absence of artistic deliberation; indeed, in Snyder's account, enterprising photographers in the 19th century crafted a patently mechanical, intentionally non-painterly approach to their camera work—optically precise, printed on glossy albumen papers—with the aim of carving out their own aesthetically distinct sector within the overall market for images. What gives most 19th-century photographs their recognizably "photographic" appearance is neither a call to function as neutral documents nor the photographer's ignorance of artistic conventions, but an ambient desire to make the photograph look like a product of technology—a look that stood for industrial progress within a milieu that valued the machine-made over the hand-made. In O'Sullivan's case, his principal task was to provide images that would satisfy the needs of the survey leaders who hired him. Snyder argues that O'Sullivan's radical views were calculated to depict the Western territories as hostile, foreign-looking *terra incognita*, where humans (if present) stand out as isolated from their surroundings.[10] The spare, anti-picturesque solutions he delivered accorded perfectly with interests of professionals making the case that these empty territories be studied, secured, and settled.

An understanding of landscape theory therefore suggests that not every photograph of land is a landscape, and not every landscape necessarily features the land. The standard definition points to places—places in the world, or places seen in pictures—which take on the quality of a thing. But "landscape" is probably better understood as that set of expectations and beliefs—about both the environment and the conventions of its representation—that we project upon the world. These conventions and expectations are subject to historical change and are culturally specific; Talbot's were a traditional set of landscape expectations projected upon his subjects, but O'Sullivan's were radically reconfigured, to the point where they are hardly recognizable by the earlier standard. American landscape photography in the 20th century and after can be usefully clarified by this notion of projection. Ansel Adams, for instance, insisted upon the purely "photographic" character of his approach, developing an ethos out of what had been the dominant 19th-century entrepreneurial idiom. Like that of others in his f/64 cohort, Adams's work in the 1930s and '40s was strikingly modernist. He stressed the primacy of "visualization": the photographer's ability to see the intended picture first (and at one and the same time) in the world and in their "mind's eye," then in the camera, and finally in the darkroom. In this scheme, the photograph is created mentally before it is realized physically; the photograph here becomes an exercise of the photographer's skill at commuting mental pictures into real ones, a process that honors talent and learned expertise (i.e., properties of the photographer) over chance and automatic recording (properties of the apparatus). Per picturesque theory, this entailed nothing if not the projection of pictorial expectations upon the world.

Yet, in the larger sense, we might ask what notion of landscape Adams overlaid upon his world. He spent his teens and early twenties in Yosemite, sent there by concerned parents as a kind of therapy for his hyperactive disposition and his inattention at school. Throughout his life, Adams embraced the notion that nature could provide the harried, urbanized citizen of the modern age with a place of spiritual refuge, and that the most beautiful natural places should be identified and preserved in the public interest for this very purpose. This was the legacy of Emerson and Thoreau, articulated by John Muir and enshrined in the National Parks Bill of 1890. The same conservationist values informed Adams's landscape photography and his activities on behalf of the environment: a National Park and an Adams photograph establish a border around a particularly inviting piece of terrain, ostensibly banishing from it what is human, allowing us to escape (at least temporarily) the intrusions of culture. Here, as Emerson urged, we might find some connection to a cosmos greater than ourselves; for the reverent Adams, art and wilderness each had the potential to make the individual whole again. Insofar as a National Park is like a garden—a protected, managed, functional container for cultivating a certain conception of nature—Adams's idea returned the viewer to Eden.

But when the premise of the projection is challenged—as it was in the late 1960s and 1970s—an entirely different kind of landscape is the result. Around this time, followers of the ecology movement broke with conservationism, reasoning that the natural environment entails both wilderness areas *and* the vacant lot next door. Pollution, pesticide runoff, the destruction of species, global warming, and rampant development affect every part of the environment, so every part needs stewardship and protection—not just the spectacular

fig. 8 **Lewis Baltz** *Model Home, Shadow Mountain*, 1977, from the portfolio *Nevada*, gelatin silver print, 8×10 in., RISD Museum: Gift from the collection of Joe Deal and Betsy Ruppa 2010.82.35.8

spots. Many of the photographers brought together for the *New Topographics* exhibition of 1975 gravitated more or less independently to a kind of landscape image indicative of this newer attitude, though they did so without overt polemical motives. Perspectives showing roadside litter, industrial parks, highway culture, and recently constructed tract homes (see fig. 8) now inverted the Adams principle of exclusion, turning straight toward human alteration to suggest an end-stage to the paradise that was America. Moreover, the exhibition noted a stylistic strategy common to the group, wherein imagery was seemingly stripped of expressivity in order to assume the appearance of being without style, a "topographic" rendering rather than landscape scenery. The work of 19th-century survey photography was again invoked, not only because of these artists' emphasis on locations in the American West, but particularly through their anti-Romantic redefinition of what a landscape photograph could be. A view of a generic building in an industrial park hardly shows land at all, let alone a vista; an image of the corner of Second Street and South Main would seem to portray real estate more than scenery. There is no denying that this recalibration of aesthetic expectations toward the social has come to predominate recent practice; however, we must now acknowledge that what gets classified as "landscape" will not follow a set of rules or conventions about subject matter or approach, but must continually evolve, because the projections we make continually incorporate, modify, and reject previous rules and conventions to produce new ones. The process by which we recast our perceptions of the world as representations guarantees that the complexity of landscape will endure as long as people do.

NOTES

1. See Nils Büttner, *Landscape Painting: A History* (New York: Abbeville, 2000), 23–31.
2. The phrase is that of J. H. Fitzgibbon, a professional photographer from St. Louis, Missouri, advertising his services in 1852. Quoted in Geoffrey Batchen, *Forget Me Not: Photography and Remembrance* (New York: Princeton Architectural Press, 2004), 36.
3. William Gilpin, *Essay on Prints* (London: Cadell and Davies, 1802), 17.
4. The camera obscura—precursor to the photographic camera—offered a similar translation of three-dimensional reality to two-dimensional image.
5. William Gilpin, *Observations on the River Wye and several parts of South Wales, etc. relative chiefly to Picturesque Beauty; made in the summer of the year 1770* (London: R. Blamire, 1782), 47.
6. In his essay "Nature," Emerson writes: "The charming landscape which I saw this morning is indubitably made up of some twenty or thirty farms. Miller owns this field, Locke that, and Manning the woodland beyond. But none of them owns the landscape. There is a property in the horizon which no man has but he whose eye can integrate all the parts, that is, the poet." Ralph Waldo Emerson, *Nature* (Boston: James Munroe and Company, 1836), 11.
7. See W.J.T. Mitchell, "Imperial Landscape," in Mitchell, ed., *Landscape and Power* (Chicago: University of Chicago Press, 1994), 12.
8. In March 1841, Talbot wrote to his friend Sir John Herschel, "I must now really transport my apparatus to some locality where picturesque objects are to be met with, such as a Cathedral, or a seaport Town, for my own neighbourhood is not particularly suited to the Artist." Quoted in Elizabeth Knazook, "A Picturesque Photographic Tour Through Scotland," *Librarian and Staff Publications*, Paper 6 (2009), http://digitalcommons.ryerson.ca/library_pubs/6.
9. Rosalind E. Krauss, "Photography's Discursive Spaces: Landscape/View," *Art Journal*, vol. 42, no. 4 (Winter 1982): 311–19.
10. Joel Snyder, "Territorial Photography," in Mitchell, 175–201.

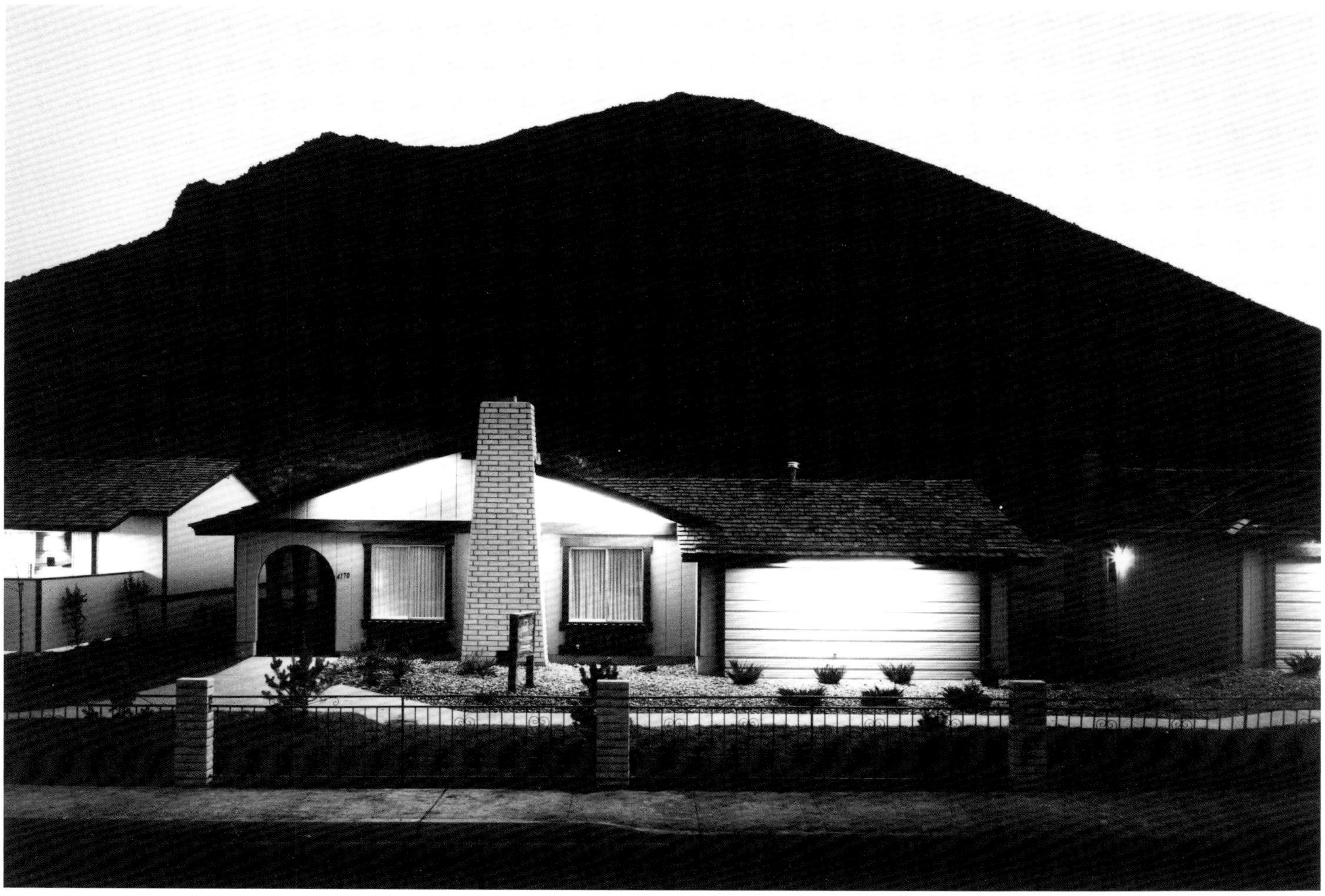

PHOTOGRAPHING NATURE, SEEING OURSELVES

Deborah Bright

As we survey the broad sweep of American landscape photography from the technology's early days to the present, it is interesting to consider how larger cultural assumptions about nature and humankind's relationship to it might have impacted the photographers' choices of subject matter and expressive treatment, as well as how the works were received by contemporary viewers. In this brief essay, I want to highlight some of the historical shifts in environmental consciousness that I see reflected in the works at hand—not to minimize each photographer's contribution to the aesthetics of photography, but to illuminate how their works also reflect changing conceptions of landscapes as bearers of cultural meaning.

If there is an overarching emotional and dramatic tension in the American Landscape Story in this exhibition, it lies along an axis between sublimity and pathos. The two concepts are related in that sublimity is a feeling of being overwhelmed by the magnitude of an experience (to the point of fear and trembling) while pathos denotes a feeling of sorrow, empathy, and tenderness for the loss of something that was once grand and noble. As my essay title suggests, in looking at photographs of landscapes we are looking into a kind of mirror that projects back to us an image of what was intelligible and meaningful to viewers at the time of their making as well as to us now as we reflect on them in the context of this exhibition.

In the era of territorial expansion and conquest by settlers of European descent, landscape photographs of the frontier (not unlike their colonial counterparts from the Middle East, North Africa, and India) emphasized the vastness of newly explored territories, their unique topographical features, and their evident lack of civilization. When visible at all, native peoples were portrayed en masse as exotic noble savages (at best), but primitive in culture

fig. 9 **Carleton Watkins** *Cape Horn, Columbia River*, 1867, albumen print, 20 ¾ × 16 ⅛ in., RISD Museum: Helen M. Danforth Acquisition Fund 1987.010

and impediments to progress. Once continental expansion had reached its limits, however, and no existential threats to white settlement remained, American landscape images began to reflect a new criticality—at turns romantic and realistic—that persists to this day. Indeed, for the last century, landscape photography has consistently mirrored Americans' anxieties about nature, or rather its imminent loss, whether due to industrialization, pollution, population growth, real estate profiteering, or bioengineering. Alternately portraying nature as a balm for the alienated modern soul or a dystopian fait accompli, modern and postmodern photographic landscapes mark a progressively disquieting understanding of humanity's relationship to the natural universe.

The role of photography as a mass communications medium that was believed to be objective cannot be underestimated in any discussion of the impact of nature photographs on popular consciousness. Attitudes toward landscapes and what they represented were shaped by a constant flow of images and commentary through a number of media portals: in the 19th century, paintings, dioramas, expositions, lantern-slide lectures, stereoviews, newspapers, and journals illustrated with line engravings; in the 20th century, direct halftone print media, modern photojournalism, film, television, and—most recently—instantaneous global image sharing through digital media. Though we see a relative handful of photographic prints on the walls of the museum, selected for their aesthetic qualities, we must also bear in mind these other ways in which landscape/nature photographs were disseminated to viewers and shaped their understanding of what they were looking at.

One of earliest works in *America in View* was made by Carleton Watkins (see fig. 9), who had followed the 1849 Gold Rush around the Horn to California and set up shop in boomtown San Francisco. Others, like Timothy O'Sullivan, William Bell, and William Henry Jackson, accompanied government-funded geological and military survey expeditions into the endless vastness of the continent, bringing back plate views and stereographs for dissemination and reproduction as line engravings and lithographs in scientific reports and illustrated newspapers.[1] Field photography in the wet-plate era (1850s–1880s) was arduous, requiring an initial outlay of funds for materials, wagon, and pack animals, as well as contending with unpredictable weather and difficult terrain. The glass plates had to be developed on site and the loss of many weeks' work in an overturned boat or mishandled crates was a constant threat. No doubt discouraged by long stretches of flat-line horizons, photographers reveled in the geological variety they found, from glaciated mountain ranges to volcanic hot springs, hanging rocks, and gorges sculpted by ancient rivers (see fig. 10).

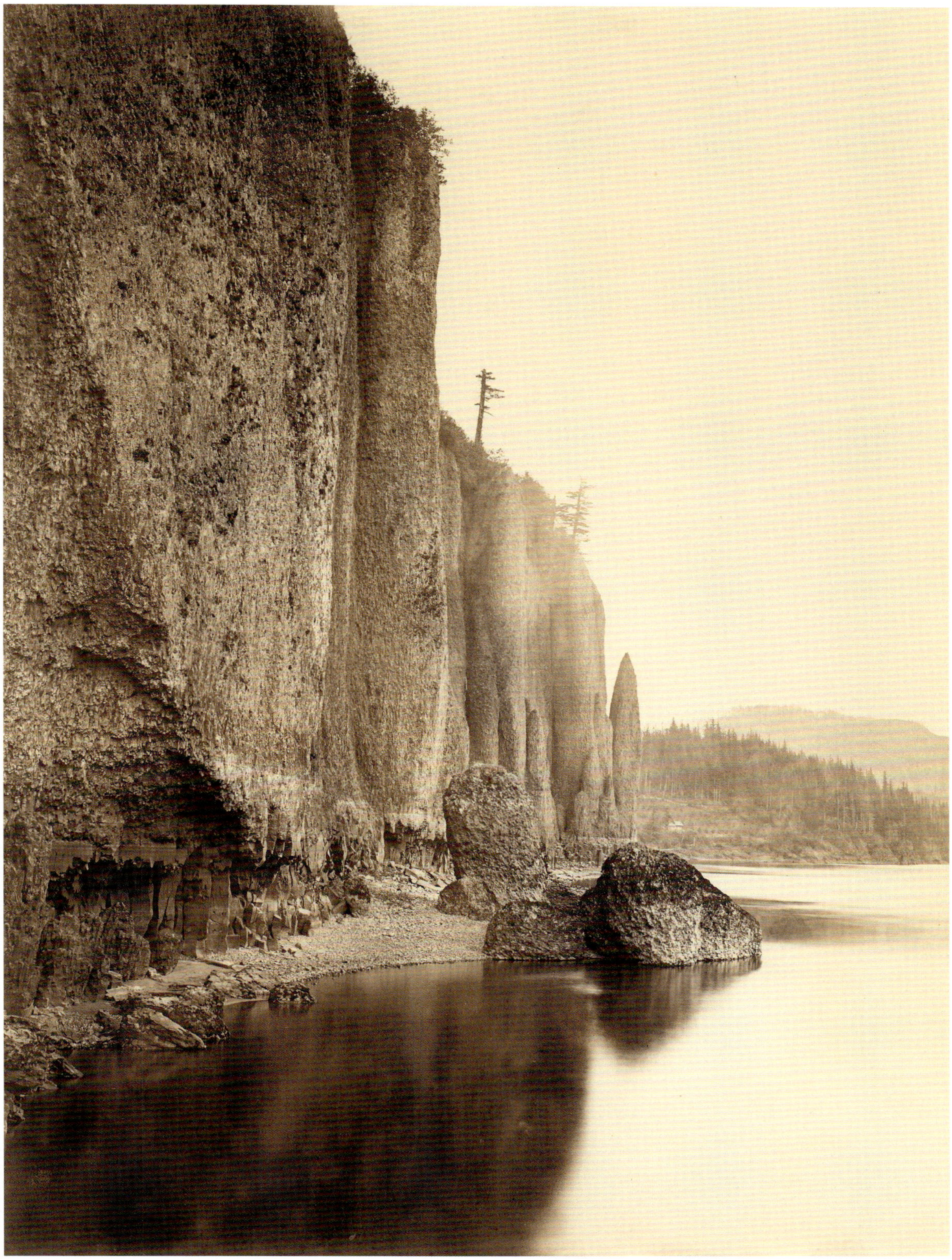

fig. 10 **Henry Hamilton Bennett** *In and about the Dells of Wisconsin: To Circle Bend, from the Navy Yard, No. 451*, from the series "Wanderings Among the Wonders and Beauties of Wisconsin Scenery," 1883, albumen print stereograph, 3⅜×7 in., RISD Museum: Anonymous gift 84.028.8

fig. 11 **William Henry Jackson** *Gardiners River Hot Springs, Diana's Baths*, 1871, from the *U.S. Geological Survey of the Territories*, albumen print, 6⅛×8 in., RISD Museum: Jesse Metcalf Fund 76.100

Along with nature's wonders, Watkins, O'Sullivan, Jackson, George Barnard, and A. J. Russell documented new railroad lines coursing through landscapes that bore eloquent witness to the bonanza of natural resources awaiting exploitation (see pl. 1). Disrupted by an exceedingly violent and costly Civil War (1861–1865) ignited by the extension of slavery into frontier states, railroad-building refocused the nation's identity and purpose. In 1869, the first Golden Spike connected the Central Pacific and Union Pacific Railroads at Promontory Point, Utah, and popular images showed transcontinental railroad-building as a glorious march of white civilization that would tame the vast uncanny spaces of the continental interior.

What strikes us now about these 19th-century views is our sense of their innocence. It is as though the photographers were capturing these places in some fixed, primordial state before settlement overran them with mining works, dams, boomtowns, asphalt, electrical pylons, resorts, suburbs, military bases, casinos, ATV tracks, and billboards. The whiff of nostalgia for a vanished Eden can be dated from 1893, when historian Frederick Jackson Turner gave his famous paper "The Significance of the Frontier in American History" at the World's Columbian Exposition in Chicago. Turner applied the ideas of natural selection to society, arguing that what made Anglo Americans so successful as a people was the development of particular character traits from their westward migration over three or four generations. A distinctly American type was forged on the frontier anvil, one who wrested productivity from uncultivated land and who was self-reliant, practical, and

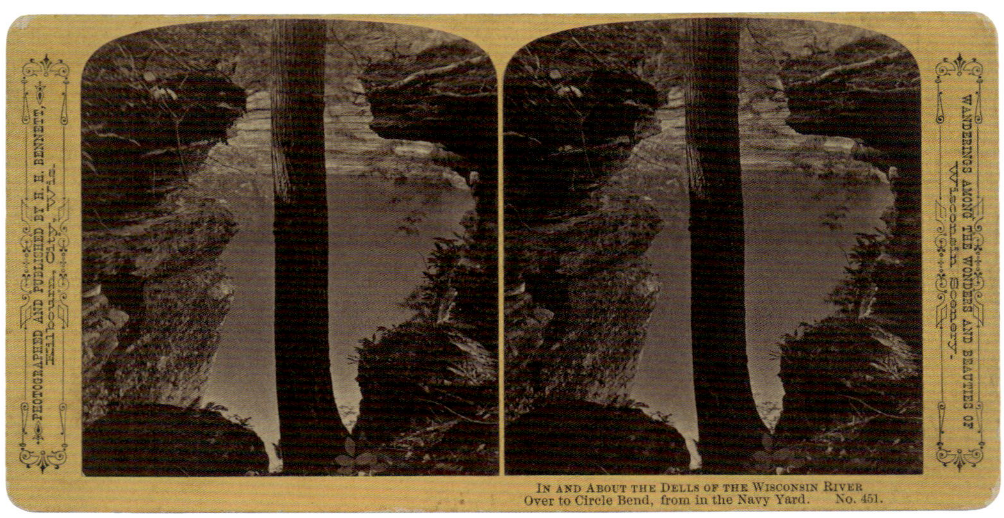

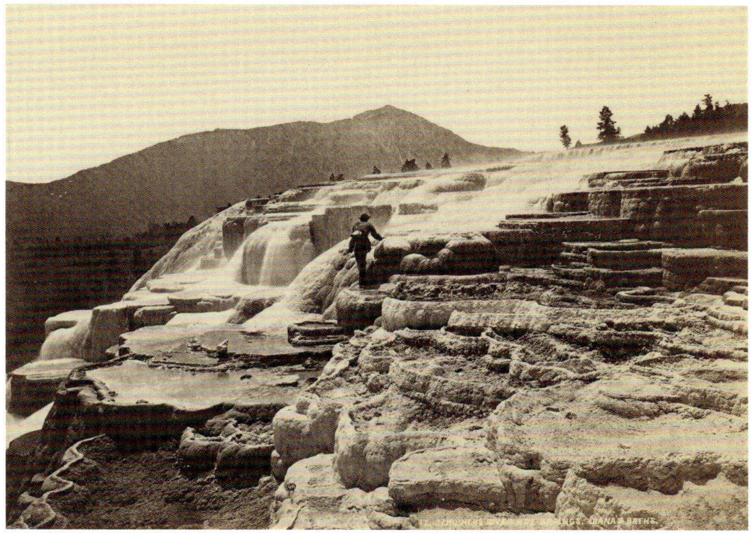

disdainful of the institutions and social hierarchies that held sway "back east."[2]

While celebrating American rugged individualism, Turner noted that the frontier days were finished, that there were no more blank spaces on the map or "Indian Territories" to claim and settle. Every useful acre of land had been surveyed, named, and turned into a potential commodity to be bought and sold. The indigenous tribes who had survived three centuries of disease, displacement, and genocidal campaigns had either assimilated to the margins of white society or been forcibly resettled on reservations under federal control. Given this context, it is easy to see how images of what appeared to be "virgin land," especially in the wilder and more dramatic western places, would have such potent psychological resonance for mass viewers, especially descendants of white settlers who now considered themselves the "native stock."

Viewing stereographs, leafing through illustrated periodicals, and touring national parks and monuments allowed viewers to imagine themselves as explorers encountering these places for the first time. Jackson's views of Yellowstone from the first Hayden Geological Survey (see fig. 11) are often credited with helping convince Congress to establish the first National Park in 1872.[3] Twenty years later, a group of journalists, lawyers, and professors from Berkeley and Stanford formed the Sierra Club, electing John Muir—an outspoken, persuasive advocate for wilderness preservation—as their first president. In 1916, Congress created the National Park Service with the mandate to "conserve the scenery and natural and historic objects and wildlife [in the parks] . . . by such means as will leave them unimpaired for the enjoyment of future generations." In 1908, sixty-nine thousand tourists visited the national parks. By 1921, annual attendance was over a million and today it tops 280 million.[4]

If there is one photographer who consciously linked Muir's preservationist ethic to the popular appeal of the West as a uniquely American Garden of Eden, it was Ansel Adams. In 1916, Adams's father bought his 14-year-old son a Brownie camera to take on a family tour of Yosemite. The Brownie was the first camera targeted to youth by George Eastman's Kodak Company, making "kodaking" a family activity. Awed by his visit, young Adams committed himself to the simultaneous pursuit of the sublime in nature and the art of photography, devouring camera club magazines and attending photographic exhibitions in his native San Francisco. At 17, he joined the Sierra Club and mastered the challenges of high altitude photography with a large-format camera. By his early twenties, Adams was making a living

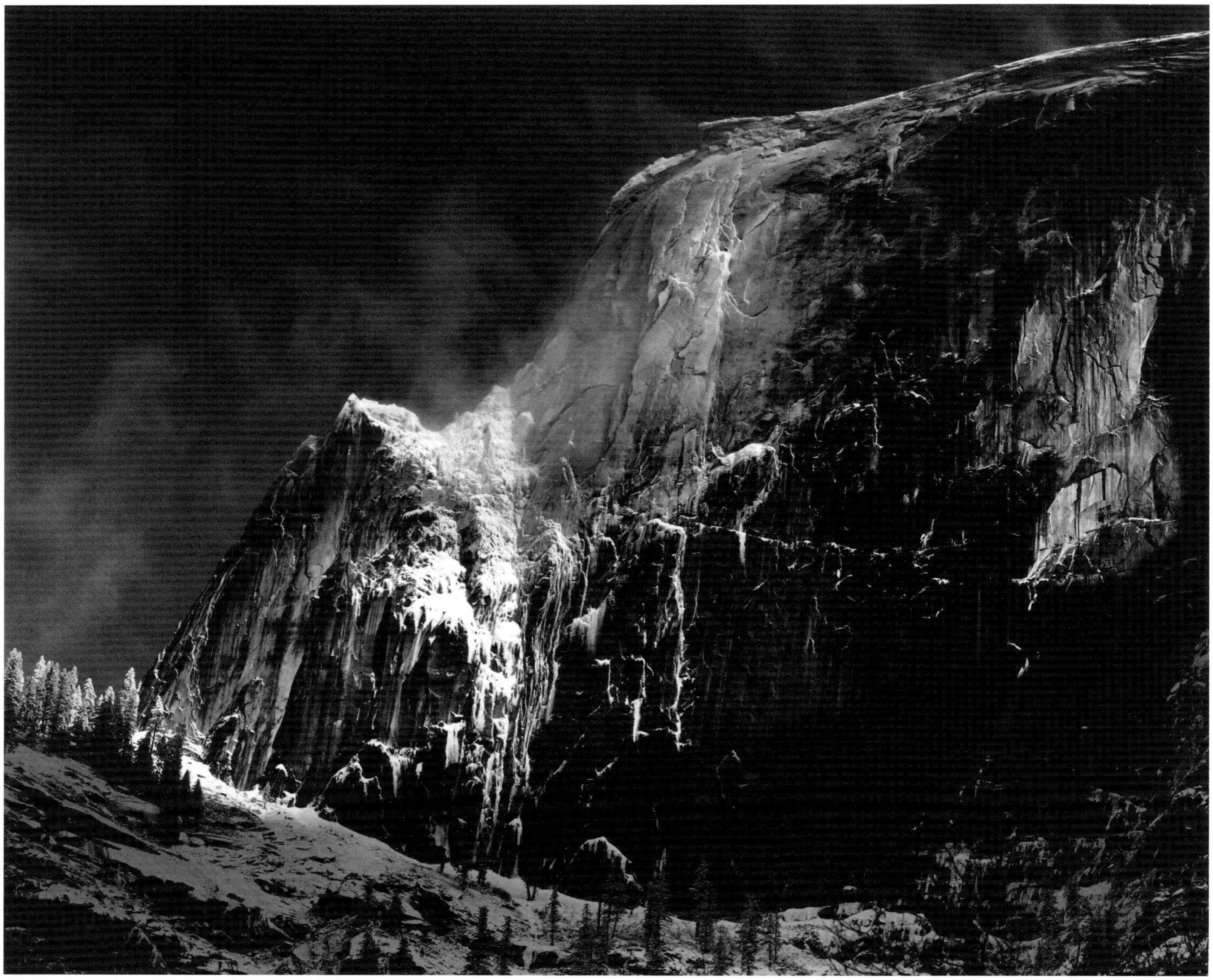

fig. 12 **Ansel Adams** *Half Dome, Blowing Snow, Yosemite National Park, California*, ca. 1955, gelatin silver print, 14 ⅛ × 18 ¾ in., RISD Museum: Museum purchase with funds from the National Endowment for the Arts 75.097

fig. 13 **Clarence H. White** *Morning*, 1905, from *Camera Work*, no. 23, July 1908, photogravure, 8×6 in., RISD Museum: Walter H. Kimball Fund 76.093

fig. 14 **Paul Strand** *Iris, Georgetown, Maine*, 1923 (printed 1975/76 by Richard Benson), gold chloride-toned silver print, 10×8 in., RISD Museum: Gift of Peter C. Jones 1987.107.2

publishing and selling his work. Images such as *Half Dome, Blowing Snow, Yosemite National Park, California*, 1955 (fig. 12), transport viewers to a realm of spiritual awe in the face of Nature's incomprehensible majesty and vastness. As did many of his peers, Adams shared the belief that the art of interpreting the natural world photographically could help restore a sense of spiritual wholeness that had become drastically attenuated in modern industrial society.

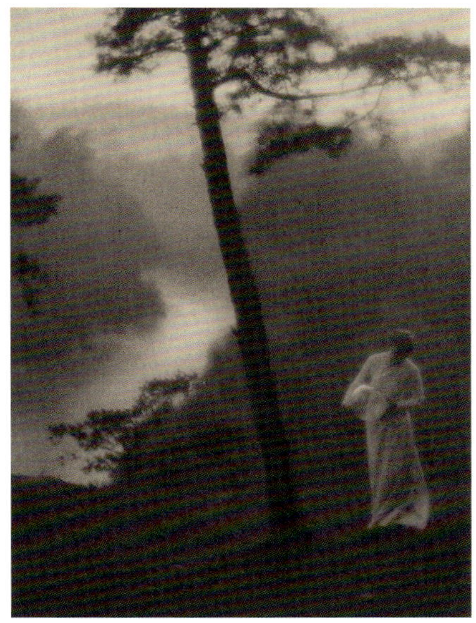

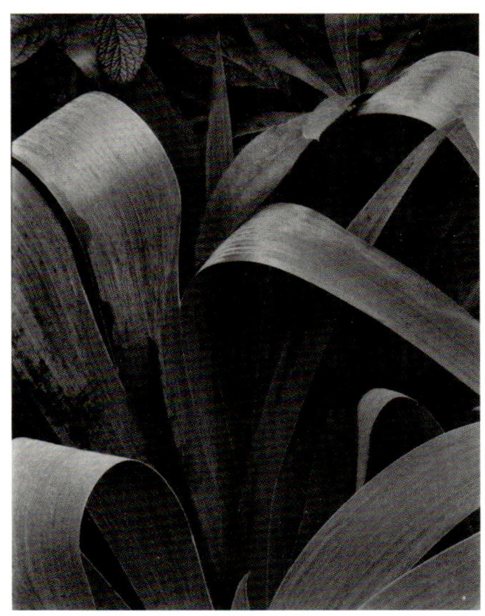

This was not a new sensibility. Turn-of-the-century Pictorialist photographers such as Gertrude Kasebier and Clarence White (see fig. 13), had drawn inspiration from Symbolist poets and Art Nouveau's turn to natural motifs as part of a widespread aesthetic revolt against the decline of taste evident in mass-produced commodities. But by the early 1920s, Paul Strand and Edward Weston abandoned the soft-focused allegorical and literary subjects of pictorial photography in favor of slices of optical reality transformed into surface pattern, rhythm, tone, and line (see fig. 14). The aim of the 1920s modernist generation inspired by Alfred Steiglitz's influential journal *Camera Work* was not to illustrate abstract concepts such as "nature" or "beauty," but to capture those instants of intensified seeing that the camera, alone, offered. One can also detect the influence of Zen Buddhism, especially among the northern California art photographers who gathered around Edward Weston in the f/64 Group. Weston's famous methodology of "previsualization" focused all attention on the act of release—literally the click of the shutter—when matter coalesced into form, and when photographer, machine, and subject became one (see pl. 11).

The Depression years of the 1930s brought renewed interest in realist documentation, temporarily eclipsing art photography's tendencies toward abstraction. Now the focus shifted to landscapes devastated by interlocking ecological catastrophes such as soil depletion and an extended period of drought that turned farms into wastelands. There was unprecedented federal patronage for photographers through the Department of Agriculture's Farm Security Administration (FSA), among other New Deal programs. FSA photographers such as Ben Shahn, Walker Evans, Dorothea Lange, and Arthur Rothstein (see fig. 15) documented conditions of environmental, economic, and social stress in rural America and remedies offered by the federal government.

The FSA Historical Section's director, Roy Stryker, was a trained social economist who urged his photographers to "get pictures of lunch rooms, filling

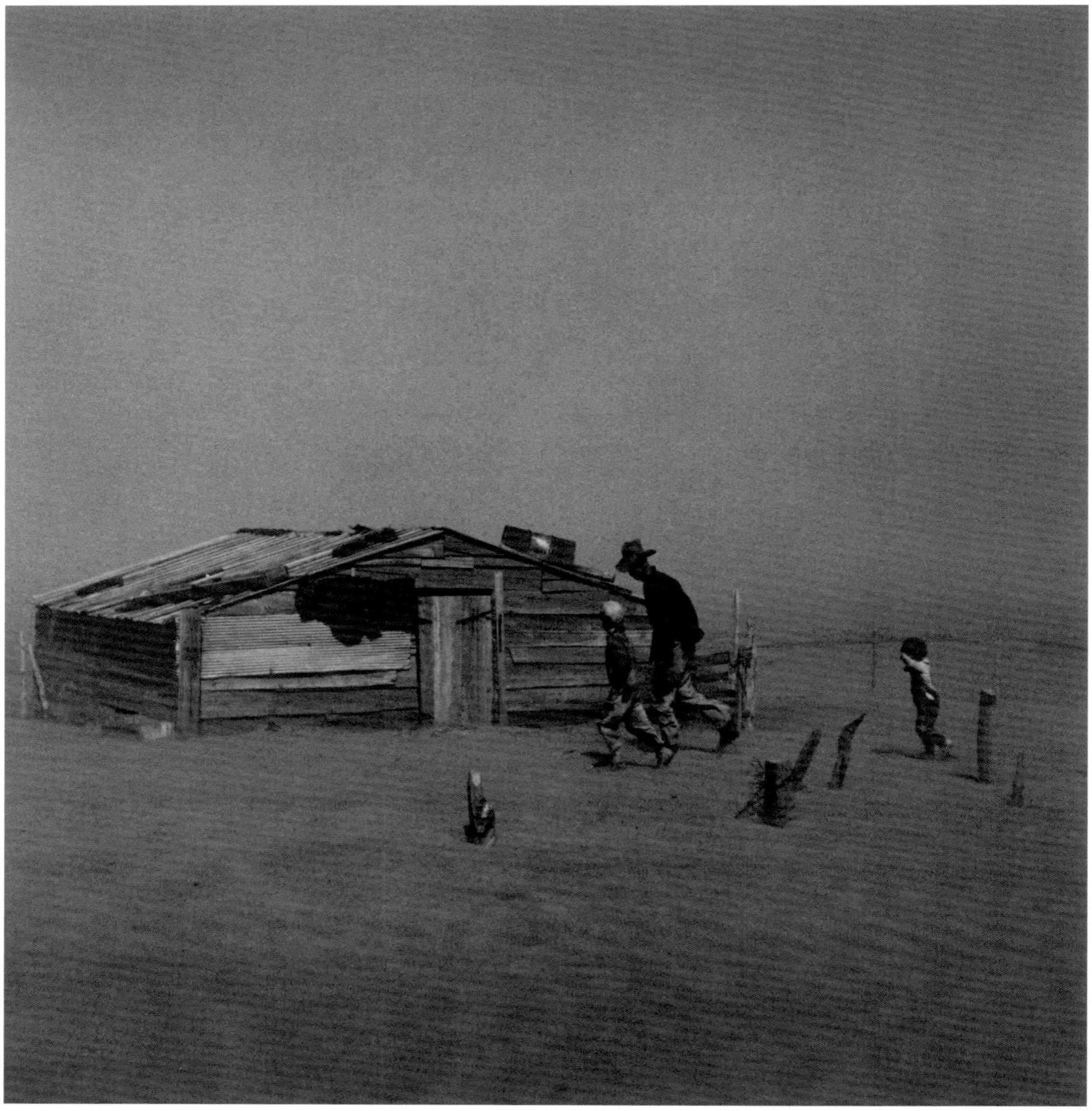

fig. 15 **Arthur Rothstein** *Father and Sons Walking in the Face of a Dust Storm, Cimarron County, Oklahoma*, 1936, gelatin silver print, 9 7/8 × 12 3/4 in., RISD Museum: Gift of Mr. and Mrs. Gilman Angier 80.088

fig. 16 **Walker Evans** *U.S. Post Office, Sprott, Alabama*, 1936 (printed 1970 by James Dow), gelatin silver print, 16 × 20 in., RISD Museum: Gift of James Dow 1971.043.11

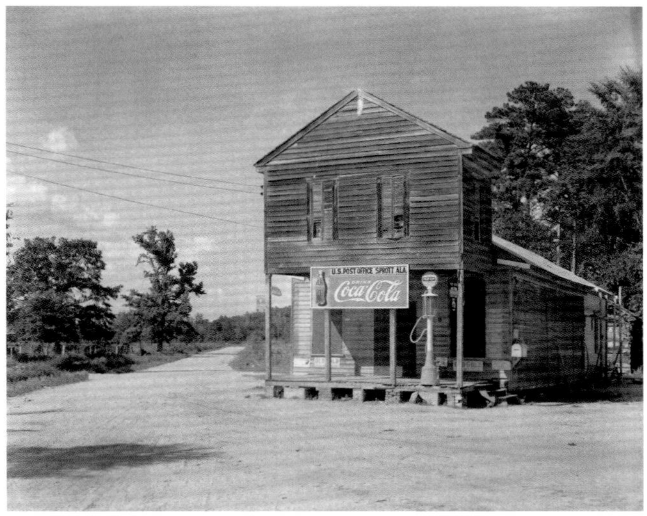

stations, advertising signs, churches and tent revivals, wall decorations in homes, backyards, men loafing under trees, people listening to the radio."[5] Inspired by the photographs of Eugene Atget that he had seen in Berenice Abbott's New York studio, Walker Evans fleshed out a new concept of the American "social landscape" in photographs such as *U.S. Post Office, Sprott, Alabama*, 1936 (fig. 16), where a weathered wooden storefront with a gas pump and mailbox—its sagging porch sporting a shiny new Coca-Cola sign—presides over a deserted intersection in the middle of the day, in the middle of nowhere. As in the best of Evans's work, vernacular architecture speaks eloquently to the humble aspirations of those who built and used it—the antithesis of the slick, corporate "Madison Avenue" world Evans grew up in and viscerally rejected.[6] Evans's reticent but socially acute documentary style would inspire FSA peers such as Russell Lee and generations of American photographers who followed.

The genocidal atrocities of the Second World War and the new cold war chess game of mutually assured nuclear destruction made Nature with a capital-*N* all the more sacred to Americans at mid-century. Oil companies and automobile manufacturers capitalized on this subconscious longing, promoting domestic tourism as patriotic to get Americans on the road in new Fairlanes, Belairs, Deluxes, Silverstreaks and Rocket 88s, fueled by cheap gas. Postwar advertising melded the technological and natural sublimes in glossy color spreads shot in spectacular locations, an unbeatable formula for selling feelings of plenitude, freedom, and security in a frightening world. Though Ansel Adams had found his photographic calling much earlier, it was in the 1950s that he became a household name. Landscapes of Nature's West, in black and white and Kodachrome, evoked myths of a simpler past when pioneers overcame hardships to build a great nation. Americans felt a renewed sense of Manifest Destiny, now on the global stage, a feeling eagerly embraced not only by corporate advertising but by politicians and the media.[7]

But some refused to be reassured as they experienced the price of postwar consensus: congressional witchhunts of homosexuals and suspected leftists, the ostracism of anyone deemed "un-American." Borrowing the improvisational style of jazz performance, Jack Kerouac typed *On the Road* (1951) in a continuous scroll—a spontaneous Beat manifesto extolling the authenticity of living life on one's own terms, at the subversive margins of the American Dream. In 1955, Robert Frank, a Swiss-American photojournalist and friend

fig. 17 **Robert Frank** *U.S. 285, New Mexico*, 1955, from *The Americans*, gelatin silver print, 13 1/2 × 9 13/16 in., courtesy Pace/MacGill Gallery, New York

of both Kerouac and Evans, received a Guggenheim Fellowship to take to the road, traveling throughout the United States and photographing its diverse social landscapes. His resulting carefully edited sequence of photographs was published as *The Americans*, first in France in 1958, then by Grove Press the following year, with an introduction by Kerouac.

Frank's photograph *U.S. 285, New Mexico*, 1955 (fig. 17), is the visual equivalent to Kerouac's paeon to the open freedom of the road and the Beat nomad's raw quest for meaning. Though it received negative reviews for its perceived disrespect to the United States and for the casualness of Frank's shooting style, *The Americans* would set the tone for photographers' responses to the American landscape in the 1960s and 1970s, notably the work of Lee Friedlander, Garry Winogrand, and Stephen Shore. Now, nature was apt to be viewed from a car window or in a rear-view mirror rather than from a hilltop. Overnight, the large-format magisterial views of Adams and Weston were replaced by a 35mm "grab-shot" style that captured the flux and contradictions of modern life with a fresh immediacy.[8] Photographers were part of that flux, restless peripatetics criss-crossing the continent on new Interstates and side roads, retrieving evidence of the "Americas" they found (see pl. 18).

In 1960 the Sierra Club responded to the threats of automotive encroachment and plans for new wilderness development by launching its series of Exhibit Format Books, beginning with Ansel Adams's *This Is the American Earth*. The U.S. Forest Service was cutting access roads into the backcountry and the Club lobbied Congress to adopt a comprehensive system of land-use classifications and hold public hearings on any plans to alter the wilderness character of public lands. In 1962, the Club published *In Wildness Is the Preservation of the World*, featuring Eliot Porter's sublime yet intimate color photographs and texts by Henry David Thoreau. The Exhibit Format Books were intended to sway public opinion in favor of preservation and bolstered the campaign for the Wilderness Act that was passed by Congress in 1964.

The 1960s and '70s also coincided with a youth-driven countercultural shift away from consumption as a programmed way of life and widespread alarm over chemical contamination sparked by Rachel Carson's 1962 exposé, *Silent Spring*. The first Earth Day in the United States took place in April 1970, a grassroots teach-in that engaged more than 20 million Americans and was heavily covered by the press, persuading Congress that environmental reform had a national constituency. That year, President Nixon signed the Clean Air Act into law, followed by the Clean Water Act two years later.

Taking their lead from both Robert Frank's and Pop Art's cool send-up of the American Dream, photographers focused their cameras on the excesses of mass consumption in

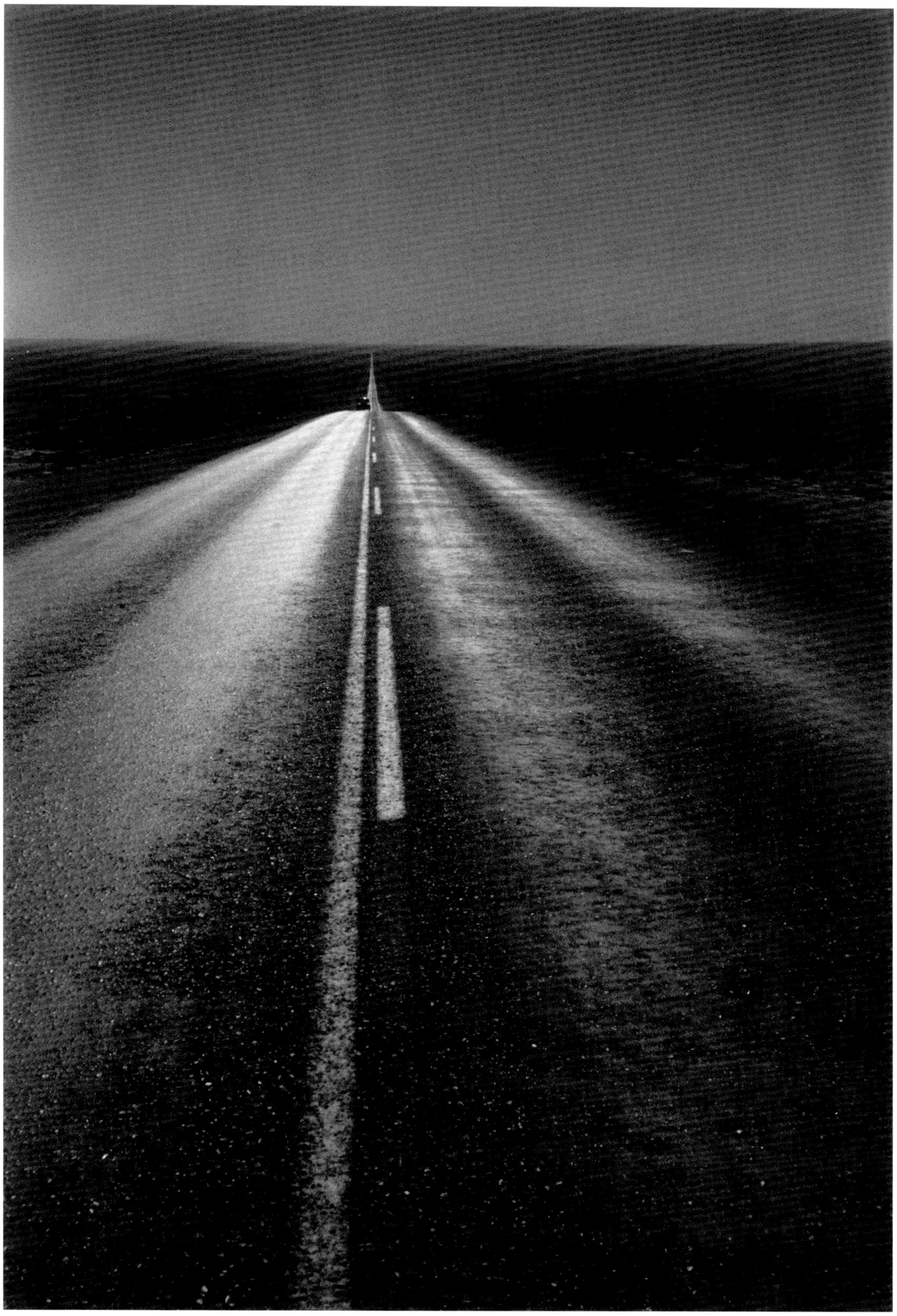

fig. 18 **Ed Ruscha** *Twentysix Gasoline Stations*, 1963, photo-offset lithograph artist's book, 7 1/16 × 5 1/2 × 3/16 in., courtesy John Hay Library, Brown University

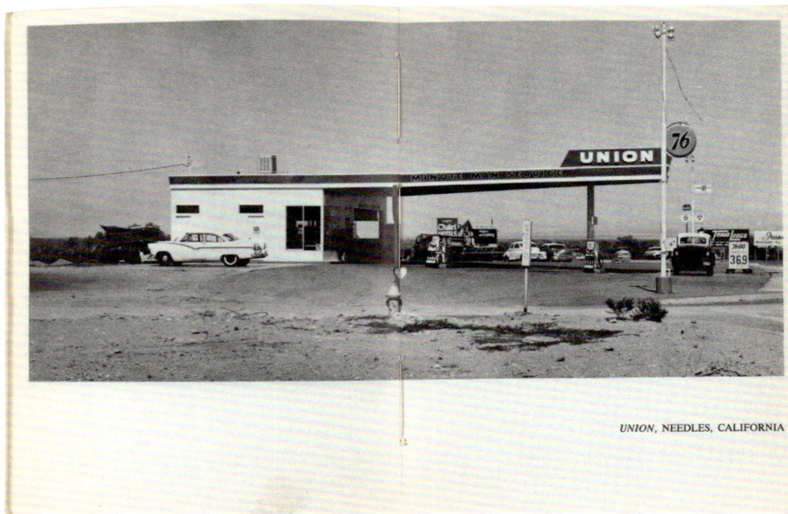

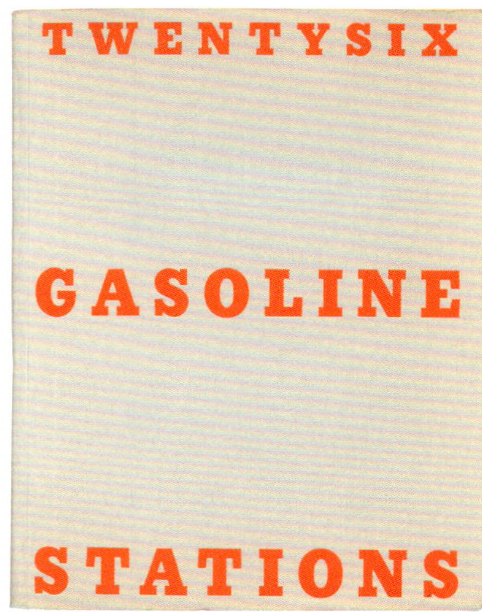

suburbia, the kitsch culture of corporate leisure and entertainment visible in the resorts of Las Vegas, Disney World, and their down-market kin, and the explosive growth of tract home subdivisions, especially in the western Sunbelt. Ed Rusha's self-published artist book *Twentysix Gasoline Stations* (1963; fig. 18), wryly documented the repetitive banality of the highway-scape between Tulsa and Los Angeles that inspired his California Pop paintings. In 1973, Bill Owens published *Suburbia*, featuring straight documentary photographs of nuclear families at home in Livermore, California, along with quotes from the subjects that were banal to the point of absurdity: "Sunday afternoon we get together. I cook the steaks and my wife makes the salad. . . . We're really happy. Our kids are healthy, we eat good food, and we have a really nice home."[9] Ironically, the complacent satisfactions of family life in 1970s suburbia are more likely to provoke nostalgia than disdain in today's viewers.

If NASA's iconic "blue marble" on the cover of the *Whole Earth Catalog* (1968–1972) represented the ultimate macro view of humanity's home planet, Joe Deal's *The Fault Zone*—photographs of the edges of new suburban development along the new interstates east of Los Angeles—showed the ground-level reality (fig. 19). No longer was it a matter of preserving the aesthetic experience of pristine wilderness—it was too late for that. What was at stake was the very survival of local ecosystems whose carrying capacities were being overwhelmed. An international crisis would soon reveal the real costs of America's cheap oil dependency. Unhappy with U.S. foreign policy in the Middle East, the oil-exporting nations of the Arabian peninsula and north Africa (OPEC) proclaimed a temporary embargo in 1973, followed by a sharp rise in prices. Gas rationing at the pump shocked the public and sent the economy into a steep recession for over a decade.

In 1975, curator William Jenkins mounted the exhibition *New Topographics: Photographs of a Man-Altered Landscape* at the George Eastman House, featuring photographs by Robert Adams, Lewis Baltz, Joe Deal, Frank Gohlke, Stephen Shore, Nicholas Nixon, and others. The show can be seen as the antithesis of the Sierra Club's Exhibit Format political advocacy. Jenkins asserted that these photographers were showing landscapes in a radically new way. Instead of following earlier aesthetic approaches informed by metaphysical, ethical, or personal ideas about humankind's relationship to nature, these photographers studiously sidestepped any visual rhetoric, sentiment, or judgment. As aesthetically neutral as real-estate snapshots, the photographers showed the facts without making a plea (see fig. 20). Nonetheless, the impact of *New Topographics* on viewers in the 1970s could not help but resonate with vigorous political debates in the press and local legislatures about the effects of the oil crisis and the ecological impacts of rampant suburban sprawl into fragile environments.

Regardless of whether the *New Topographics* photographers were personally invested in environmental politics, their photographs departed from their 20th-century predecessors in their implicit critique of the notion of nature as a refuge from the ills of industrial life. The accelerating degradation of the environment had become an inescapable reality; there was no longer any land or water source in the United States unaffected by human encroachment. The old dichotomies that had previously structured commonly held assumptions—nature vs. culture; urban vs. rural; human vs. non-human; first world vs. third world; private vs. public—were coming apart.

In 1981 the Sierra Club published *Dead Tech: A Guide to the Archaeology of Tomorrow*, originally released in Germany with photographs by Manfred Hamm. Hamm's images were organized by subject: military ruins, automobile graveyards, sunken harbors, abandoned factories, and so on. As a Sierra Club publication, *Dead Tech* was unabashedly a propaganda book that emphasized the long-term environmental hazards of industrial and military production at the very moment the United States was exporting much of its toxic manufacturing and waste disposal to impoverished nations with few, if any, environmental restrictions. The lid was blown off this ugly reality in 1984 when a gas leak at a Union Carbide (now Dow Chemical) plant killed over three thousand men, women, and children in Bhopal, India. Environmental regulation in advanced capitalist nations had pushed corporate polluters over southern borders and across oceans, into the lives of those unable to defend themselves.

The exportation of dirty industries abroad did not bring an environmental utopia to the United States. Aside from depressing wages and weakening unions (a plus for multinational corporations), capital flight devastated local economies and turned once-thriving communities into ghost towns. New England had suffered disinvestment earlier as the largest textile mills had relocated to the non-unionized South by mid-century. Fifty years later, photographers Salvatore Mancini, Scott Lapham, and Michael Cevoli trained their cameras on the former manufacturing landscapes of Rhode Island and Massachusetts when mill buildings that could not be repurposed for the newer economy were being demolished or left to

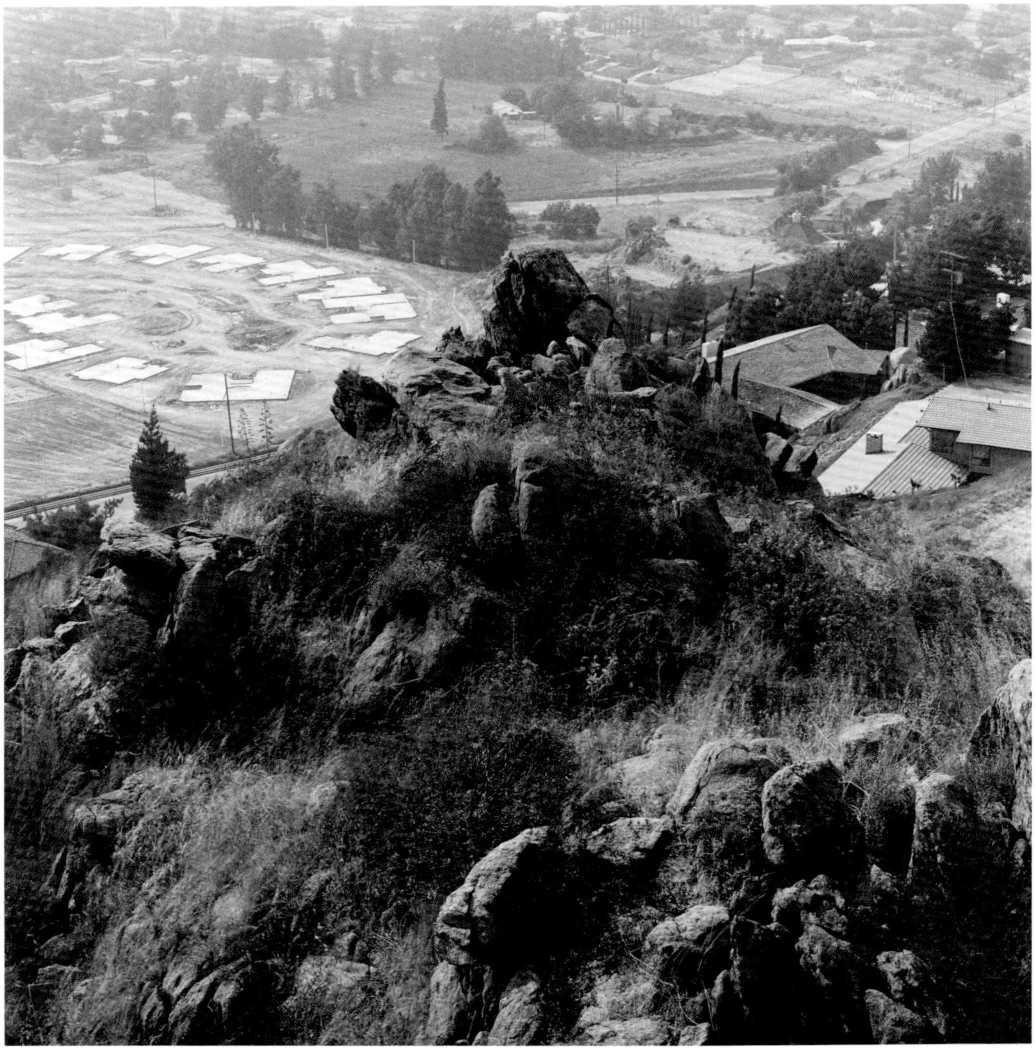

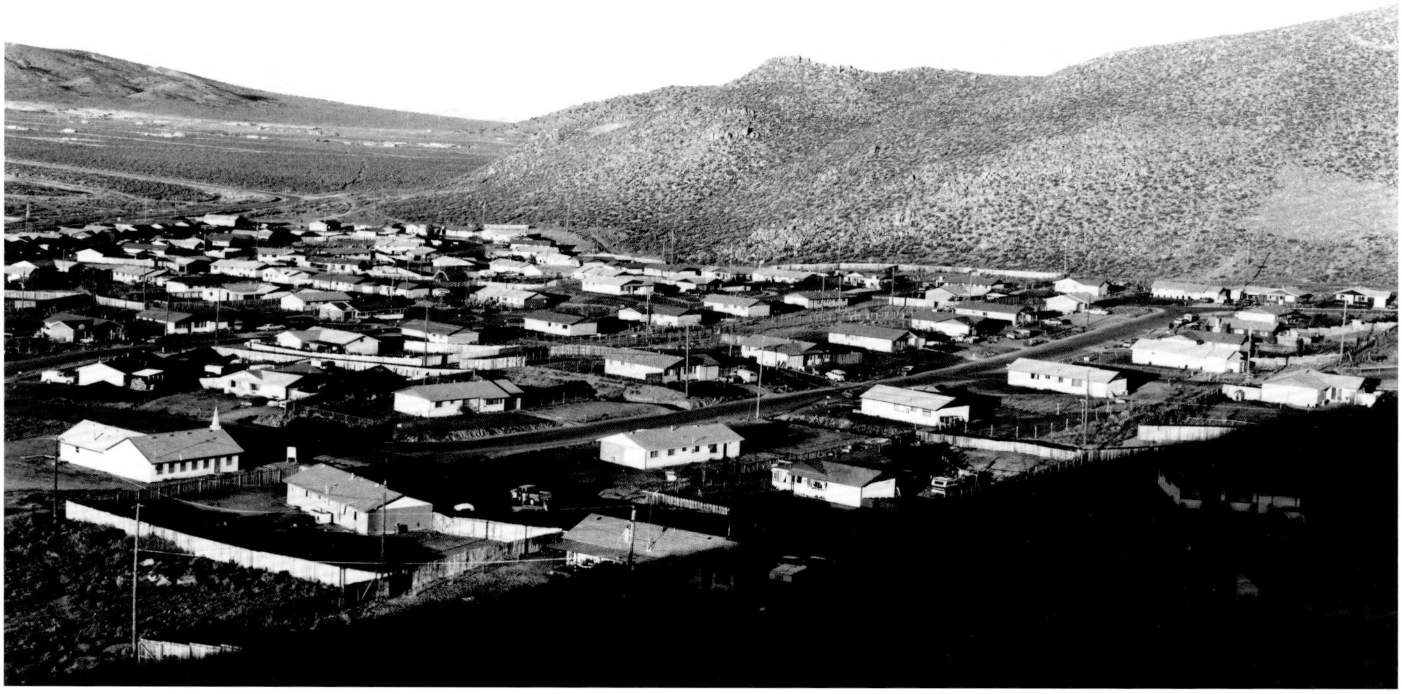

fig. 19 Joe Deal *Colton, California*, 1978, from *The Fault Zone*, 1981, gold-toned gelatin silver print, 15×15 in., RISD Museum: Museum purchase, Georgianna Sayles Aldrich Fund and Gift of James D. and Diana D. Burke 2003.76.19

fig. 20 Lewis Baltz *Lemmon Valley, Looking North*, 1977, from *Nevada*, gelatin silver print, 8×10 in., RISD Museum: Gift from the collection of Joe Deal and Betsy Ruppa 2010.82.35.11

fig. 21 **Scott Lapham** *Providence Cold Storage #1, Demolished 1999*, 1999, gelatin silver print, 16×20 in., RISD Museum: Gift from the Collection of Dr. and Mrs. Joseph A. Chazan 2005.132.5

fig. 22 **Edward Burtynsky** *OMYA #51, Calcium Carbonate Waste Area, Proctor, Vermont*, 1991, digital color chromogenic print, mount: 34×41 in., Courtesy Howard Greenberg Gallery, New York

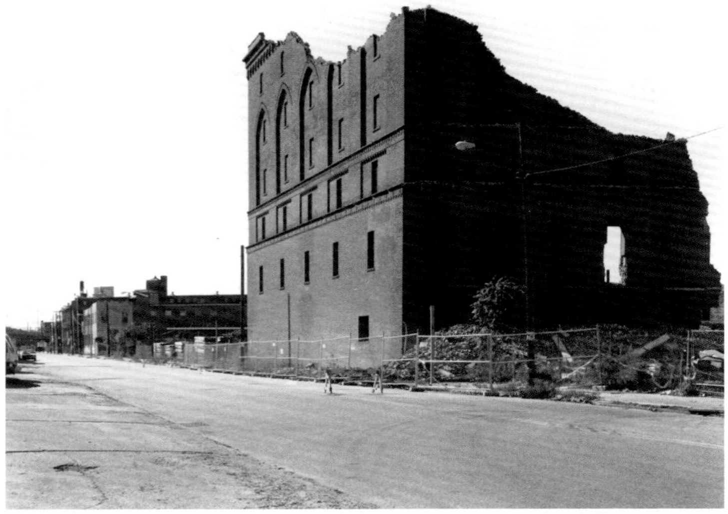

crumble (see fig. 21). The old industrial landscapes of New England may appear deceptively green and lush with vegetation, but the subsoils and groundwater are saturated with contaminants. After the Love Canal scandal in Niagara Falls, NY, Congress established the Superfund program (1980), charging the EPA with locating, investigating, and cleaning up the most hazardous toxic waste sites.[10]

The 1980s opened with a well-funded (and ongoing) backlash against environmental reform, epitomized by President Reagan's appointment of James Watt as Secretary of the Interior. Watt had led the Sagebrush Rebellion by western developers, ranchers, and energy corporations against government regulation and the establishment of the EPA. Meanwhile, a string of international disasters made headlines, including Three Mile Island, Bhopal, Chernobyl, and the Exxon Valdez oil spill. Scientific reports on acid rain, deforestation of the Amazon basin, desertification, ozone depletion, and global warming raised broad international concern. The scandalous deal-making and crony capitalism that rocked the EPA under Reagan and successive GOP administrations, along with the repeated refusal of the United States to respect international protocols on energy consumption, galvanized new waves of political activism, including grassroots direct-action groups such as Earth First!, whose members chained themselves to trees in national forests to prevent logging.

The *New Topographics* aesthetic of deadpan observation had embraced color in the modestly scaled photographs of Stephen Shore, who brought to the "Great American Road Trip" tradition of Frank, Friedlander, and Winogrand a Pop sensibility left over from his youthful days as a member of Warhol's Factory (see pl. 21). While many of today's landscape photographers trace their roots to *New Topographics*, photographers such as Richard Misrach and Edward Burtynsky have perfected what one might call the "topographic sublime." Burtynsky's photographs are straightforward documents of industrially impacted landscapes on truly superhuman scales, beginning with his series on Vermont's flooded marble quarries (1991–1992; see fig. 22), and continuing with his extended documentation of global sites of extractive and recycled waste mining and the decade-long building of China's Three Gorges Dam, which displaced entire communities. Burtynsky reprises the magisterial view tradition, using large-format cameras and high,

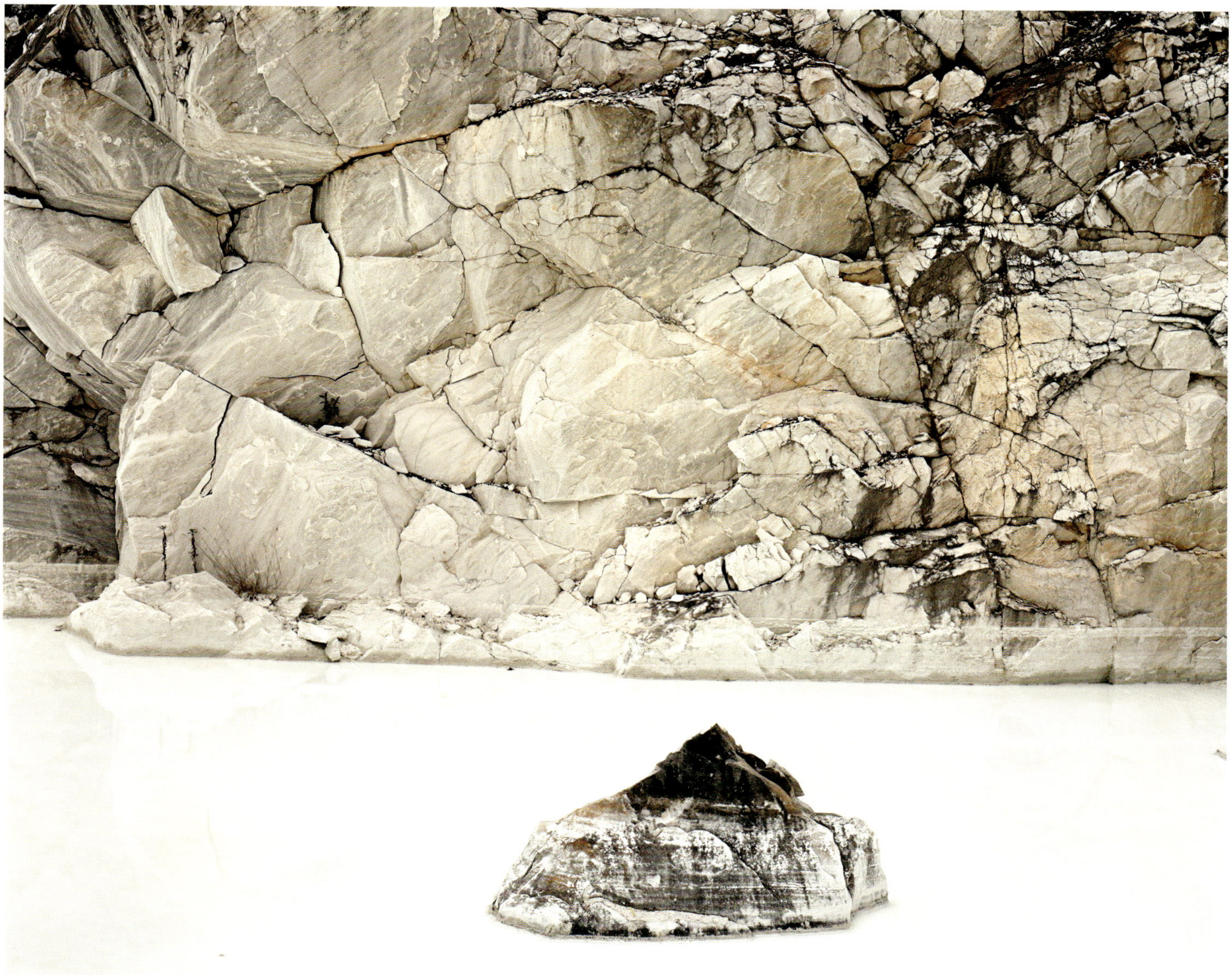

often aerial, vantage points. In this sense, he is less the inheritor of Lewis Baltz than of Albert Bierstadt. Unlike the *New Topographics* photographers, who tended to work close to home, Burtynsky seeks out global locations that are inherently spectacular, and his large-scale exhibition prints immerse viewers in a phantasmagoria of visual stimuli. Of all of the post–*New Topographics* landscape photographers working today, Burtynsky has been the most consistent in his focus on the massive transformations of environments wrought by modern engineering, technology, and the demands of global commerce.[11]

The topographic style of the 1970s was also very influential on the German School photographers, a number of whom studied at the Kunstakademie Düsseldorf with Hilla and Bernd Becher, whose precisely framed typological photographs of industrial structures were introduced to American audiences in *New Topographics*. Thomas Struth, a Düsseldorf graduate, photographed in Yosemite National Park for his 1991–1992 series *Paradise* (see fig. 23). In setting up his 8 × 10 view camera in some of the remaining old-growth forests around the world, Struth was not making any ecological, romantic, or socio-economic statement but rather confronting the viewer with a dense jungle of tree trunks, branches, and foliage. His stated intention with his mural-scale photographs was to inspire feelings of loss of direction and confusion—reminding us, perhaps, of how

fig. 23 **Thomas Struth** *Untitled*, 2004, from the portfolio *Paradise*, color inkjet print, 13×19 in., RISD Museum: Mary B. Jackson Fund 2006.11

ignorant we modern consumers have become about finding our way home—to nature or any other imagined paradise.[12]

If Struth deploys topographic realism to provoke disorientation when confronted with a "wall of nature" that does not yield to our mastering gaze, a very different feeling is elicited by other influential photographers—one that directly challenges the emotionally distanced (some would say masculine) style of *New Topographics* and much of the German School. Sentimentality is a culturally feminized emotion that expresses a private and tender response to what is beheld, rather than sublime awe or detachment. Sentimentality solicits a modest feeling, not a grandiose one. While the sentimental is most evident in the portraiture of such artists as Nan Goldin and Wolfgang Tillmans, it is also present in contemporary landscape tableaus composed by artists such as Justin Kimball, whose *Deep Hole, New Hampshire*, 2002 (pl. 48), updates a durable theme from the western canon (Giorgione, Manet, Eakins): youths enjoying communal leisure in a local arcadia.

Sentimentality's postmodern affect derives from its sense of déjà vu, reminding us that we've seen this movie before. Is it Hitchcock or Billy Wilder? We can't quite put our finger on it, but the scene appears both uncanny and deeply familiar. German photographer Uta Barth, who has been living and working in Los Angeles for many years, captures this feeling in her gauzy landscape fragments and interiors that are as spare in their detail as Struth's are charged. Her choice to radically soften the camera's focus removes all signs of site specificity and veils the scene in a dream-like haze. *Field #14*, 1996 (pl. 42), shows a literal *terrain vague*, a nondescript suburban landscape rendered in an almost monochromatic palette. It is a non-place as viewed through a heavily fogged window, or perhaps tears.

As we survey the possibilities of landscape expression in the present, we recognize that we can satisfy our curiosity to see what "America" (or anywhere else) looks like by roaming Google Maps as well as highways and airports. In his 2010 artist book *A New American Picture*, Doug Rickard selected and digitally enhanced images taken by Google Street View's automated cameras of blighted neighborhoods across the United States, places that would have been difficult, even dangerous, to photograph in person. Rickard's virtual road trip is a dystopian high-tech update of the genre, showing streetscapes of communities ravaged by capital flight and government neglect (see fig. 24). Trevor Paglen, a trained geographer as well as a writer and visual artist, used the Internet extensively to research what he calls the "black world"—secret military and CIA sites whose existence

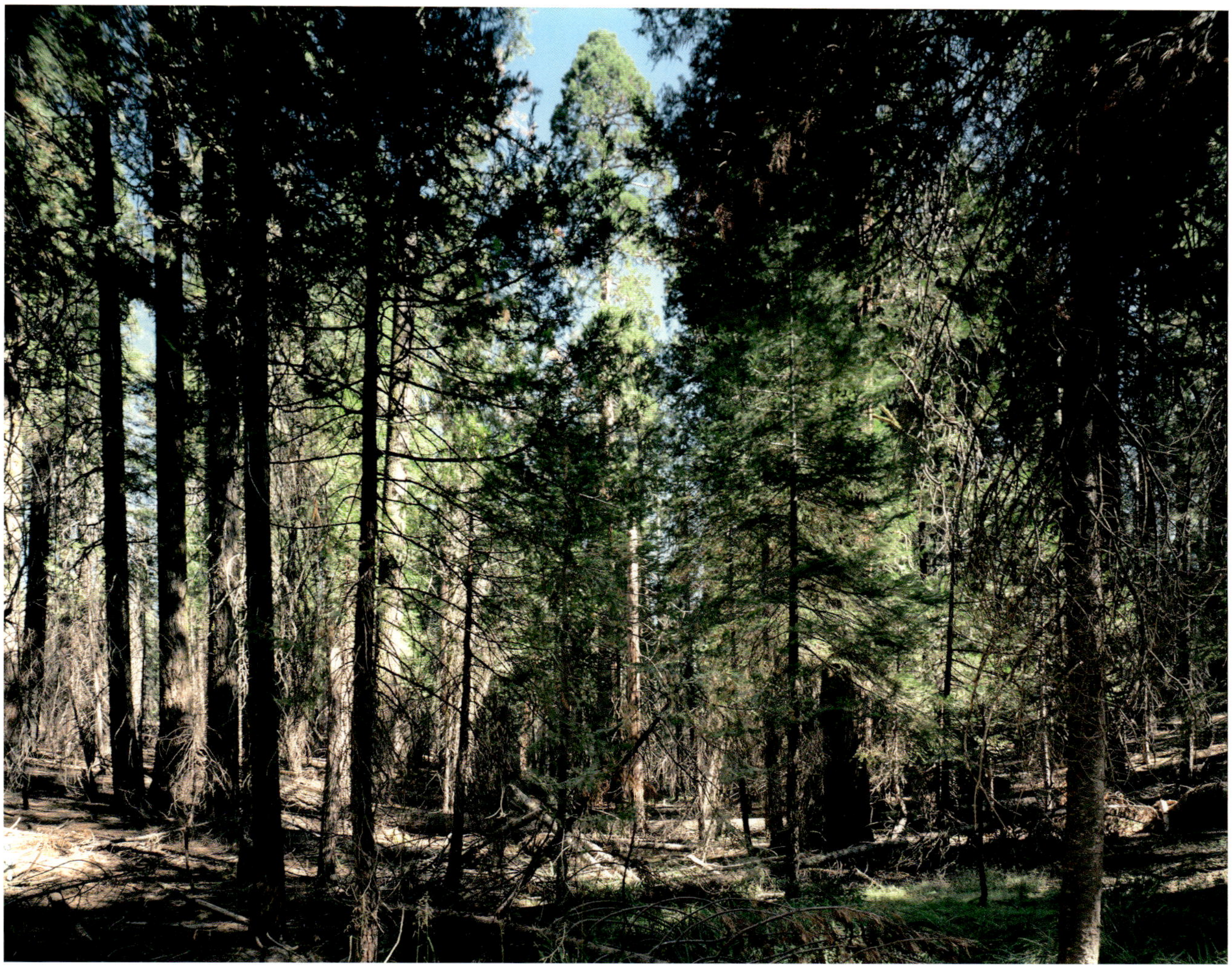

fig. 24 **Doug Rickard** *#82.948842, Detroit, MI, 2009*, 2010, from the series "A New American Picture," color inkjet print, 26×41½ in., RISD Museum: Mary B. Jackson Fund 2012.41

the government officially denies. Availing himself of an extremely high-powered telescopic camera used by astronomers, Paglen captured blurry visual evidence of militarized installations buffered by vast areas of restricted desert. Ironically, both Rickard and Paglan use cutting-edge technological tools to reveal landscapes that most Americans would prefer *not* to see or know anything about.

Tracing the relationships between photographic aesthetics and cultural shifts in American attitudes toward the environment is only one way of thinking about the histories of American landscape photography, but a particularly productive one. Though Turner's Thesis is long buried, the notion of a unique national character shaped by the frontier experience continues its myth-making work in the entertainment media and political speech, notably in debates about the security of national borders from both actual and imaginary outside threats. Despite billions spent on high-tech missile defense systems, surveillance satellites, electronic fences, airport body scanners, security cameras, and gated communities, many Americans feel neither safe nor secure. Even the weather seems ominous as rising temperatures are blamed for more violent storms, droughts, heat waves, and growing water shortages. Oceans are becoming more acidic, endangering aquatic life; the earth is running out of easily extractable fossil fuels; the food chain is increasingly subject to chemical and genetic intervention. Perhaps this accounts for the pervasive sense in contemporary American photography that a national landscape that once offered its citizens the promise of unlimited abundance, freedom, and opportunity has turned into a disquieting hall of mirrors.

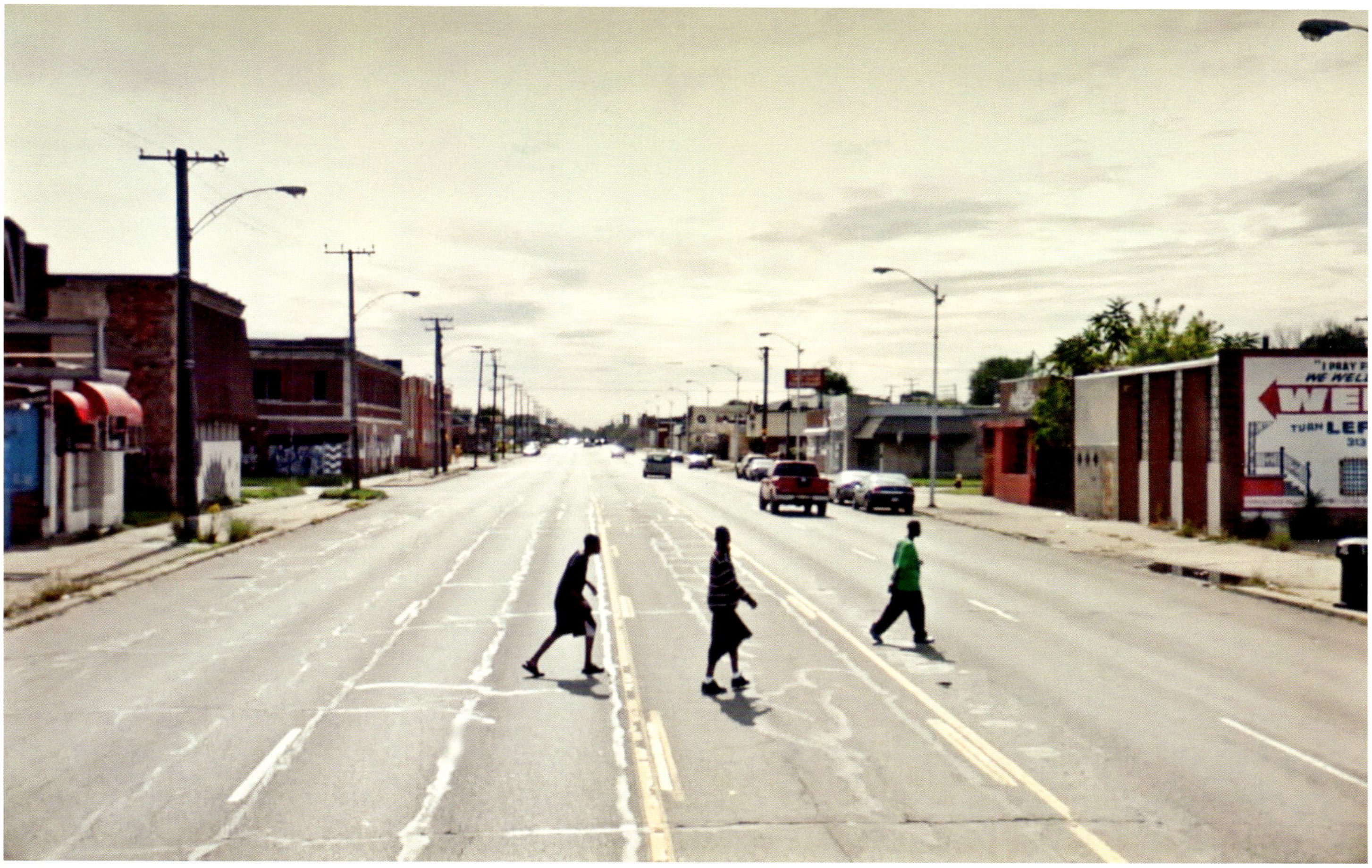

NOTES

1. The earliest surviving photographic documentation from an expeditionary survey are several daguerreotypes made by William Mayhew on Lt. Israel Woodruff's 1850 survey of the northern boundary of the Creek Nation in the Oklahoma Territory. The Muscogee Creek nation was one of a number of native tribes forcibly relocated from ancestral homelands in the Southeast after the Indian Removal Act of 1830 opened twenty-five million acres to white settlement. Woodruff's images show the survey party in camp rather than the landscape itself.
2. See Frederick Jackson Turner, *The Frontier in American History* (New York: Henry Holt & Company, 1921). Turner's heroic frontier American types were popularized in dime novels and Buffalo Bill's Wild West Show, followed by motion picture and television Westerns. Invariably, the heroes were American-born, white, and male, and we recognize an unbroken Hollywood lineage from John Wayne in *Stagecoach* (1939) to Daniel Day-Lewis in *There Will Be Blood* (2007). Despite the efforts of historians to highlight the equally critical roles played by Native Americans, women, Hispanos, Mestizos, Chinese and Japanese immigrants, and African-Americans in the histories of the West, the stock drama of the frontier (of any frontier, for that matter) almost always turns on testing the character of Anglo-American masculinity.
3. Peter Bacon Hales, *William Henry Jackson and the Transformation of the American Landscape* (Philadelphia: Temple University Press, 1988), 108.
4. 2010 Annual Summary Report, National Park Service website http://www.nature.nps.gov/stats/viewReport.cfm?selectedReport=SystemSummaryReport.cfm.
5. As quoted in Stuart Cohen, *The Likes of Us: America in the Eyes of the Farm Security Administration* (Jaffrey, NH: David R. Godine, 2008), 25.
6. Walker Evans's father was a copywriter and executive for several large advertising agencies in the Midwest, a world his artistic and literary son rejected as phony and inauthentic. See Belinda Rathbone, *Walker Evans: A Biography* (New York: Mariner Books, 1995).
7. See Deborah Bright, "Victory Gardens: The Public Landscape of Postwar America," *Views* (Spring 1990).
8. The 1952 publication of Henri Cartier-Bresson's *The Decisive Moment* also played an important role in advancing the rapid snapshot-style aesthetic.
9. Bill Owens, *Suburbia* (San Francisco: Straight Arrow Press, 1973), n.p.
10. As of 2010, there were 1,280 Superfund sites listed on the EPA's National Priority List, mostly concentrated in the Northeast and Upper Midwest. Assessing responsibility for the damage often sets off years of litigation with the designated polluters over who actually pays for the cleanup.
11. Another significant offshoot of *New Topographics*, not represented in this exhibition, was the 1994 founding of the Center for Land Use Interpretation (CLUI) by Matthew Coolidge (www.clui.org). CLUI's aim was to be an educational resource and databank for images of land use and development updated continually through a global network of participating photographers. Its projects to date have been interdisciplinary and eclectic, ranging from guided tours that are turned into online videos to books, exhibitions, and residencies. It remains to be seen how much of CLUI's original mission will be overtaken by Google Maps and other information-aggregating sites.
12. Hans Rudolf Reust, "Thomas Struth: Talks About His 'Paradise' Series," *Artforum* (May 2002), 151.

LANDSCAPE AS STAGE

Jan Howard

Joe Deal's *Kite, Chino Hills, California*, 1984 (fig. 25), captures an adult and child flying a kite in a bit of open space left in a new development. The driveway already in place makes for a convenient drive-up recreational area. Off in the distance to the right the residential growth that will soon cover this piece of land is visible through the atmospheric smog; off in the distance to the left are still untouched hills. Deal often found his picture, as here, at the edge of the built and unbuilt landscape. He was among ten artists included in *New Topographics: Photographs of a Man-Altered Landscape*, the influential 1975 exhibition that identified a tendency among photographers to acknowledge rather than deny the reality of development in the landscape.

Inspired by conceptual art, Deal generally developed his work in series, choosing a particular location and adhering to a strict visual formula. For the first ten years of his career his landscapes were square format, viewed from above, lacking a horizon, and empty of people (see pages 4, 12, 44, 90, and 91). *Kite, Chino Hills, California*, from the series "Subdividing the Inland Basin," marks a shift to the 4 × 5 camera's rectangle framing a sky and horizon. The series also includes people—evidence of a rapidly exploding community near the intersection of the Pomona and Orange freeways. As ordinary as these figures seem, they are exceptional. While photographers associated with *New Topographics* recorded the impact of humans on the landscape, the vast majority of their pictures are devoid of people. Deal, who often said he never wanted to see the pile of a particular kind of picture grow too large, continually explored ways to expand the definition of landscape photography. Placing people at the center of his landscapes did just that, opening up his pictures to a narrative reading and infusing them with an air of theatricality.

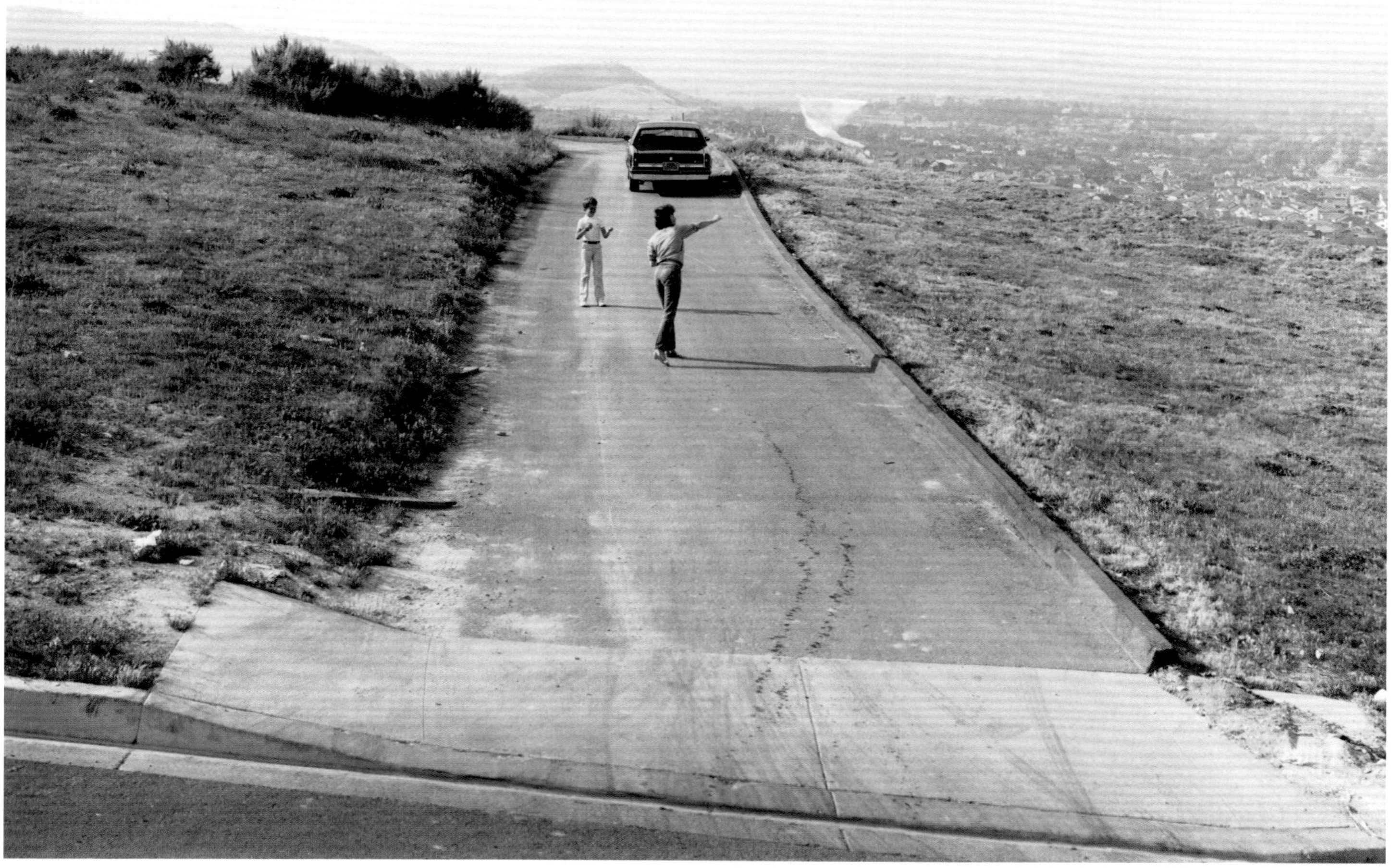

fig. 25 **Joe Deal** *Kite, Chino Hills, California*, 1984, from the series "Subdividing the Inland Basin," gelatin silver print, RISD Museum: Gift of the Artist 2003.104.2

fig. 26 **Anne Brigman** *Soul of the Blasted Pine*, 1908, from *Camera Work*, no. 25, January 1909, photogravure, 6⅛ × 8¼ in., Collection Susan Ehrens

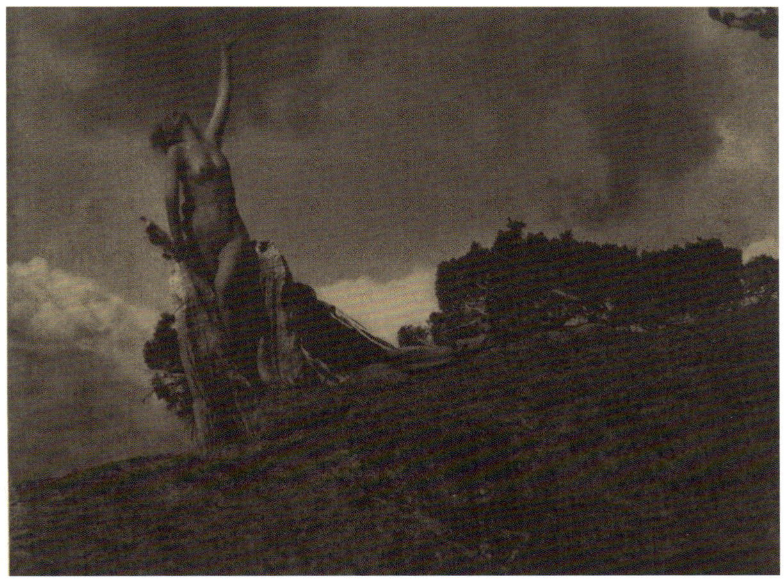

Such an approach had been used sporadically in photography throughout its history, perhaps most commonly in the Pictorialist era, when Anne Brigman choreographed nudes in the High Sierra, creating liberating gestures that countered the restrictions in women's lives at the time (see fig. 26).[1] In the 1980s theatricality took center stage, so to speak, as artists such as Cindy Sherman and Laurie Simmons—born into the first generation raised in a camera-based world of television, advertising, and film—situated obviously staged figures (real and surrogate) in charged settings. At the same time, artists such as Tina Barney, Philip-Lorca diCorcia, and Jeff Wall created photographs in which the featured people might have been staged in the site but still bore a plausible, if sometimes ambiguous, relationship to reality. Recent landscape photography with dramatic or narrative ends, in keeping with shifts in contemporary photography more generally, often explores this tension between fiction and reality.[2] *Kite, Chino Hills, California*, is not at all fabricated, but that doesn't mean its driveway is not a stage. Deal understood the tension at the edge of development well enough to be prepared for the scene that played out in front of him. The exhilaration of kite flying and the promise of a new home juxtaposed with a road to nowhere under a polluted sky offered a compelling narrative with no need for intervention. Whether fabricated or not, contemporary American landscape photography, when it places figures on the stage of the outdoors, reflects our complicated relationship with both authenticity and the landscape, telling compelling stories about nature, artifice, and life as we know it—or seek to understand it—today.

Gregory Crewdson, among the most prominent artists associated with fabricating photographs, has described himself as an "American realist landscape photographer" even though he creates pictures with characters, crew, and equipment one would expect on location for a major film. Scouting for a place to stage local people is a key step in the construction of his photographs, in which the physical characteristics of the landscape are essential to suggesting psychological states.[3] The large-scale color photographs in his series "Beneath the Roses," for example, were made in and around beleaguered small

fig. 27 **Gregory Crewdson** *Untitled* (Cement Canal), 2007, color inkjet print, 58½×89½ in., Courtesy Gagosian Gallery, New York

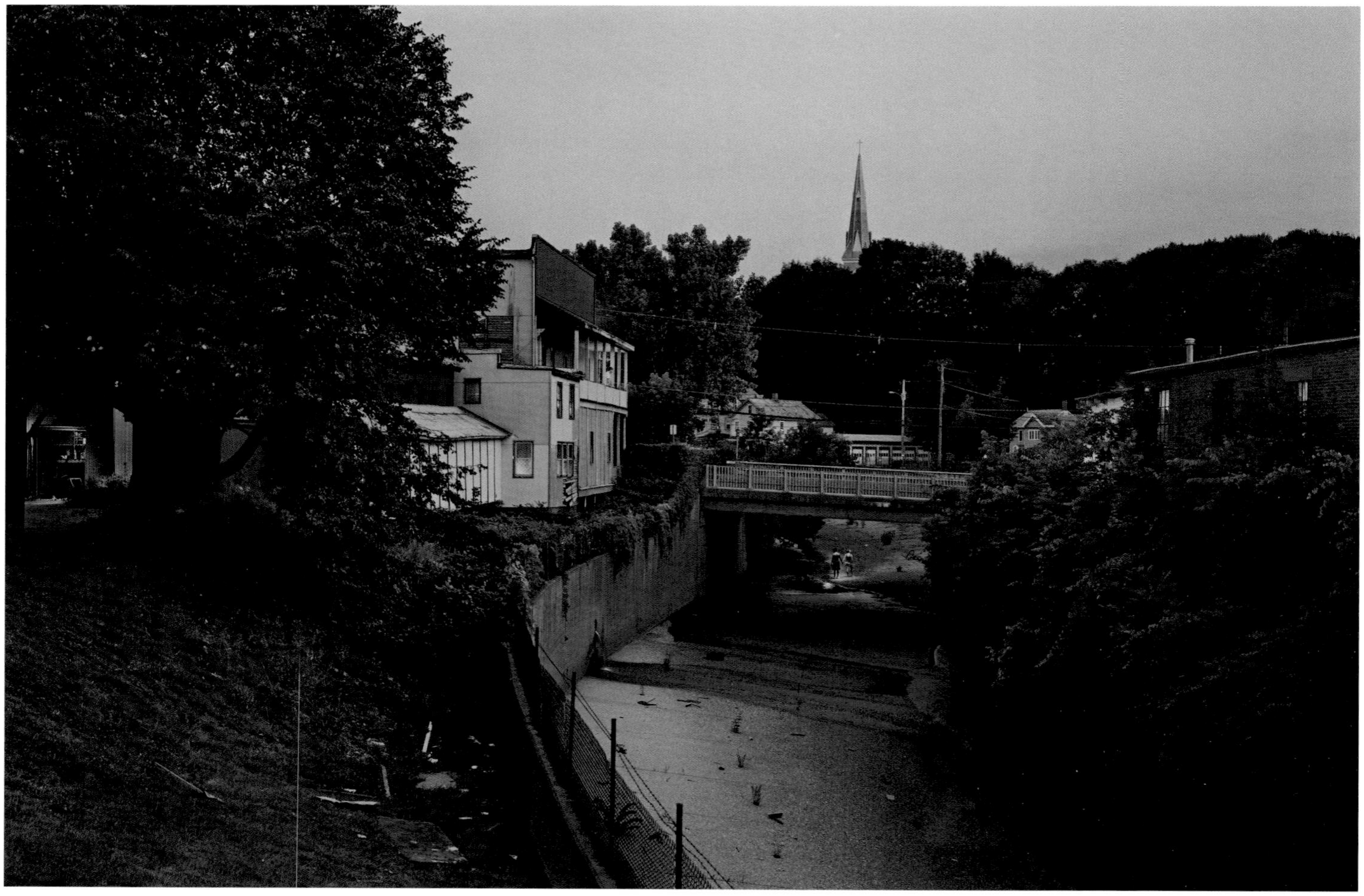

towns under a darkening, portentous sky. In *Untitled* (Cement Canal), 2007 (fig. 27), the iconic New England church steeple is still a focal point of the town, but a trash-strewn storm culvert rather than a bucolic stream runs through it. In the distance a couple holding hands walks through the canal, spotlit in an incongruously idyllic vignette. A man looks out from a balcony above them. Each element foretells ill fate, reflecting the disquieting narrative within once-thriving small-town America.

A similar rust-belt landscape provides the context for Justine Kurland's narrative series "Runaway Girls."[4] Rooted in historical landscape painting and photography, Kurland's narratives are suggested by the landscape itself.[5] The artist drove cross-country in search of settings for her fictive story about fugitive teenagers. Once she chose her location, she recruited local adolescent models, asked them to envision how the picture would play out, and documented their unpredictable responses. The neglected space under a New Jersey highway overpass was an ideal spot for three girls to act out *Smoke Bombs*, 2000 (pl. 47). The figurative grouping recalls paintings of pastoral scenes, and the danger of the girls' pursuit in this dicey no man's land is temporarily suspended in the hazy romantic fantasy of escape. The strong light streaming across the scene and the overall beauty of the composition suggests a desire to pursue the sublime even in the most degraded landscapes.

Like Kurland, Alec Soth develops a narrative storyline that often stems from exploring a particular place or kind of landscape. For his "Broken Manual" series, which centers on individuals who have dropped out of society to live in the wilderness, Soth traveled across the United States in search of their incredibly challenging off-the-grid environments.[6] Many of the images in this series picture inventive dwellings, but where Soth was able to find the inhabitants he coaxed them into the compositions. In *2008_08z10031*, 2008 (fig. 28), a small figure silhouetted within a crudely made geodesic dome atop a boulder stands overlooking a vast surreal desert landscape of rock, cactus, and a bare tree. The eccentricity, harshness, and beauty of the California desert, where this man had lived for many years when Soth photographed him, speak to the complexity of his alternative existence. With his back toward the viewer, he recalls the awe-inspired figures overlooking the vast and unknowable landscapes in Casper David Friedrich's 19th-century paintings, and yet perhaps this brutal landscape is more reassuring than the "civilized" one he left behind.

Intermingling portraits and still lifes with landscapes, Laura McPhee connects place to individual lives and personal stories. Her series "River of No Return," set in Idaho's Sawtooth Valley, addresses complex environmental questions about living in an area

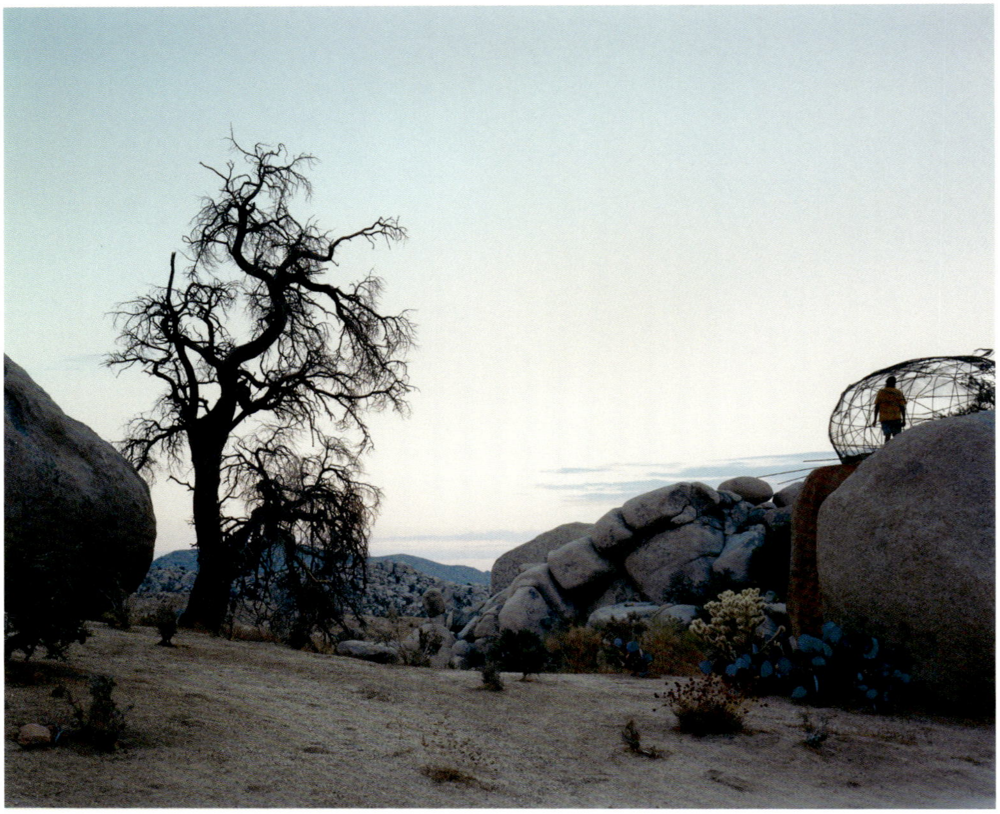

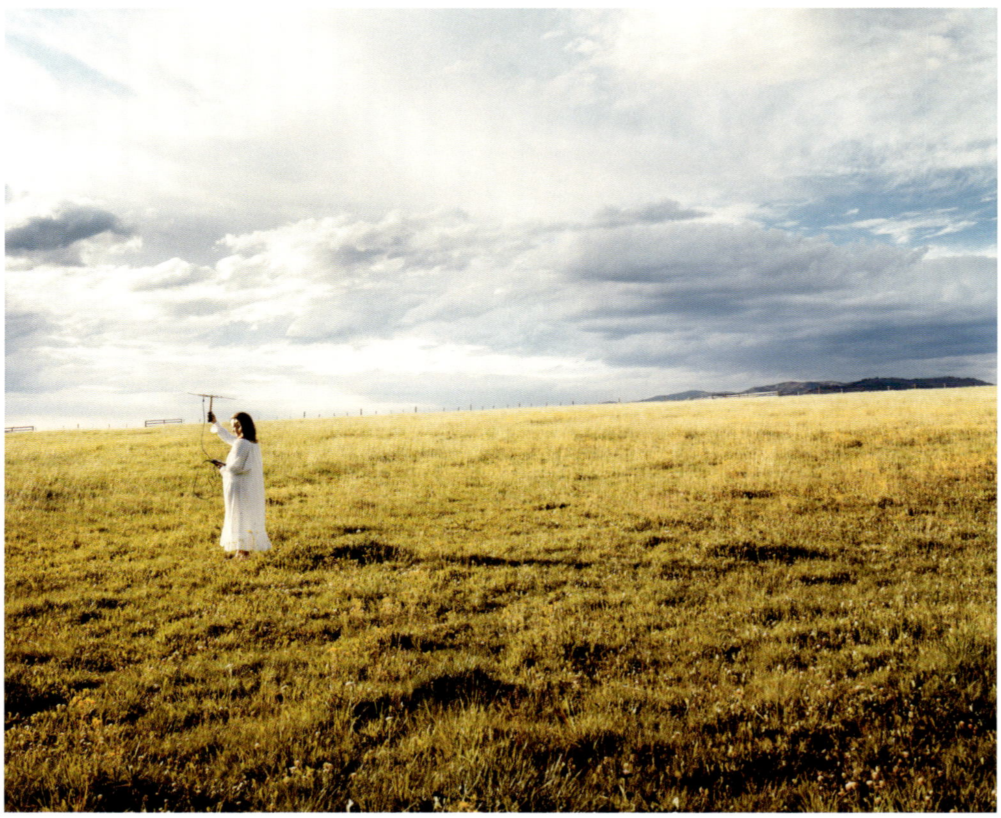

fig. 28 **Alec Soth** *2008_08zl0031*, 2008, from the series "Broken Manual," color inkjet print, 32×40 in., RISD Museum: Mary Ann Lippitt Acquisition Fund 2012.39

fig. 29 **Laura McPhee** *Judy Tracking Radio-Collared Wolves from Her Yard, Summer Range, H-Hook Ranch, Custer County, Idaho*, 2004, from the series "River of No Return," color chromogenic print, 30×40 in., RISD Museum: Purchased with funds donated by Donald Stanton and Helen M. Danforth Acquisition Fund 2008.54

where human occupancy is barely sustained. *Judy Tracking Radio-Collared Wolves from Her Yard, Summer Range, H-Hook Ranch, Custer County, Idaho*, 2004 (fig. 29), gives away the mystery of the image in its title, but on first encounter one still imagines that McPhee must have invented this mystical woman in a white nightgown, standing alone in a golden field and raising an instrument to the expansive sky. Rather, Judy is entirely real, part of a family of scientists McPhee got to know and photograph. The pictured ritual is Judy's regular morning chore—it keeps the family and animals safe from wolves, which were controversially reintroduced to the area. Struck by the enigma and drama of this act, McPhee had Judy restage it for her camera.[7] While the image speaks to daily life in the Sawtooth Valley and to political issues surrounding the management of the land, it also suggests that our relationship to the land could still be sacred.

Capturing slices of life, as Deal did, is about both knowing where to look and being ready for what French photographer Henri Cartier-Bresson called the "decisive moment" when it happens. Street photography, which dominated the medium from just after World War I into the 1970s, made use of the hand-held 35mm camera to quickly make pictures, generally catching people unaware and producing images seemingly without artifice. Justin Kimball's experience as a street photographer taught him to anticipate people's actions but Kimball combines his street skills with a slower, medium-format camera to both capture reality and make the viewer question whether the result is in fact reality. Kimball's series "Where We Find Ourselves" explores the fantasy of finding wilderness in state and national parks and instead finding only other people looking for it too. *Deep Hole, New Hampshire*, 2002 (pl. 48), captures light filtering through the trees as a dozen young men and women distribute themselves among rocky outcroppings, poised for adventure in the water below. The scene seems familiar and resonant. We suspect it must be staged as we recognize its historical precedent in the quiet drama of Thomas Eakins's swimmers. Indeed, that reference is exactly what drew Kimball to the picture as it played out in front of him, along with the palpable sense of elation in the youths' encounter with the landscape, no matter the deteriorating state of the site due to its heavy use.[8]

Long interested in the subject of landscape and its relationship to community, Catherine Opie chose one of most ubiquitous and recognizable landscape constructions in America for her series "Football Landscapes." Seen through her eyes, the football field becomes an outdoor public stage where communities gather and ideas of masculinity, camaraderie, teamwork, and leadership play out. The "Football Landscapes" were shot during games on high-school football fields across the United States, but they do not record exceptional feats or plays in the game as one might expect. Rather, Opie edited her pictures to foreground the choreography that metaphorically spoke to the boys' relationships to each other and the arena in which they perform.[9] In *Football Landscape #12 (Alice vs. W. B. Ray, Corpus Christi, TX)*, 2008 (fig. 30), Opie's distant position behind the goalpost seems to emphasize the enormity of the stage and, accordingly, the expectations for and among these adolescents as they play out the competitive glamour and spectacle of the sport.

The path from the playing field to the battlefield is often short, and it would be no surprise if some of Opie's subjects found themselves pictured in An-My Lê's "29 Palms." Lê's series appears to document soldiers deployed in the Middle East, but instead records staged maneuvers at the Marine training camp in California for which her series is titled. The harshness of the intense light and mountainous desert terrain and the documentary style of her black-and-white prints all sustain the fiction that these soldiers are in Iraq and Afghanistan rather than California. In making *29 Palms: Captain Folsom*, 2003–2004 (fig. 31), and other works in the series, Lê distanced herself from her subjects both physically and emotionally. Shooting with a large-format camera from a height and remove that captures the vast theater of activity in the landscape, she describes the scene with remarkable yet cool and detached detail. Photographing staged combat, Lê ultimately stages a dialogue about a distant war with huge consequences for American culture and lives.

Elsewhere in this catalogue Douglas Nickel describes the evolution of landscape as a genre, beginning with the removal of the figure from painted compositions in the 1500s. Today, contemporary American landscape photography is redefining the genre yet again by reintroducing the figure. The landscape, so fraught—as Deborah Bright describes in her essay in these pages—with environmental, cultural, and political issues, is both a stage for figures acting out their relationships with nature and a central character in its own drama. The photographs discussed here begin to suggest the rich territory that has opened up for American landscape photography with the inclusion of the figure, especially as it mines the tension between fiction and reality. Now, we can only await landscape photography's next act.

NOTES

1. See Susan Ehrens, *A Poetic Vision: The Photographs of Anne Brigman* (Santa Barbara, CA: Santa Barbara Museum of Art, 1995).
2. See Susan Bright, *Art Photography Now* (New York: Aperture, 2005), and Eric Lutz, *An Orchestrated Vision: The Theater of Contemporary Photography* (St. Louis, MO: St. Louis Art Museum, 2012).
3. Stephan Berg, "The Dark Side of the American Dream," in *Gregory Crewdson 1985–2005* (Ostfildern-Ruit: Hatje Cantz Verlag, 2005), 11.
4. Kurland was a graduate student of Crewdson's at Yale University, where Collier Schorr, Laurie Simmons, and others who construct imagery for the camera also taught.
5. Kurland described her process during a talk at RISD on February 28, 2012, as part of the Photography Department's T. C. Colley Lecture series. See also Meghan Dailey, "A Thousand Words: Justine Kurland," *Artforum* (April 2000), 119.
6. The project began as a commission from the High Museum in Atlanta, "Picturing the South," but soon evolved into "Broken Manual." See Siri Engberg, ed., *From Here to There: Alec Soth's America* (Minneapolis: Walker Art Center, 2010).
7. See Joanne Lukitsh, "Place Above All Else: Laura McPhee's *River of No Return*," and McPhee's interview with Dabney Hailey in *River of No Return: Photographs of Laura McPhee* (New Haven: Yale University Press, 2008).
8. In conversation with the author, April 4, 2012.
9. In conversation with the author at the exhibition *Catherine Opie: High School Football*, Mitchell-Innes & Nash, New York, March 9, 2011.

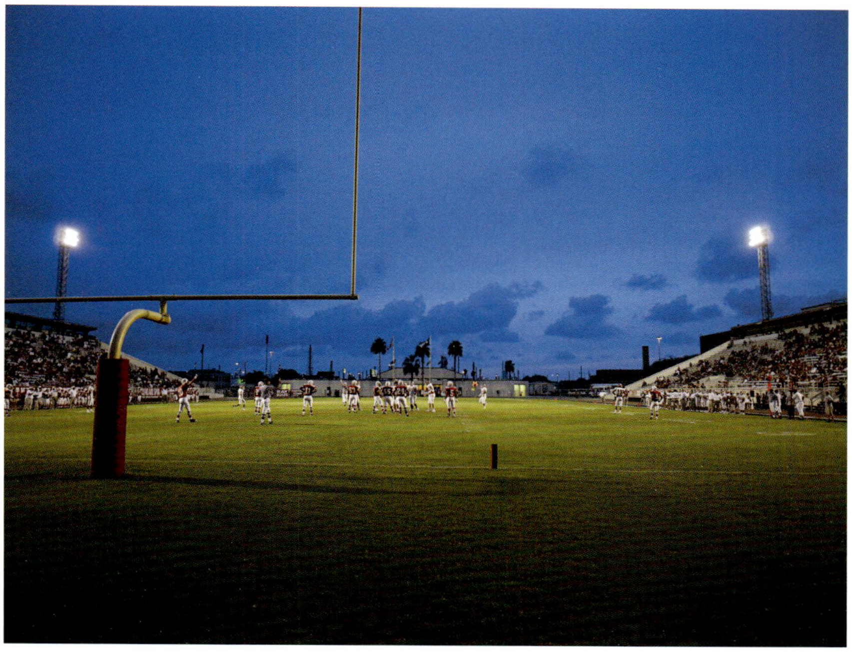

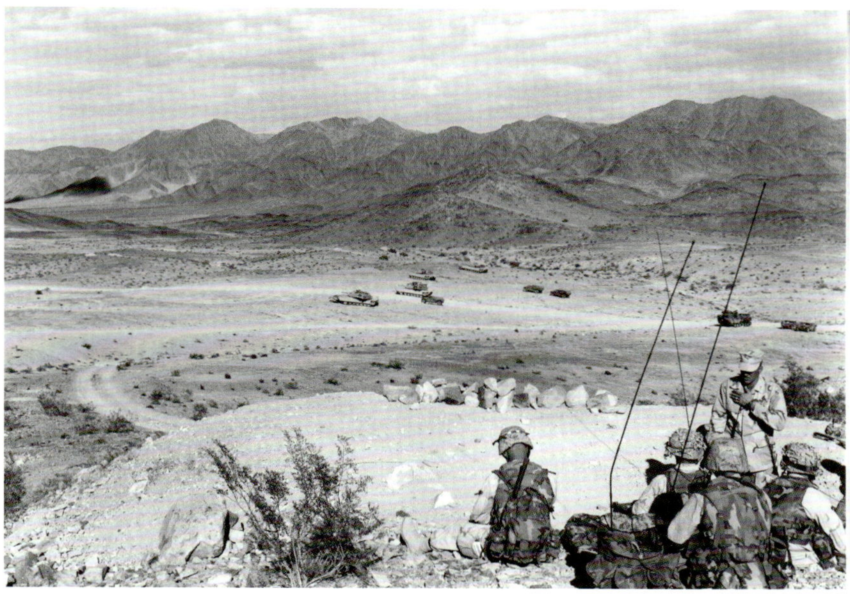

fig. 30 Catherine Opie *Football Landscape #12 (Alice vs. W. B. Ray, Corpus Christi, TX)*, 2008, color chromogenic print, 48×64 in., Courtesy of the Artist and Mitchell-Innes & Nash

fig. 31 An-My Lê *29 Palms: Captain Folsom*, 2003-2004, gelatin silver print, 26×37½ in., RISD Museum: Helen M. Danforth Acquisition Fund 2007.7.2

PLATES

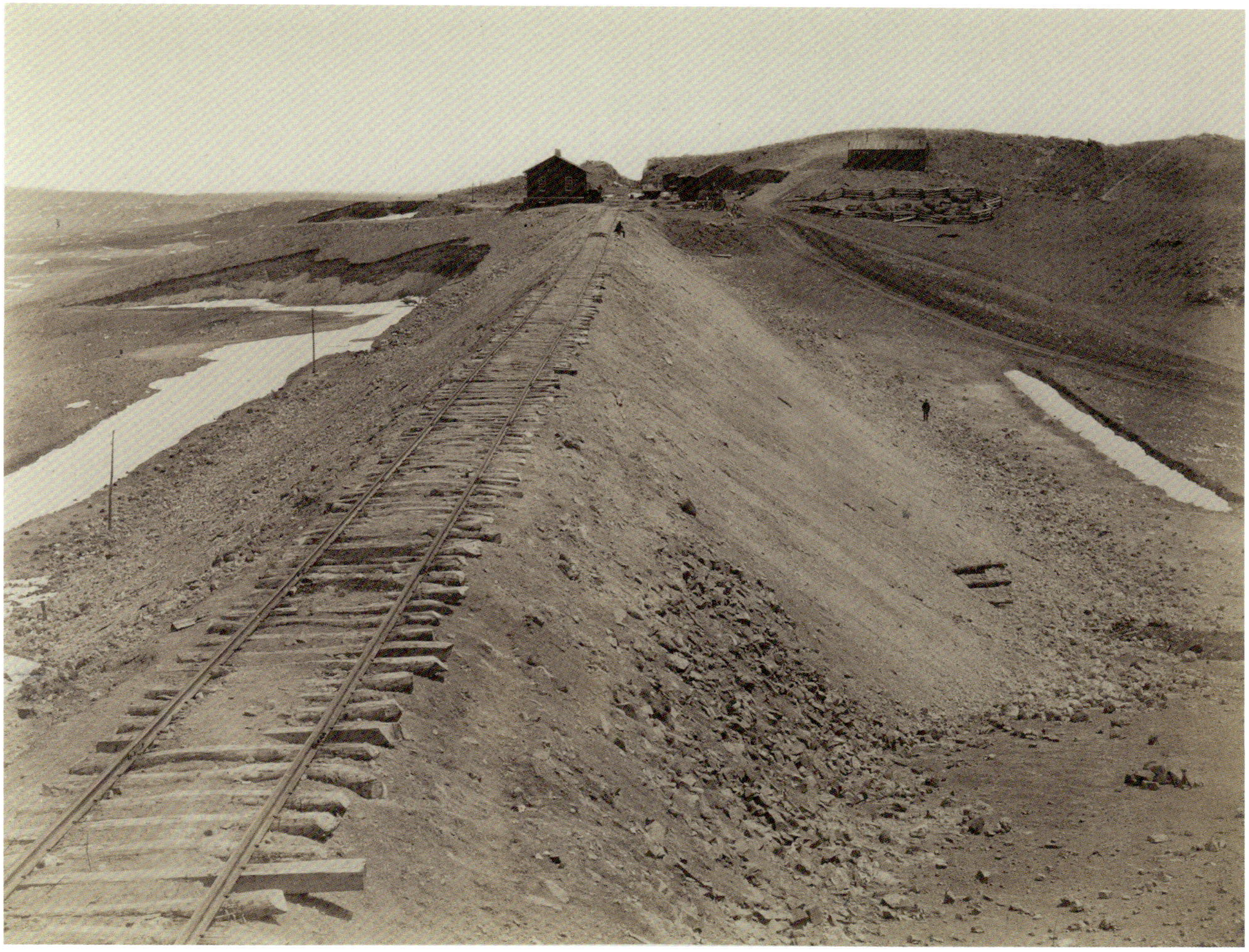

pl. 1 A. J. Russell, *No. 2, Granite Cañon from the Water Tank*, 1869

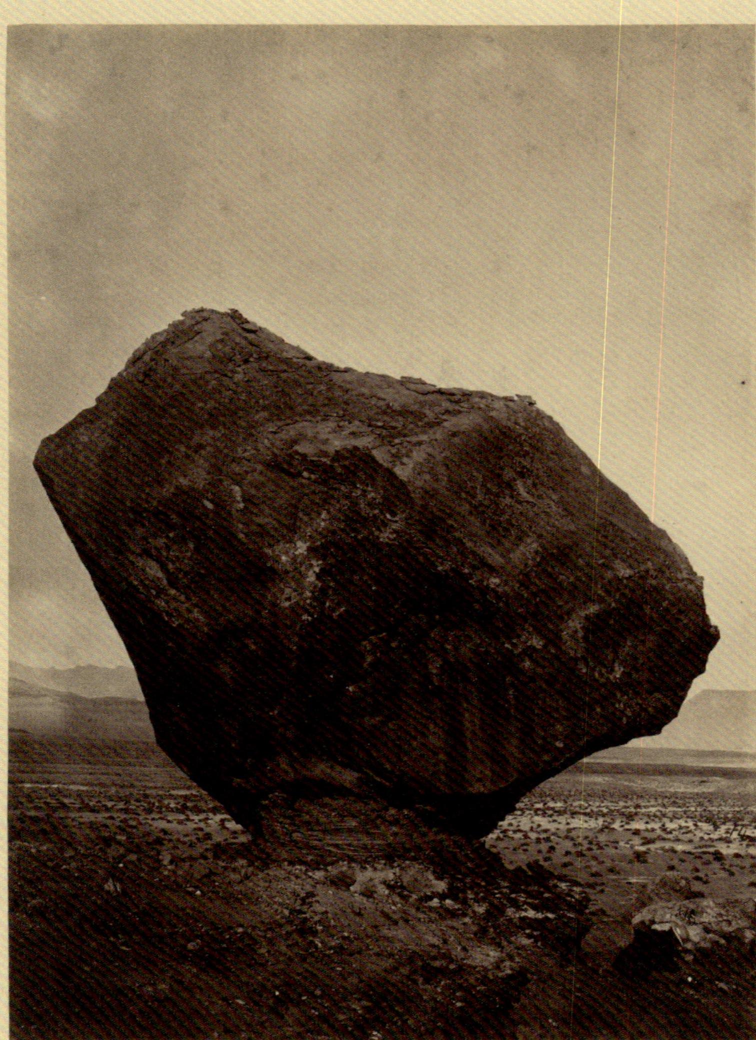

PERCHED ROCK, ROCKER CREEK, ARIZONA.

pl. 2 William H. Bell, *Perched Rock, Rocker Creek, Arizona*, 1872

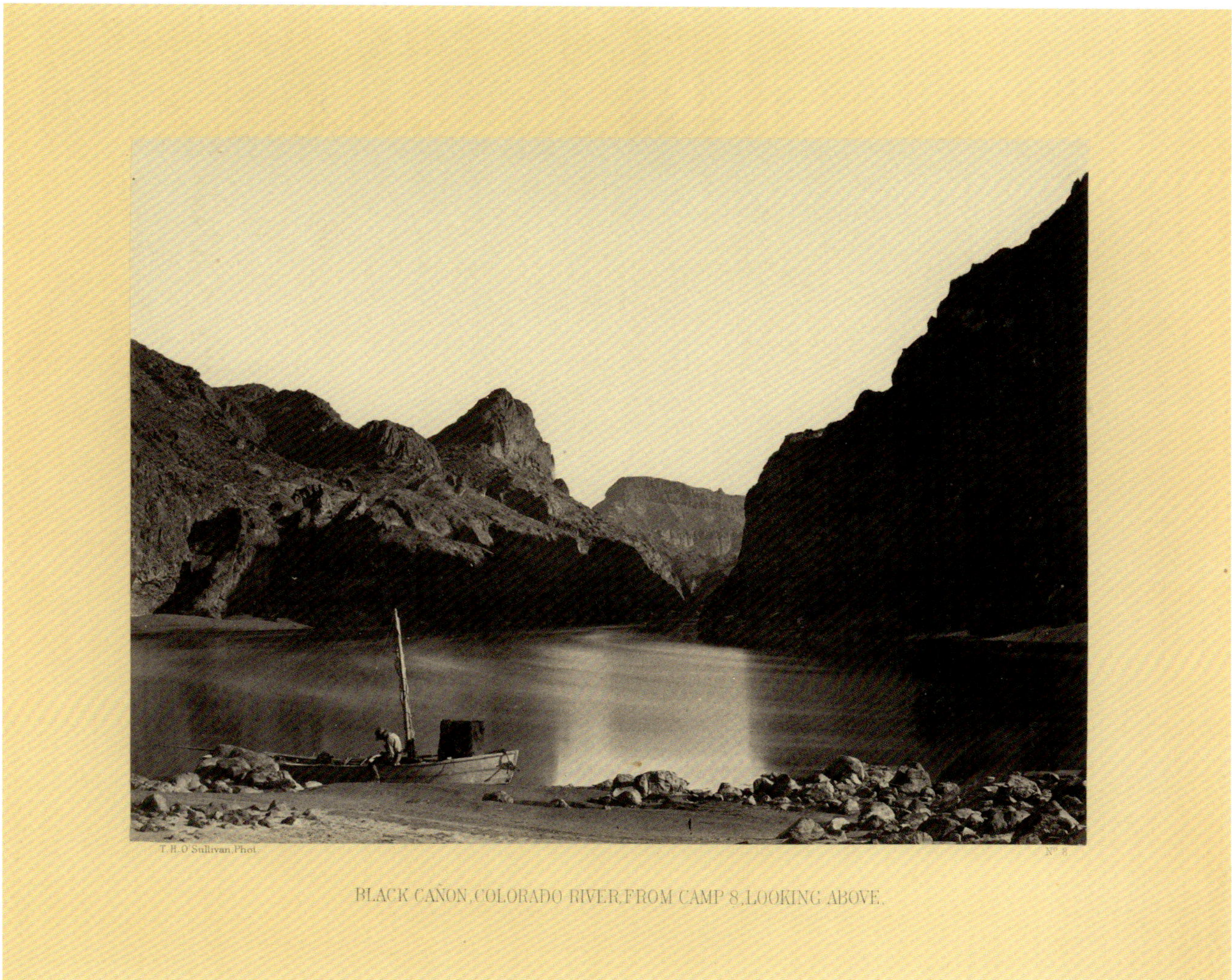

pl. 3 Timothy O'Sullivan, *Black Cañon, Colorado River, from Camp 8, Looking Above*, 1871

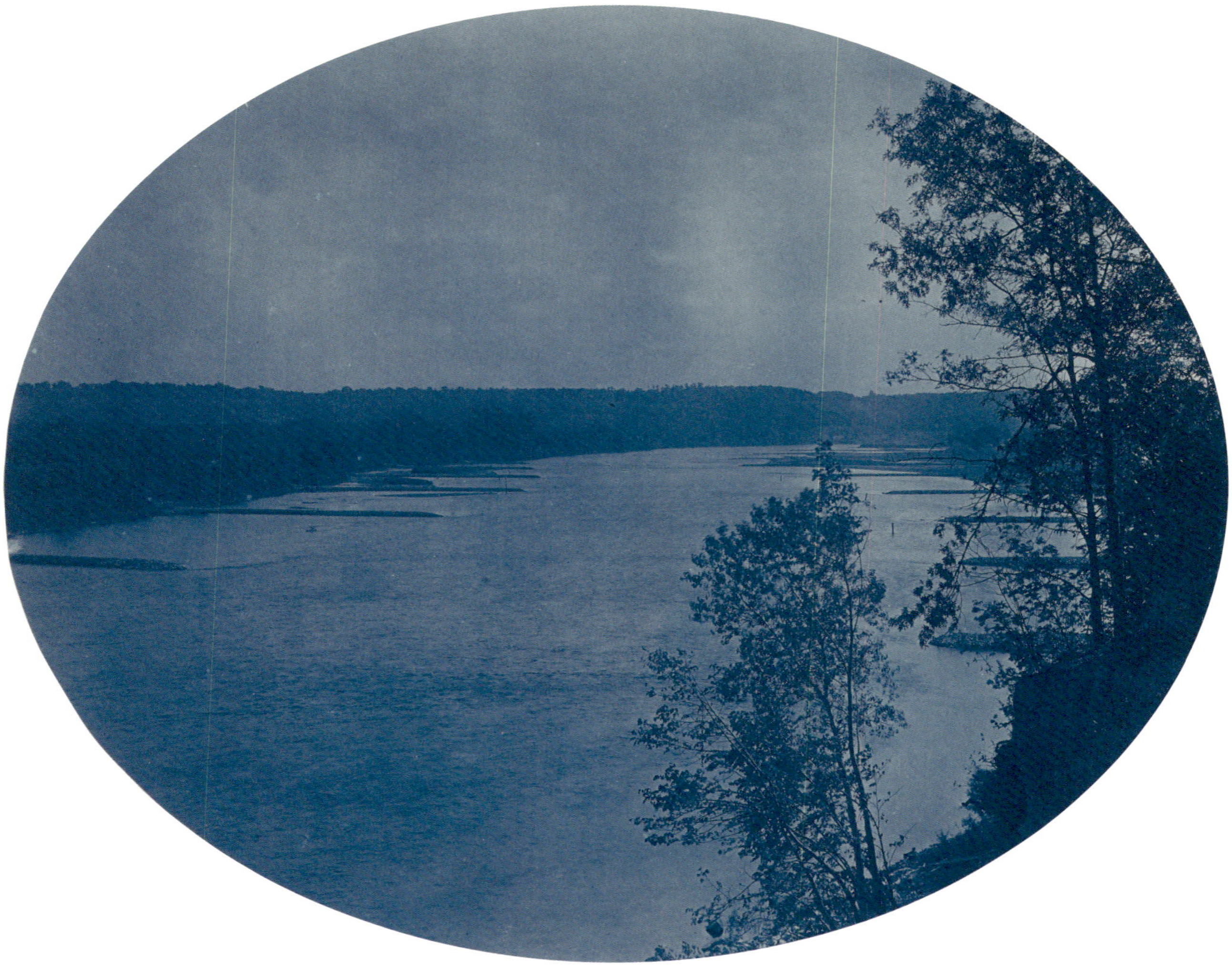

pl. 4 Henry Bosse, *From Foot of Boulanger Slough Looking Downstream*, 1891

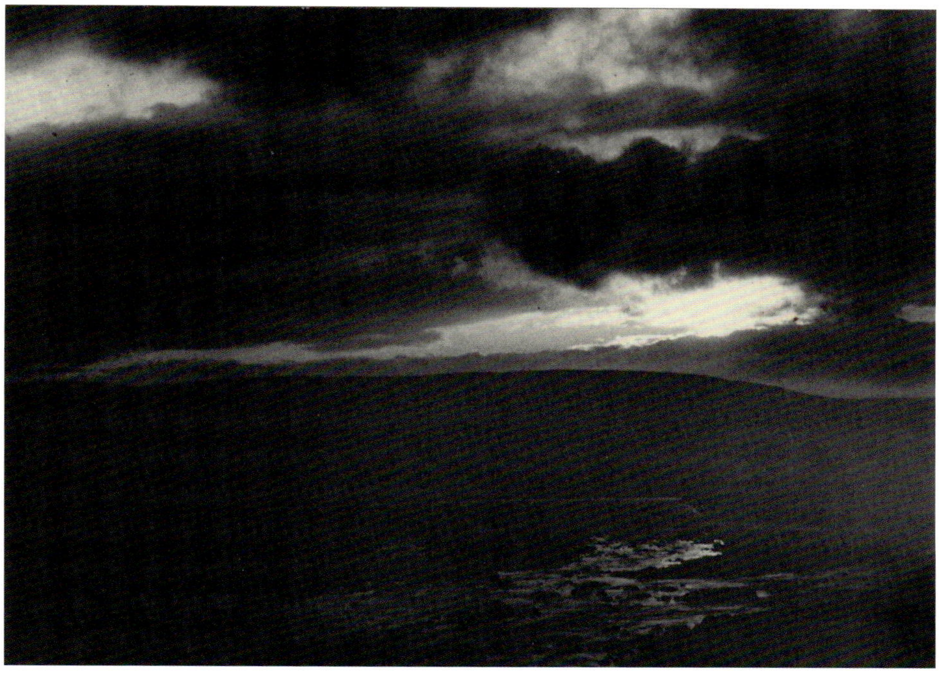

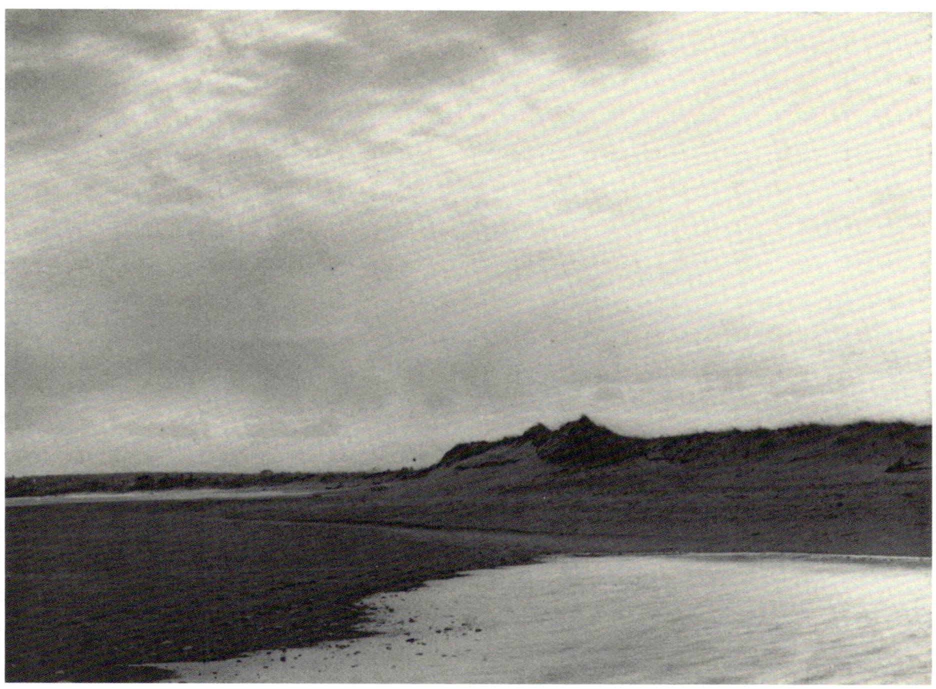

pls. 5 and 6 Christopher Grant La Farge, *Bay at Sunset* and *Wesquage Beach Inlet*, ca. 1900

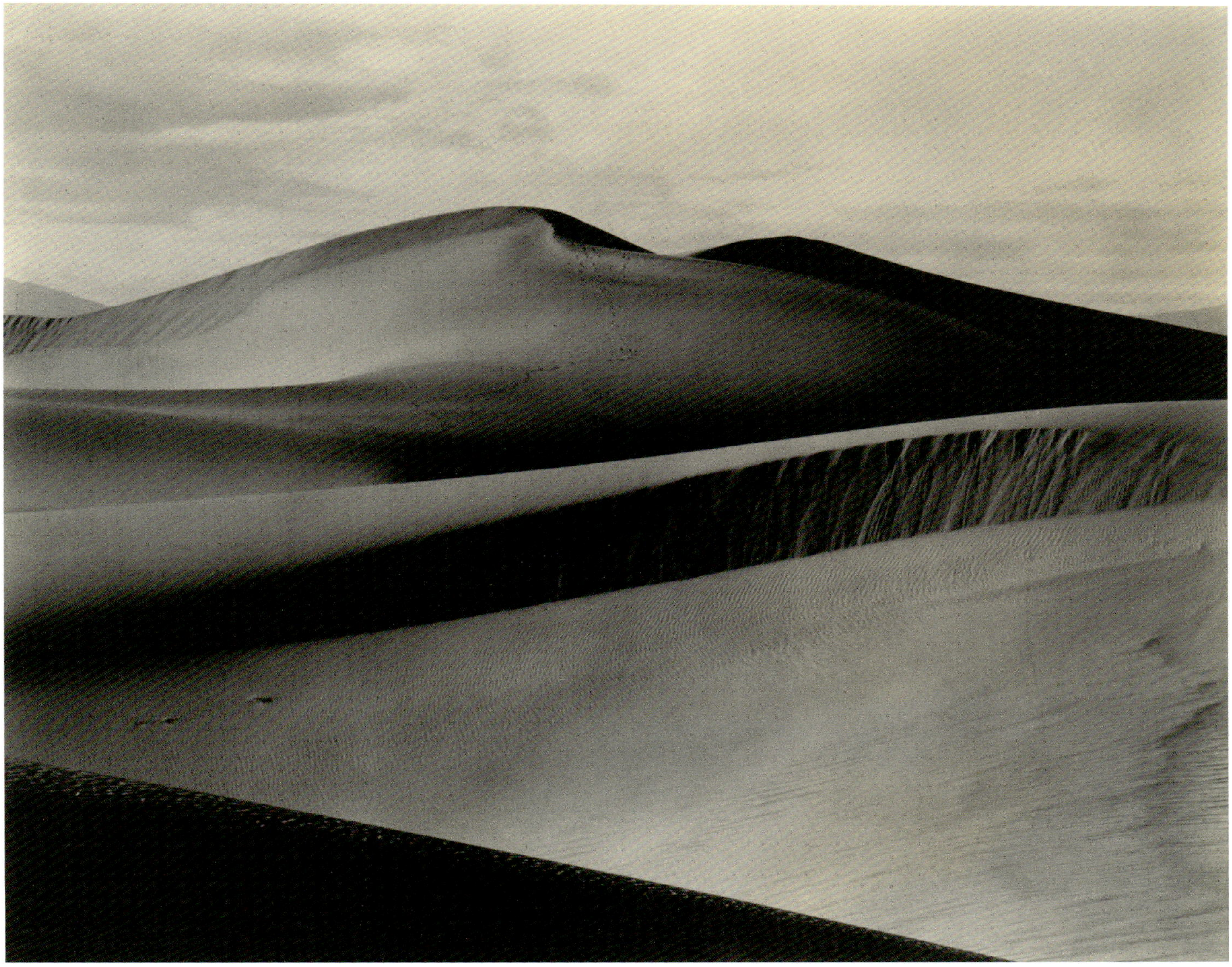

pl. 7 Willard Van Dyke, *Death Valley Dunes*, 1930

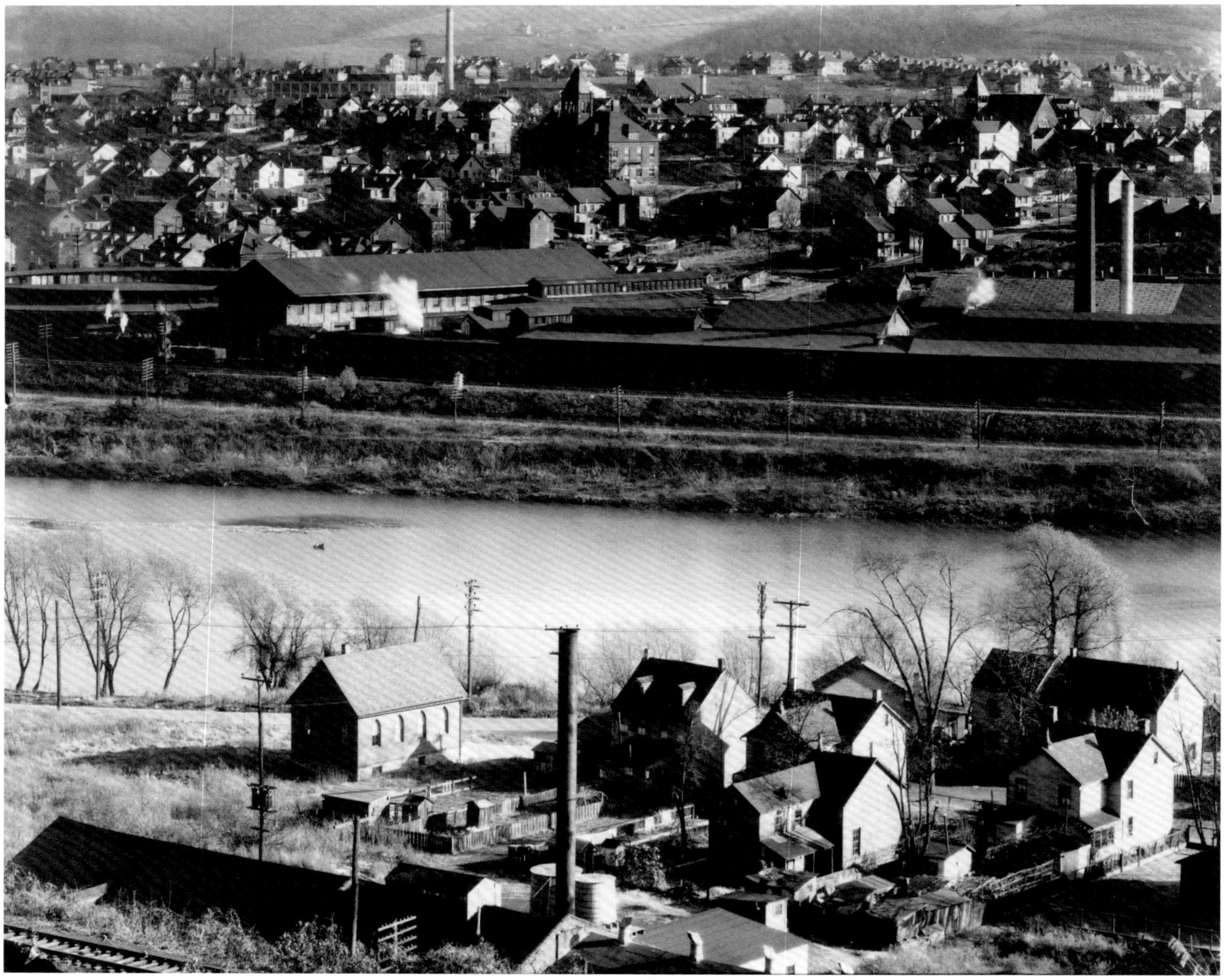

pl. 8 Walker Evans, *View of Easton, Pennsylvania*, 1936

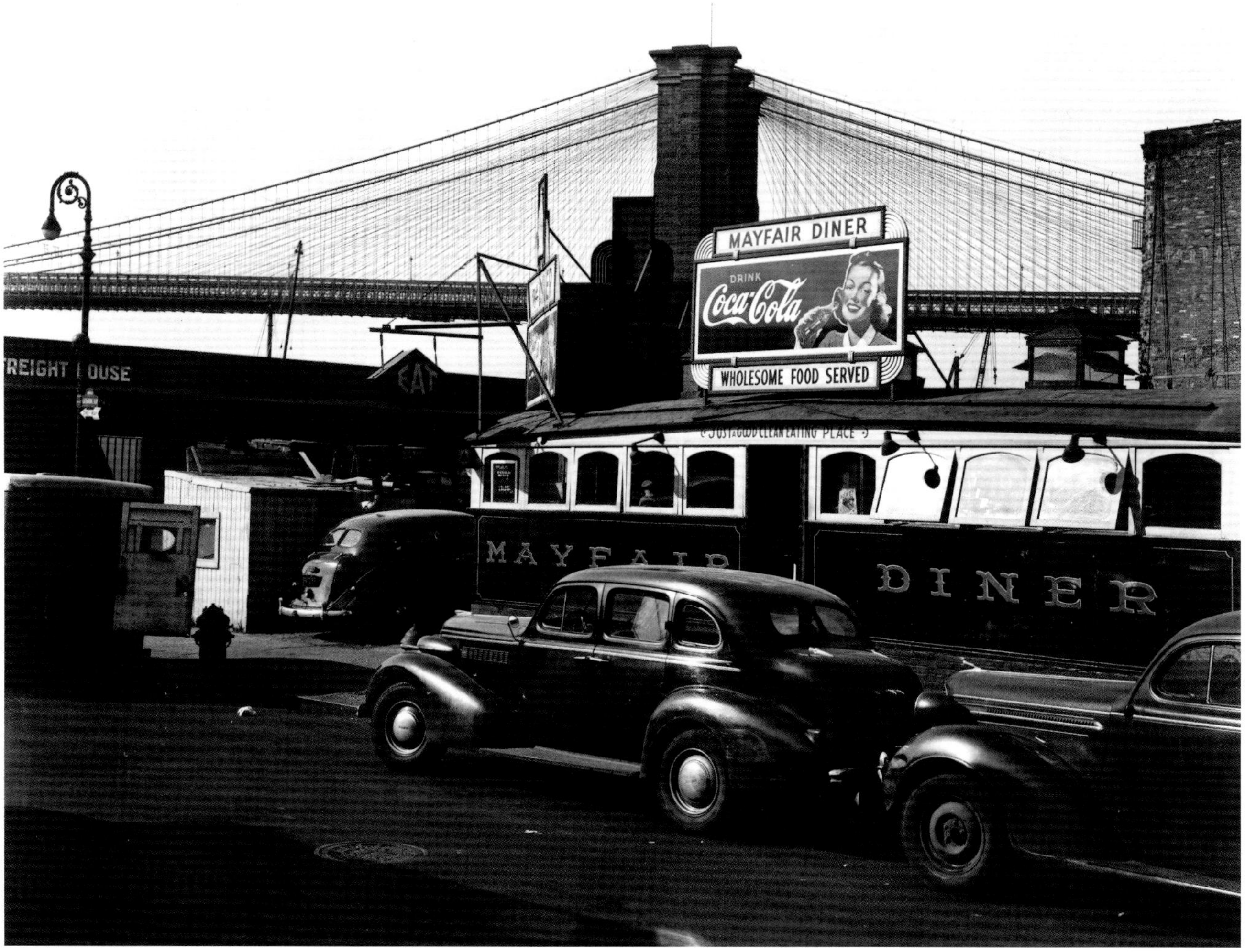

pl. 9 Brett Weston, Untitled (Brooklyn Bridge), 1943

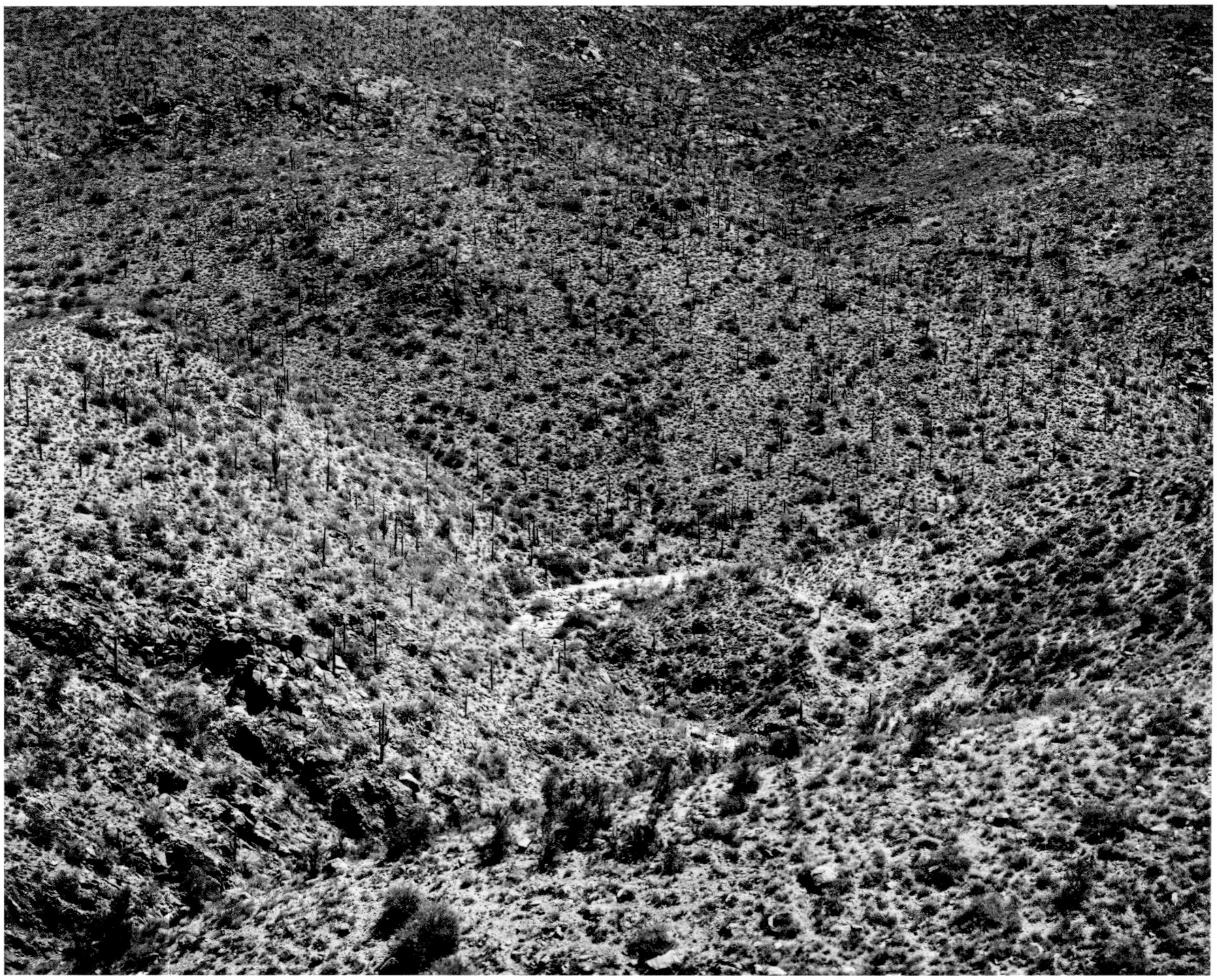

pl.10 Frederick Sommer, *Arizona Landscape*, 1943

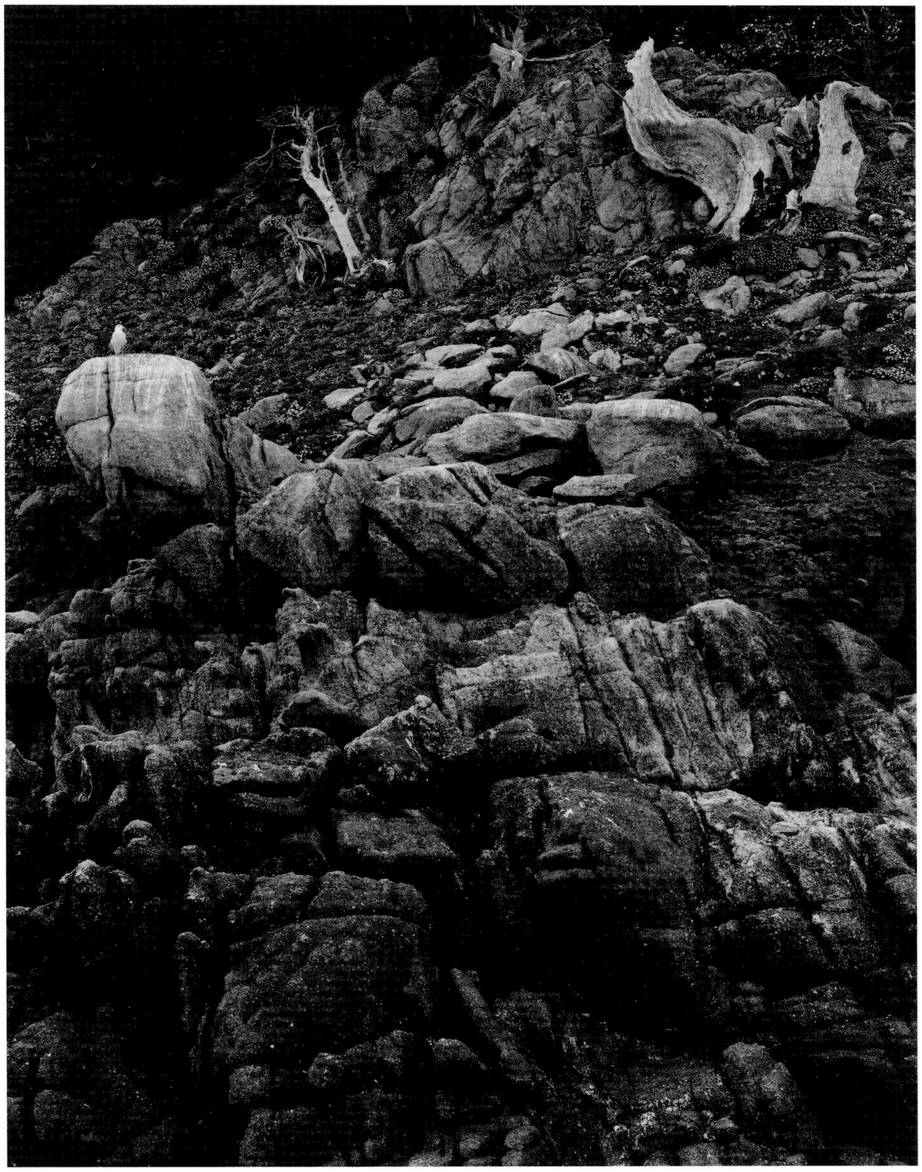

pl. 11 Edward Weston, *Cliff with Seagull, Point Lobos*, 1946

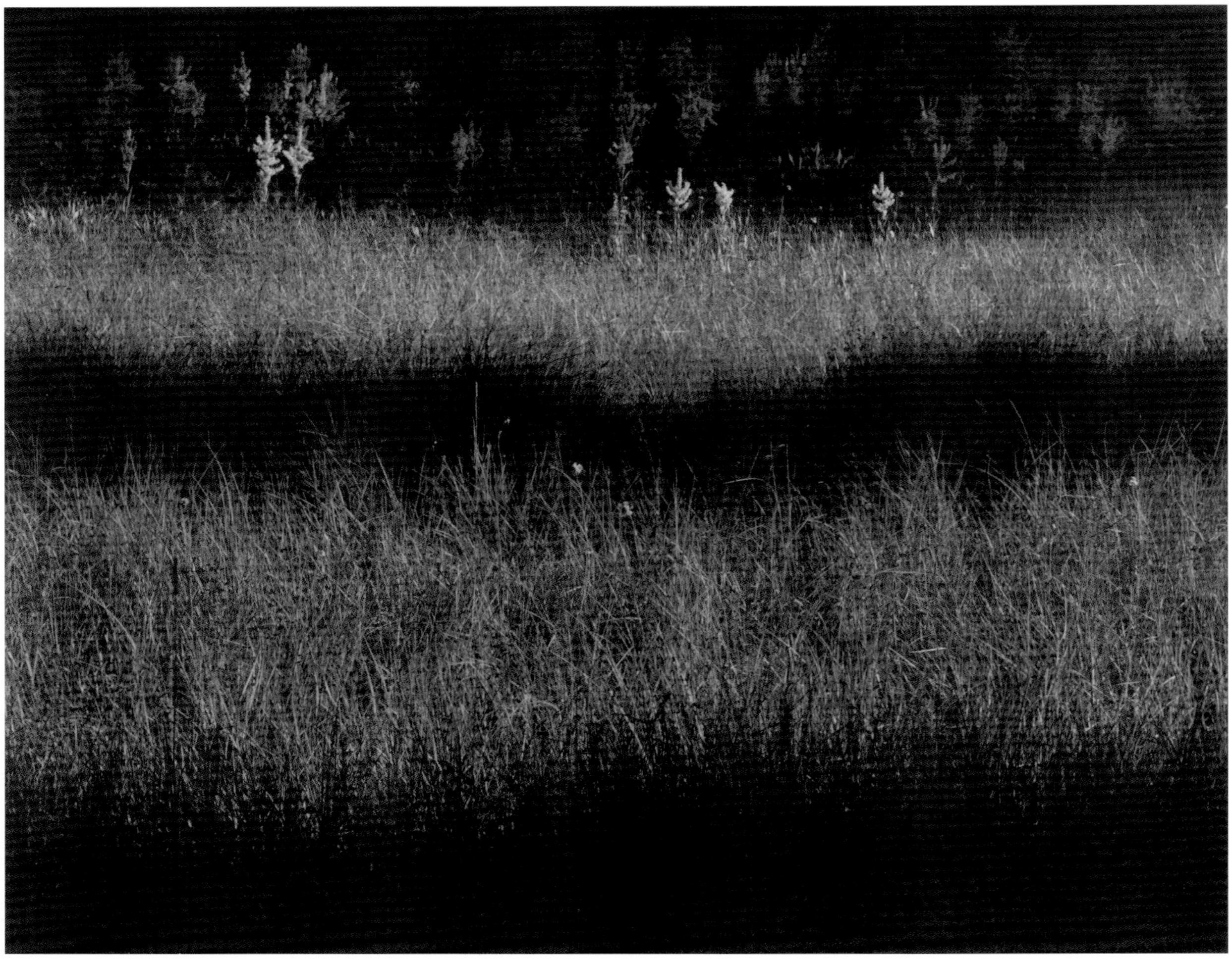

pl.12 Oliver Gagliani, *Untitled*, 1948

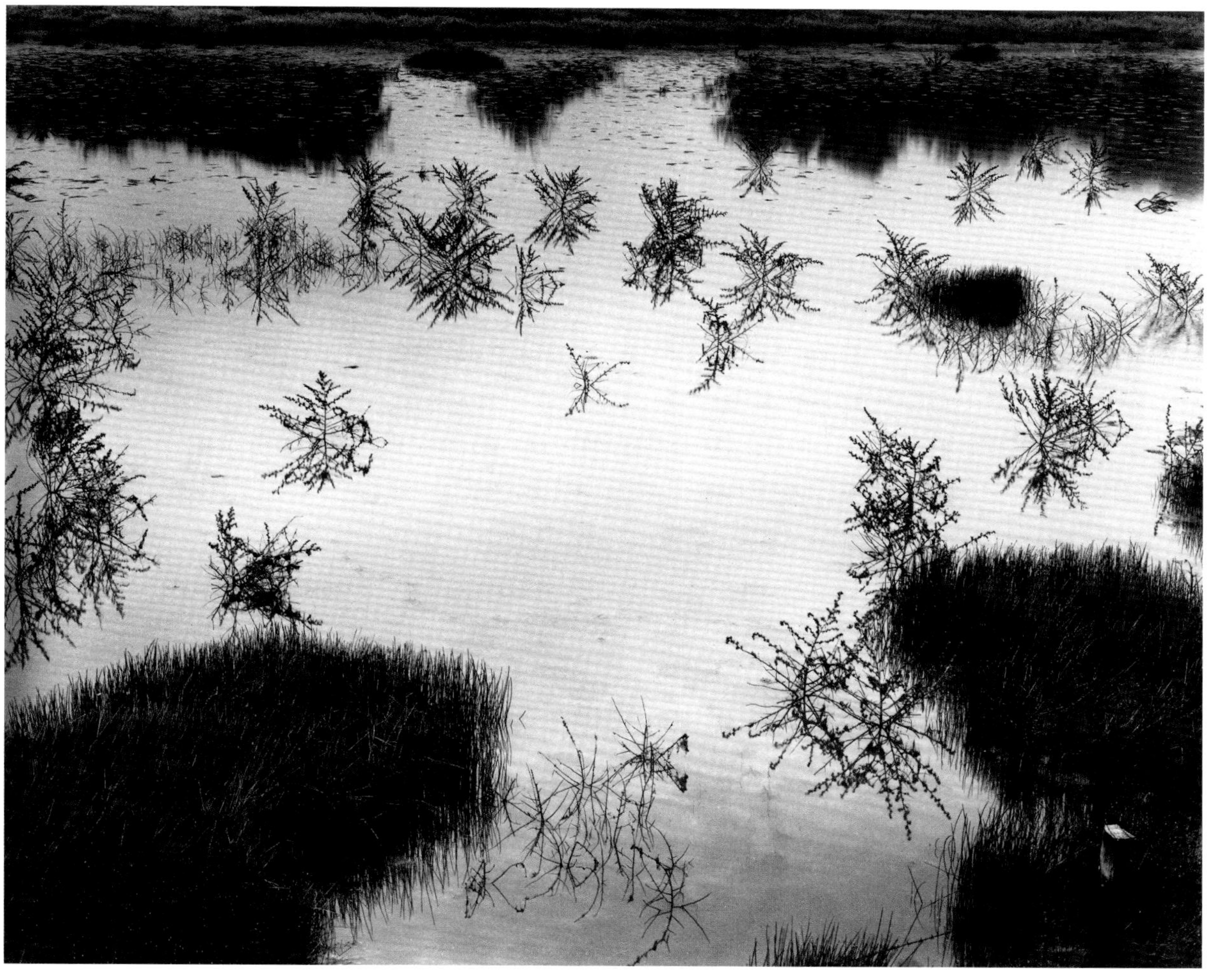

pl. 13 Brett Weston, *Pond*, 1950

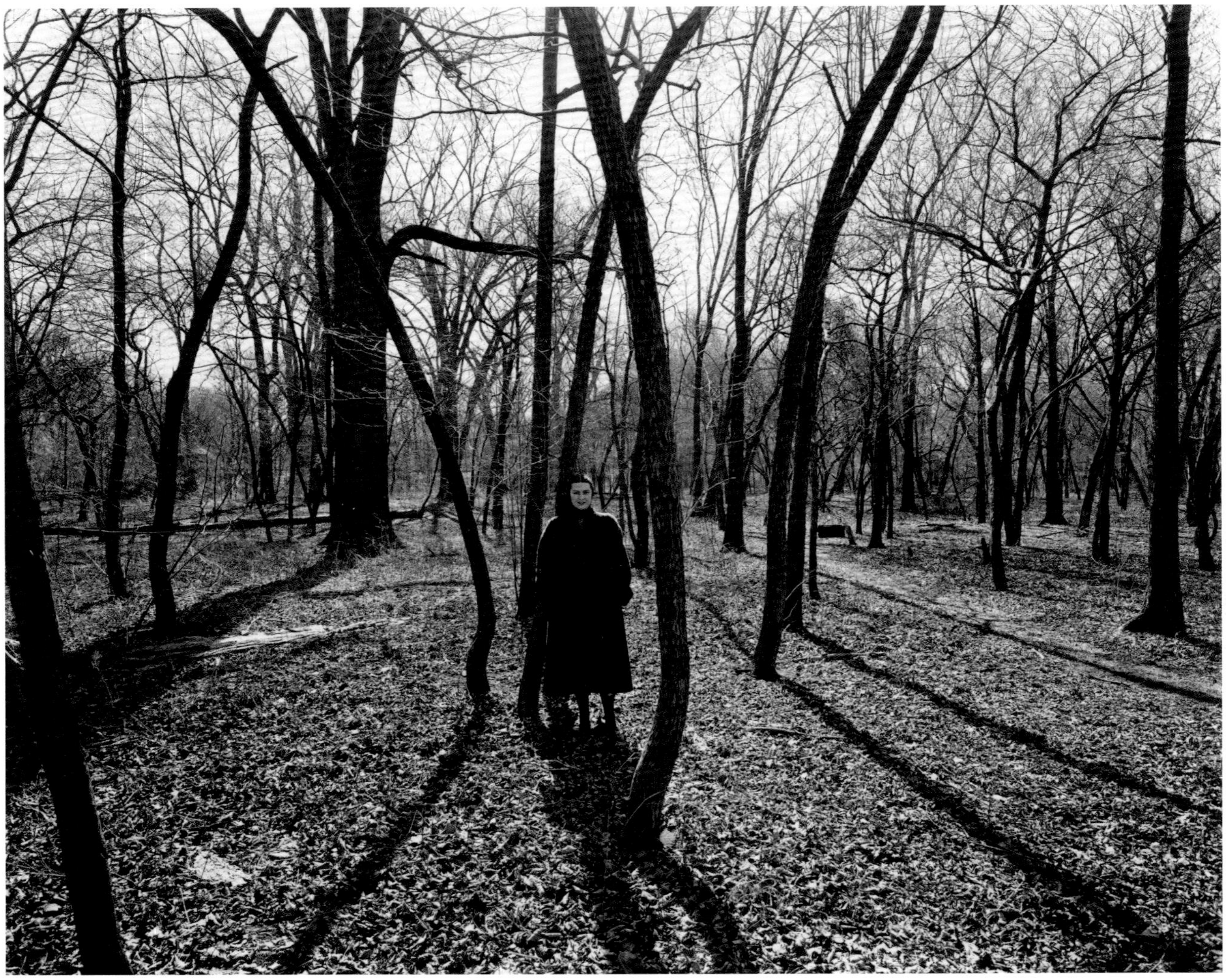

pl.14 Harry Callahan, *Eleanor, Chicago*, 1952

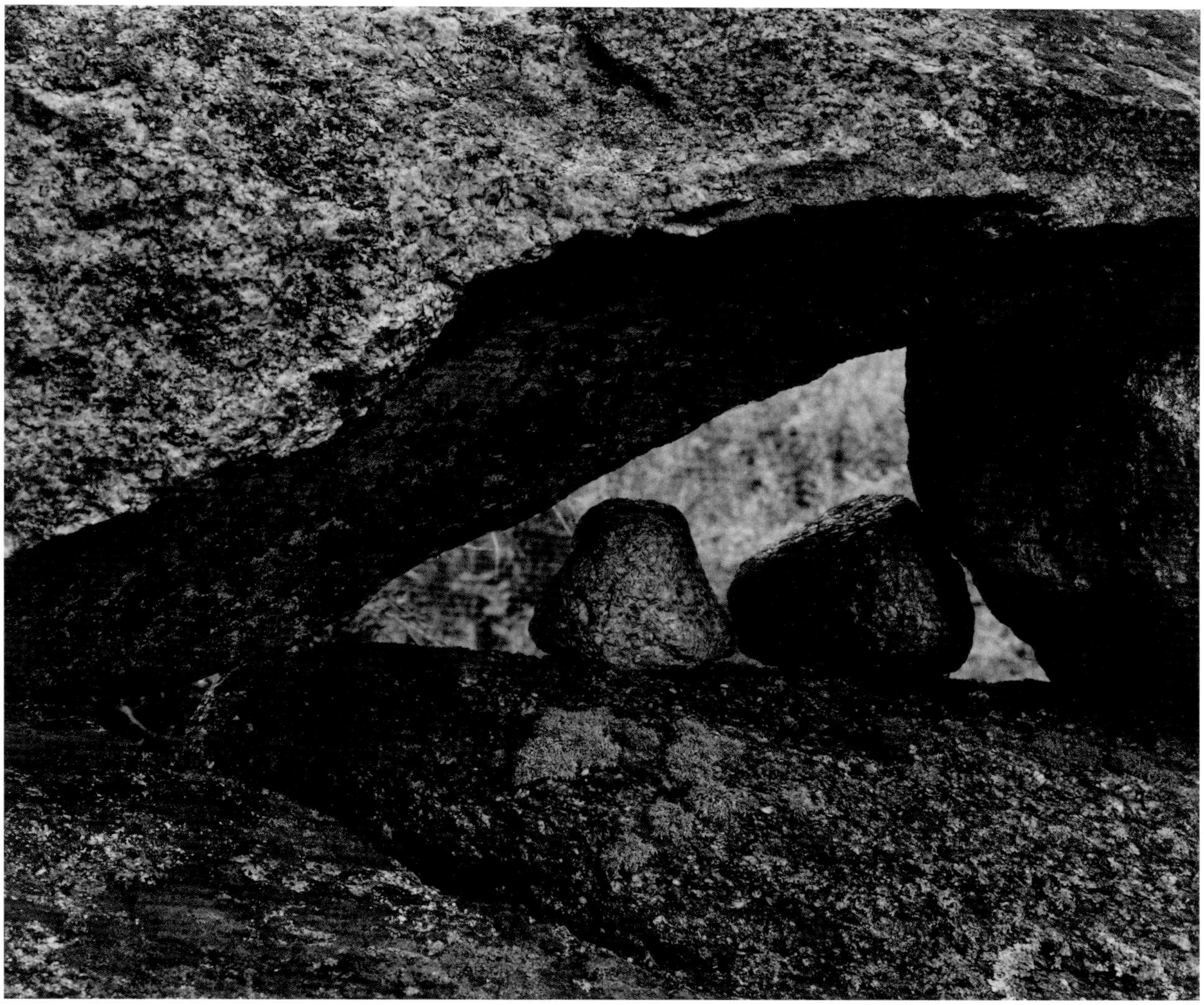

pl.15 Aaron Siskind, *Martha's Vineyard 114B*, 1954

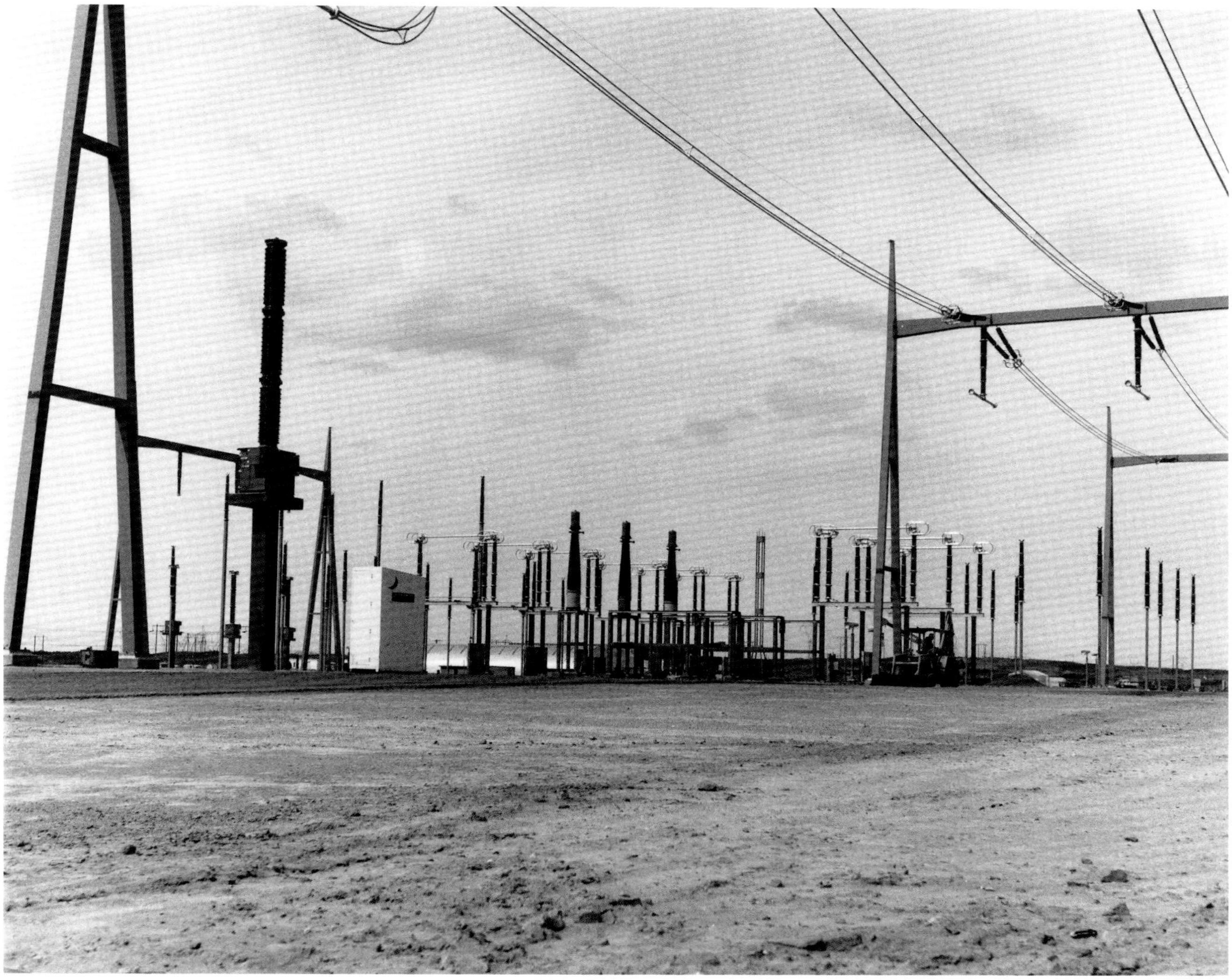

pl.16 Ralston Crawford, *High Tension Lines*, ca. 1950

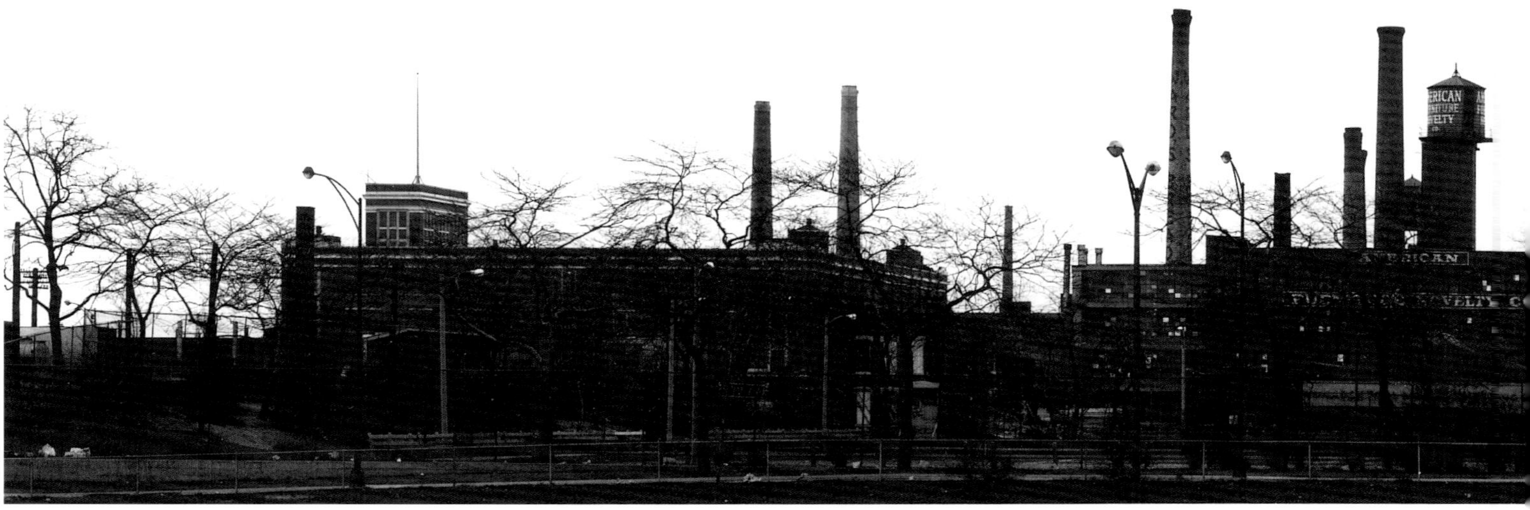
AMERICAN

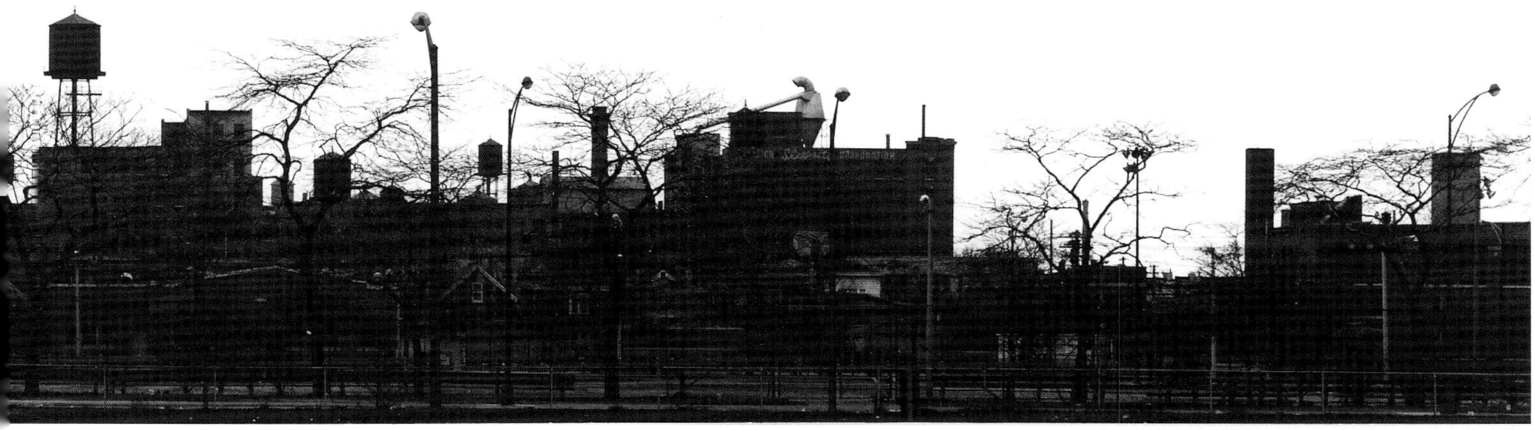

pl.17 Art Sinsabaugh, *Chicago Landscape, #24*, 1964

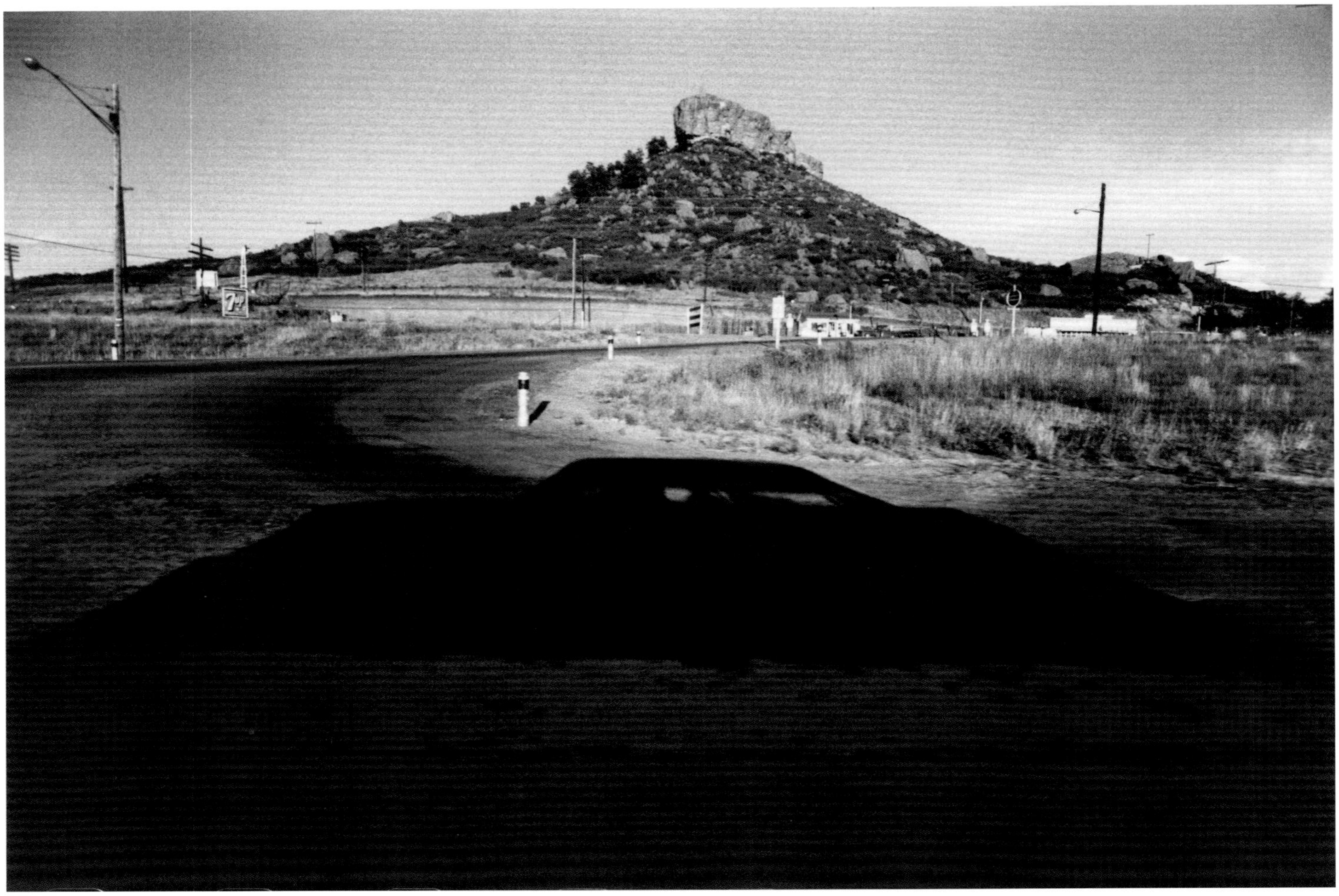

pl. 18 Garry Winogrand, *Castle Rock, Colorado*, 1960

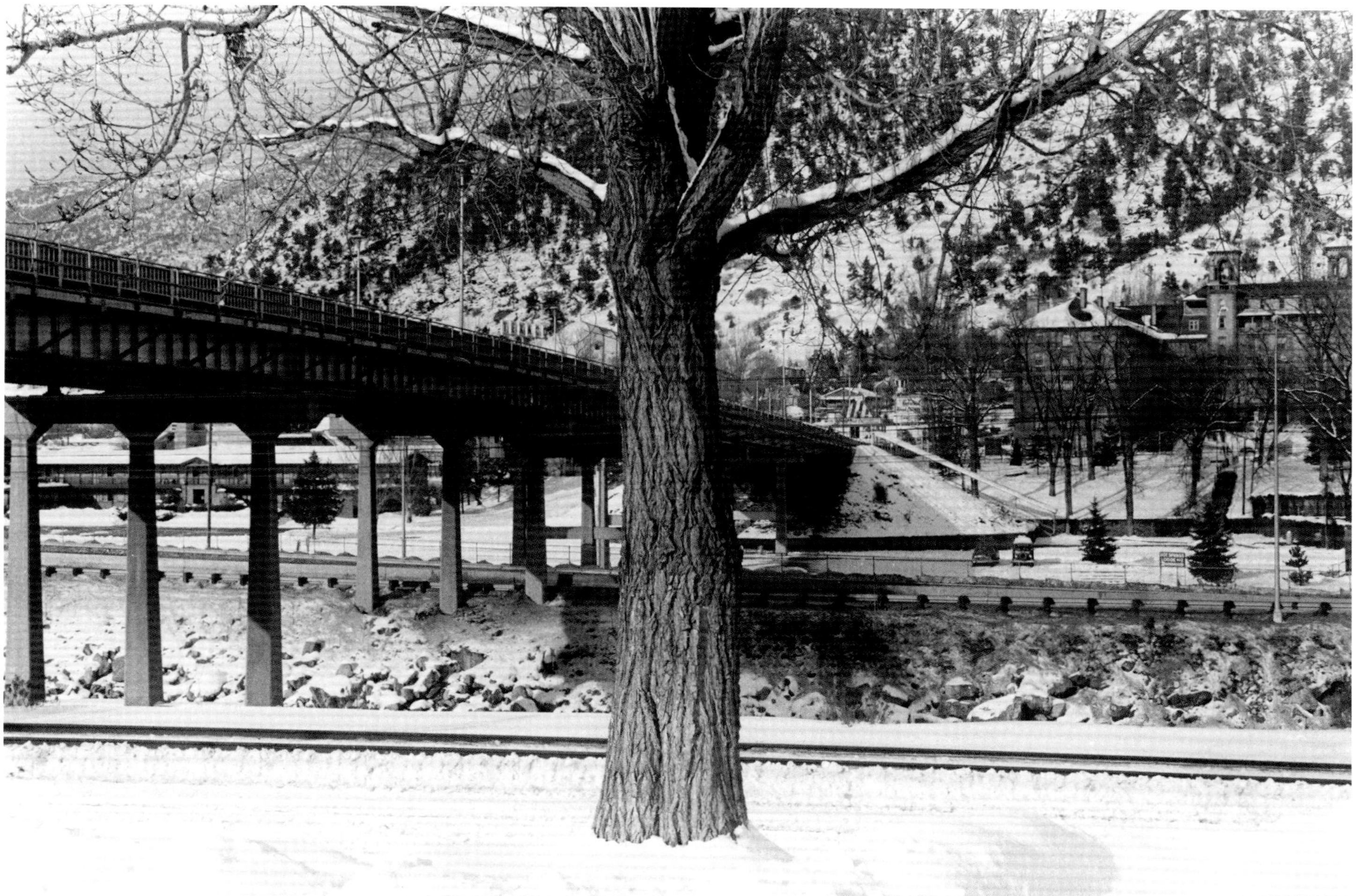

pl.19 Gary Metz, *Untitled*, 1973

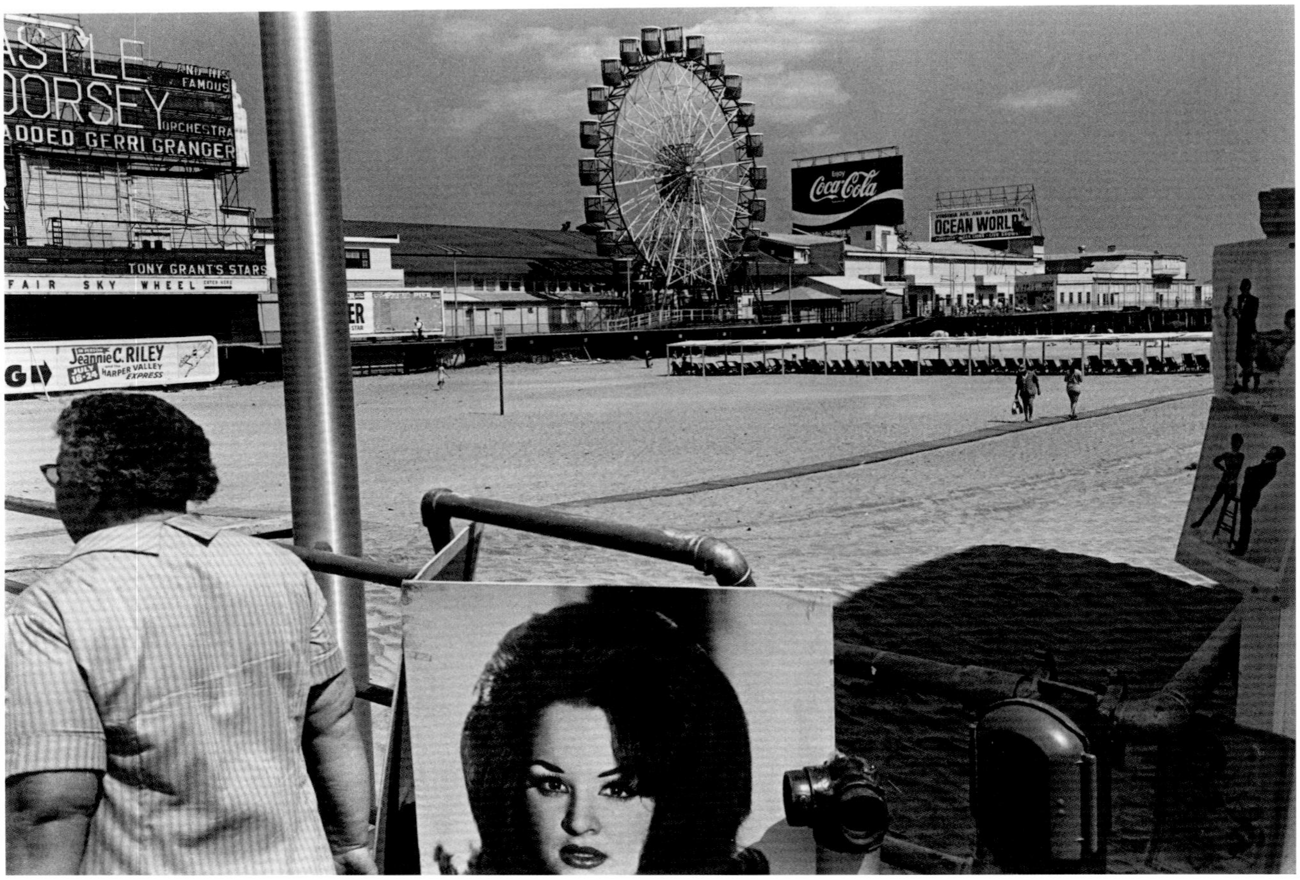

pl. 20 Lee Friedlander, *Atlantic City, New Jersey*, 1971

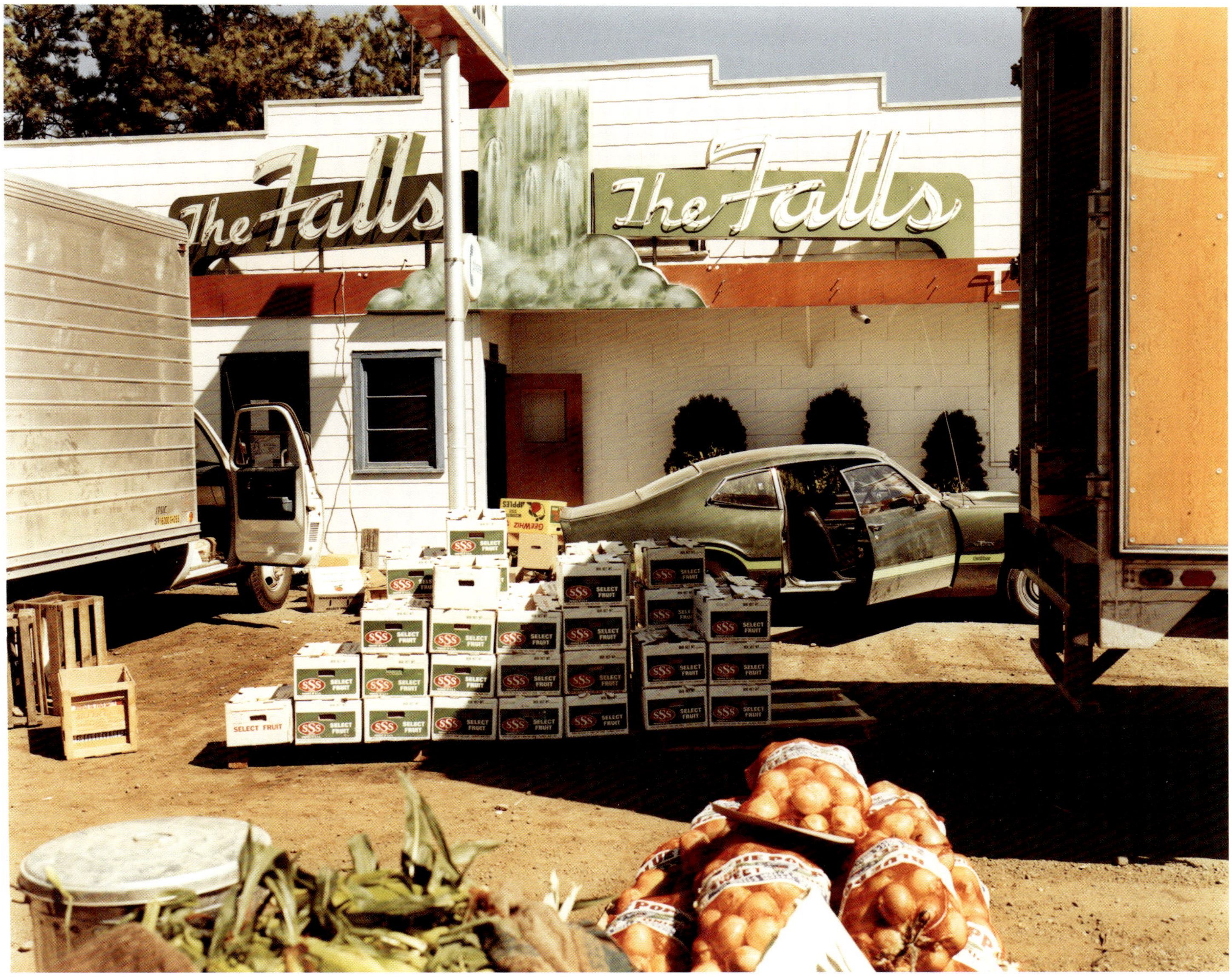

pl. 21 Stephen Shore, *U.S. 10, Post Falls, Idaho*, 1974

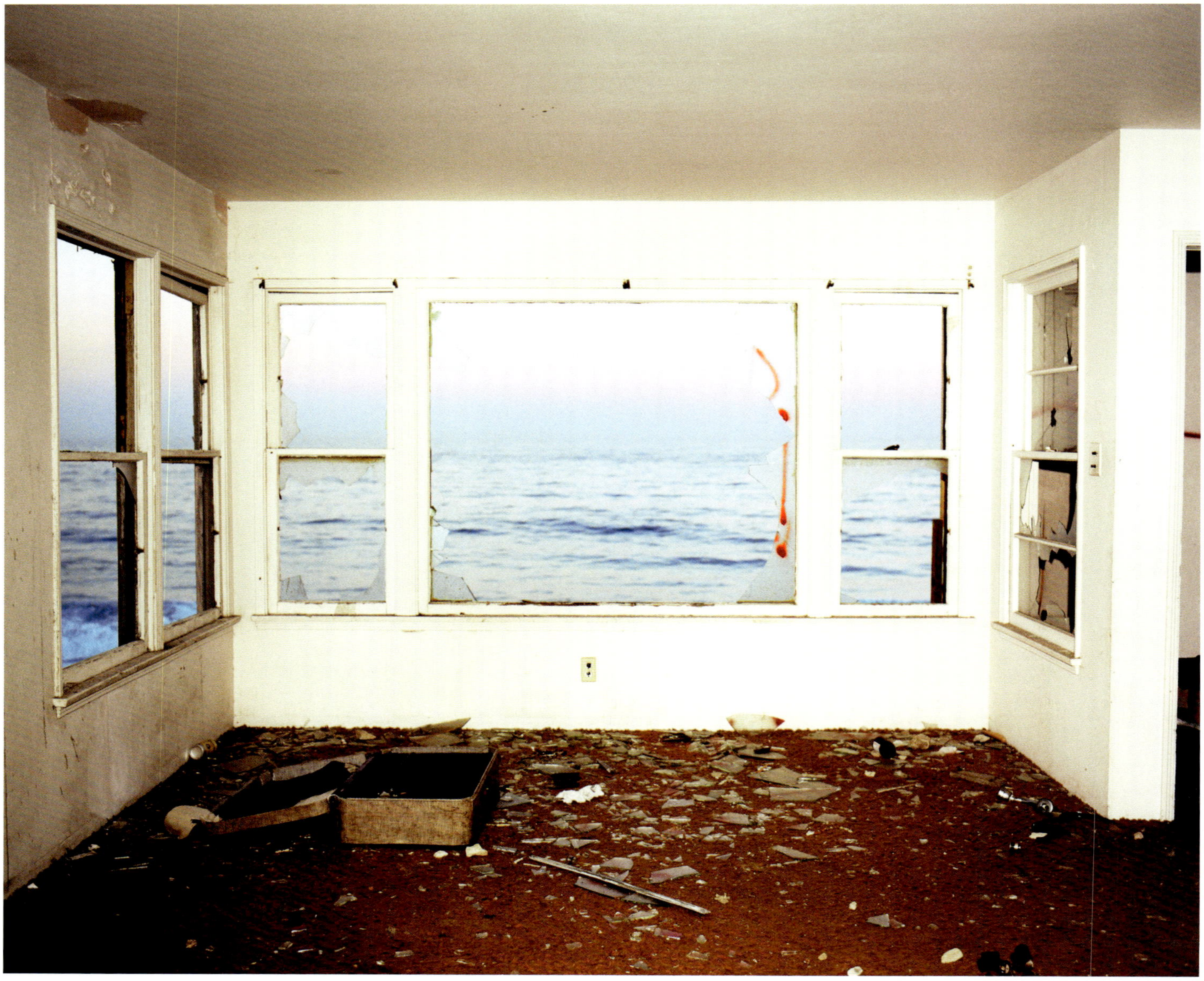

pl. 22 John Divola, *Zuma #8*, 1977

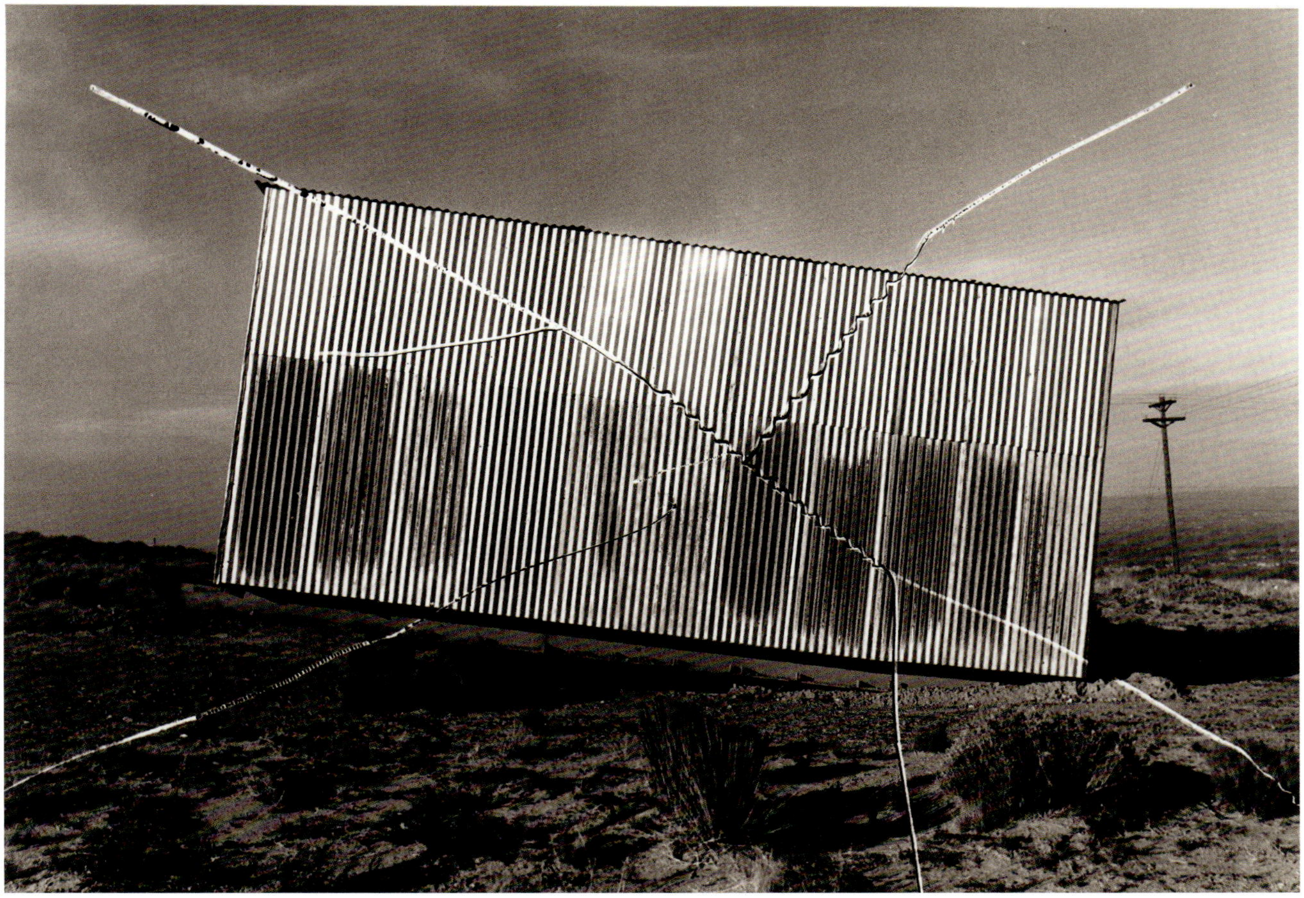

pl. 23 Thomas Barrow, *f/t/s Cancellations—Horizon Rib*, 1974

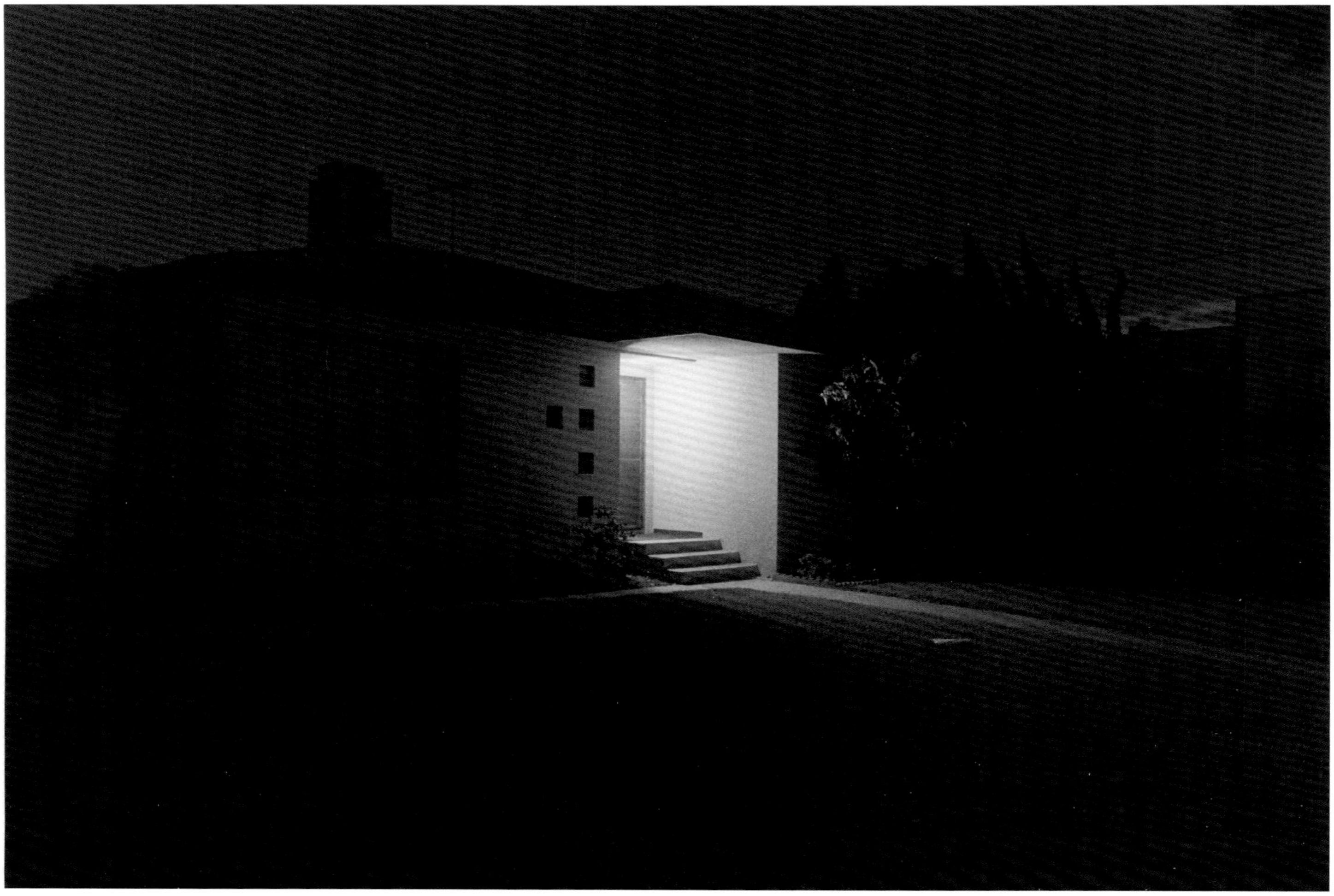

pl. 24 Henry Wessel, *Night Walk #28*, 1995

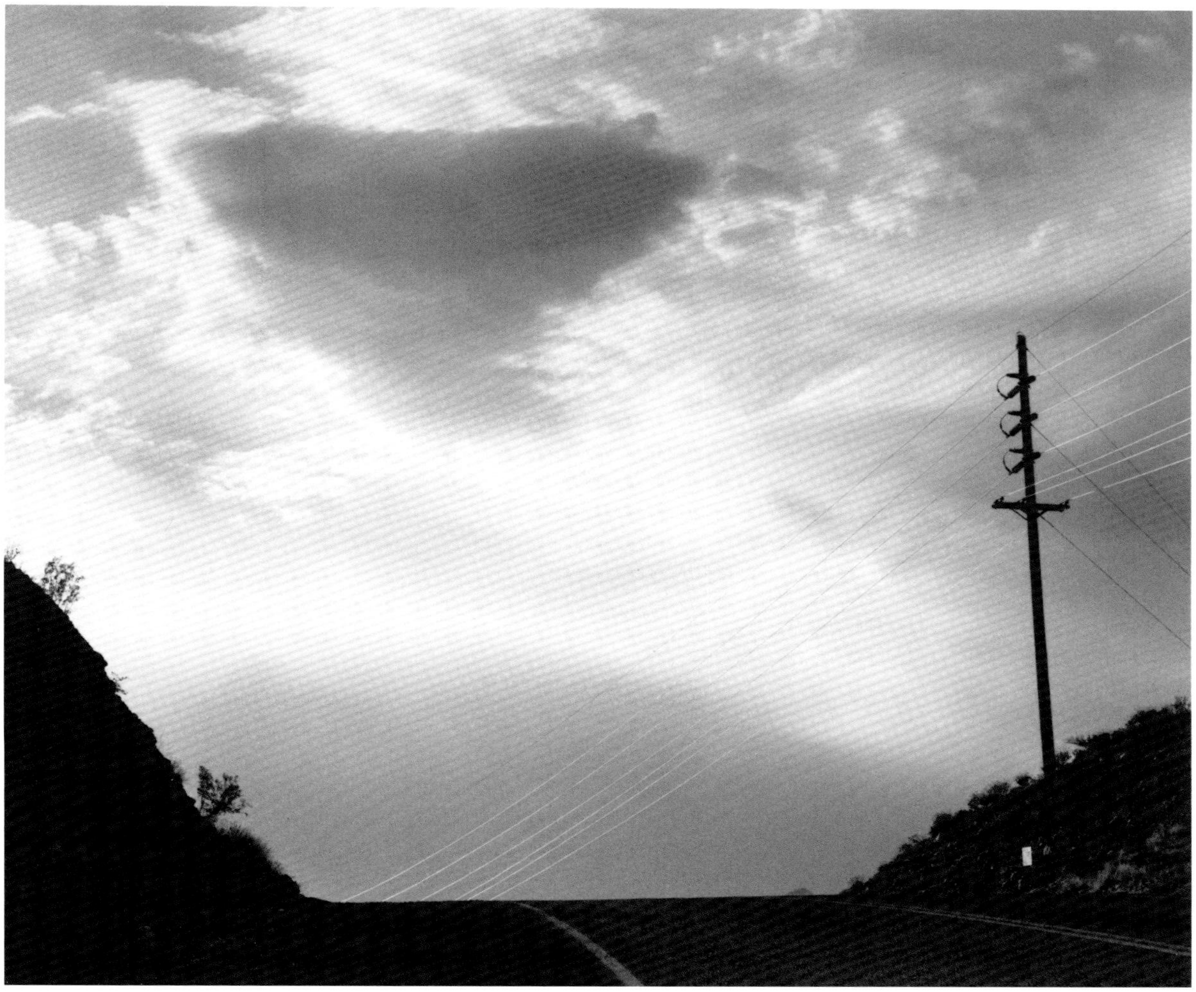

pl. 25 Harold Jones, *With Emmet*, 1978

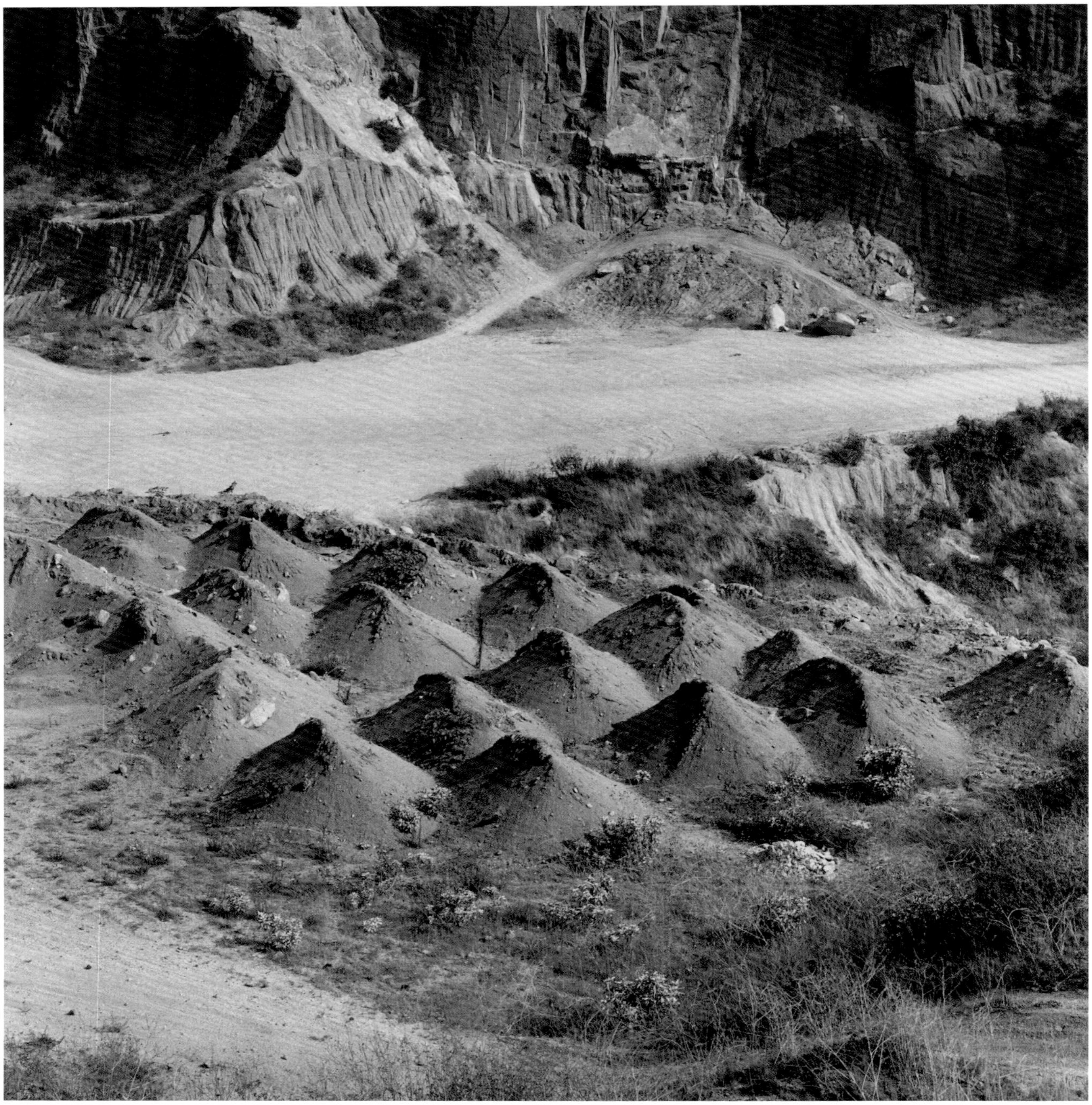

pl. 26 Joe Deal, *San Bernadino, California*, 1978, from *The Fault Zone*

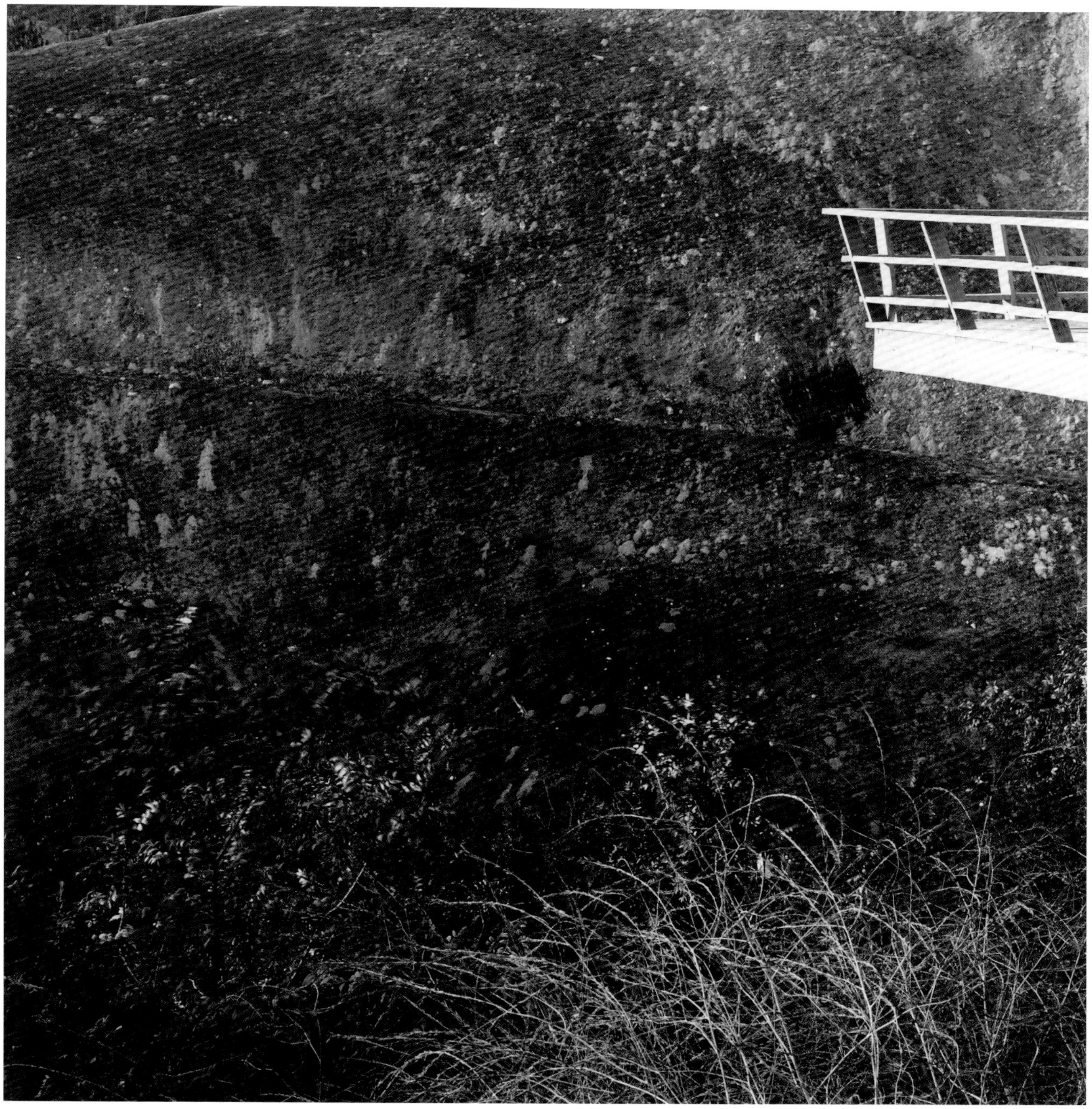

pl. 27 Joe Deal, *Glendale, California*, 1979, from *The Fault Zone*

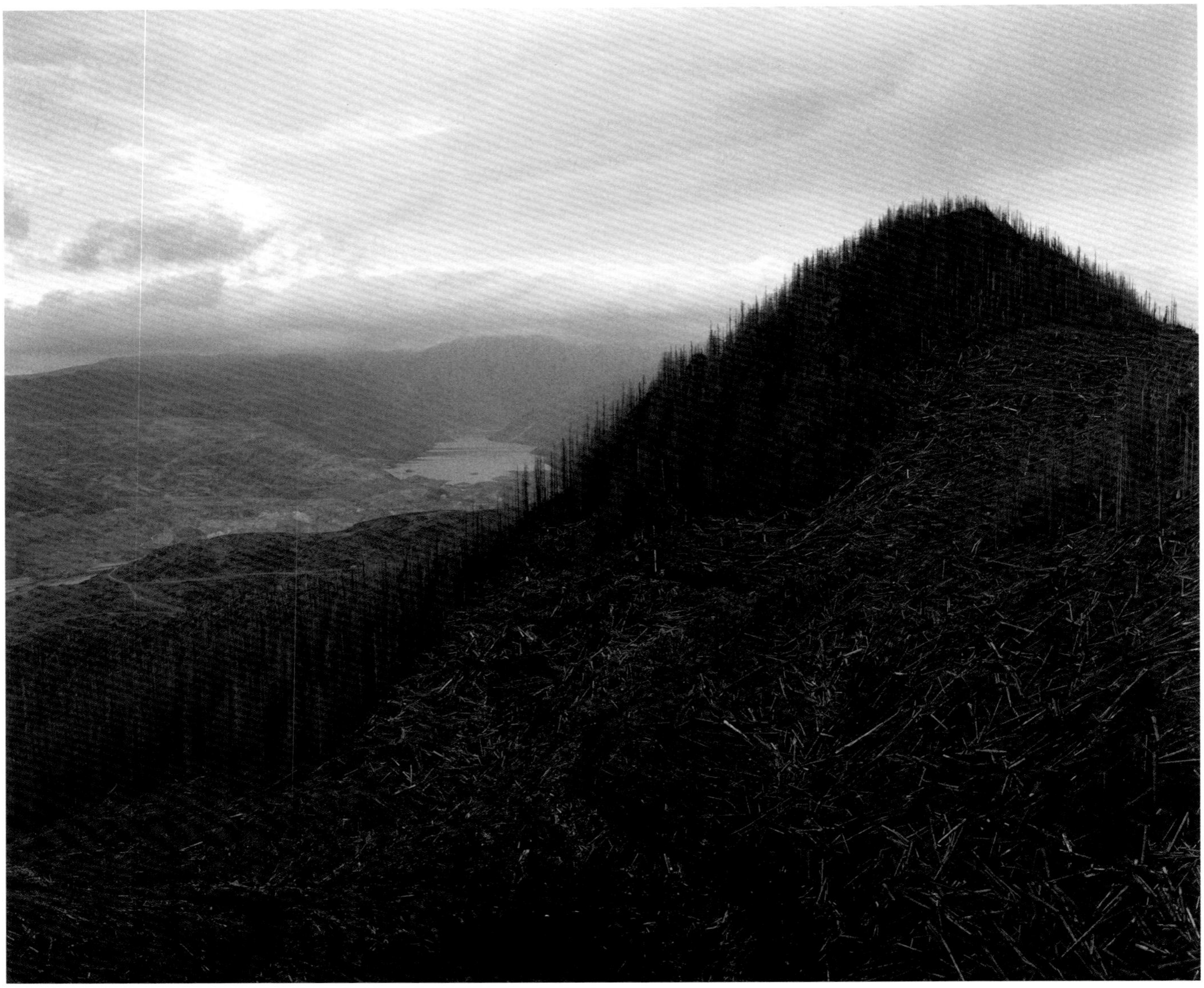

pl. 28 Frank Gohlke, *Salvaging dead timber on Spud Mountain—looking NE at Coldwater Lake from a point 7.5 miles NW of Mt. St. Helens, Washington*, 1982

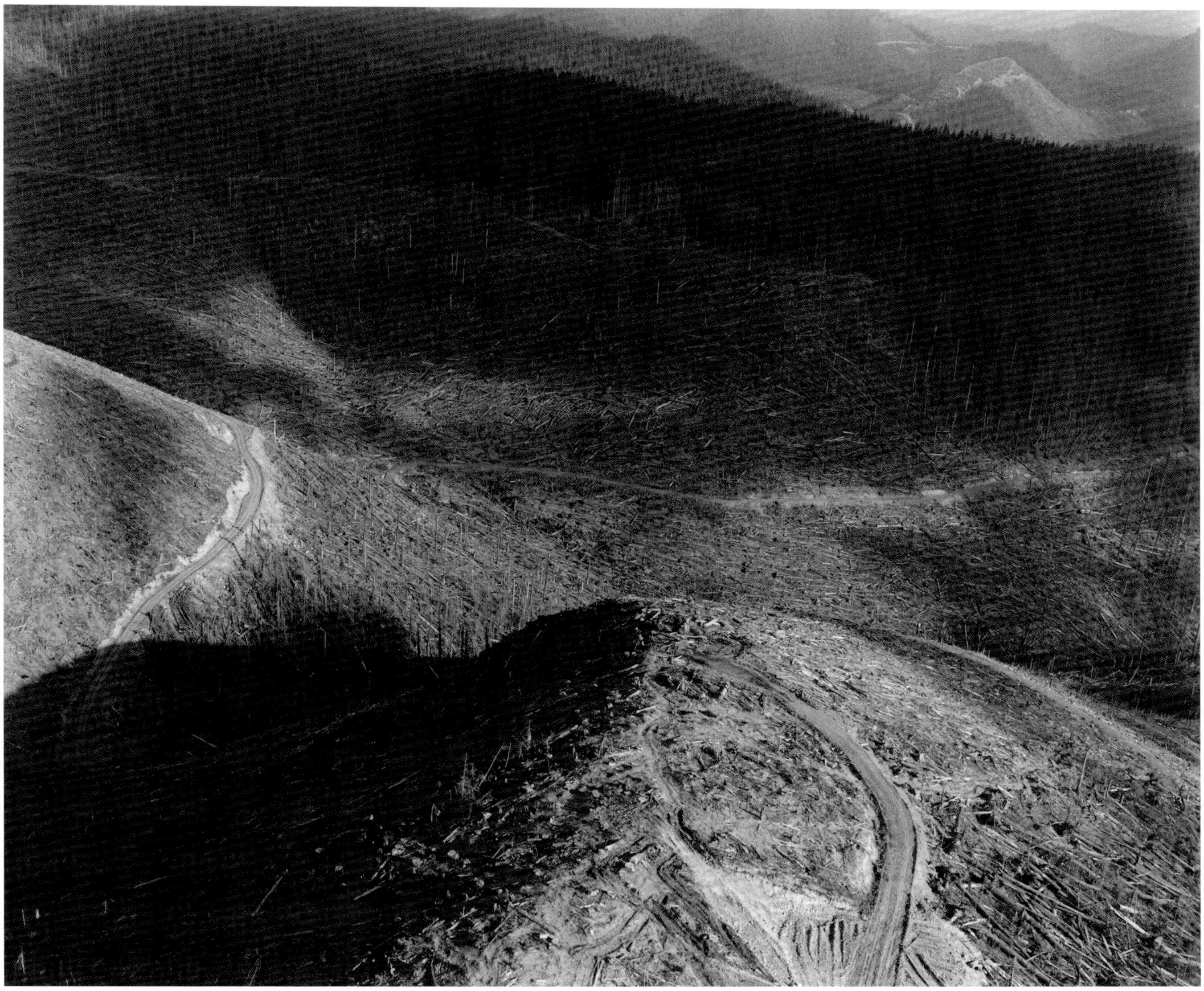

pl. 29 Frank Gohlke, *Aerial View: Edge of eruption impact zone showing blown-down, standing dead and living trees. Salvage in progress. Approximately 14 miles NW of Mount St. Helens, Washington*, 1981

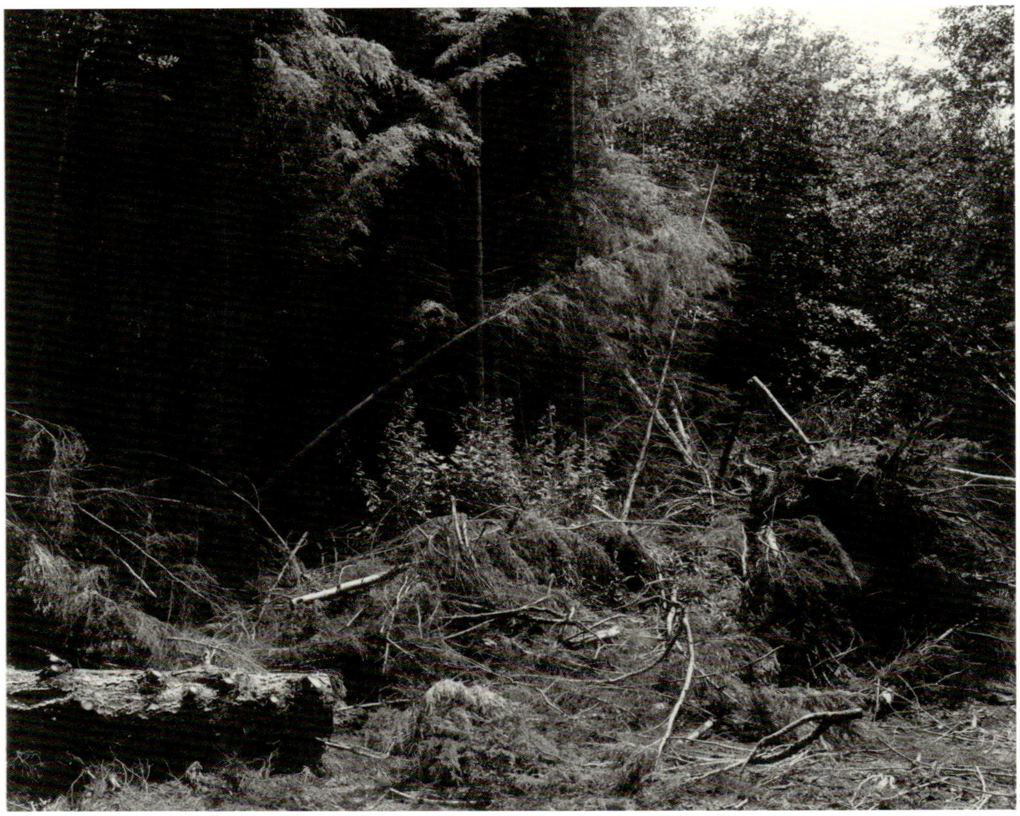

pl. 30 Robert Adams, *Bulldozed Slash, Tillamook County, Oregon*, 1976

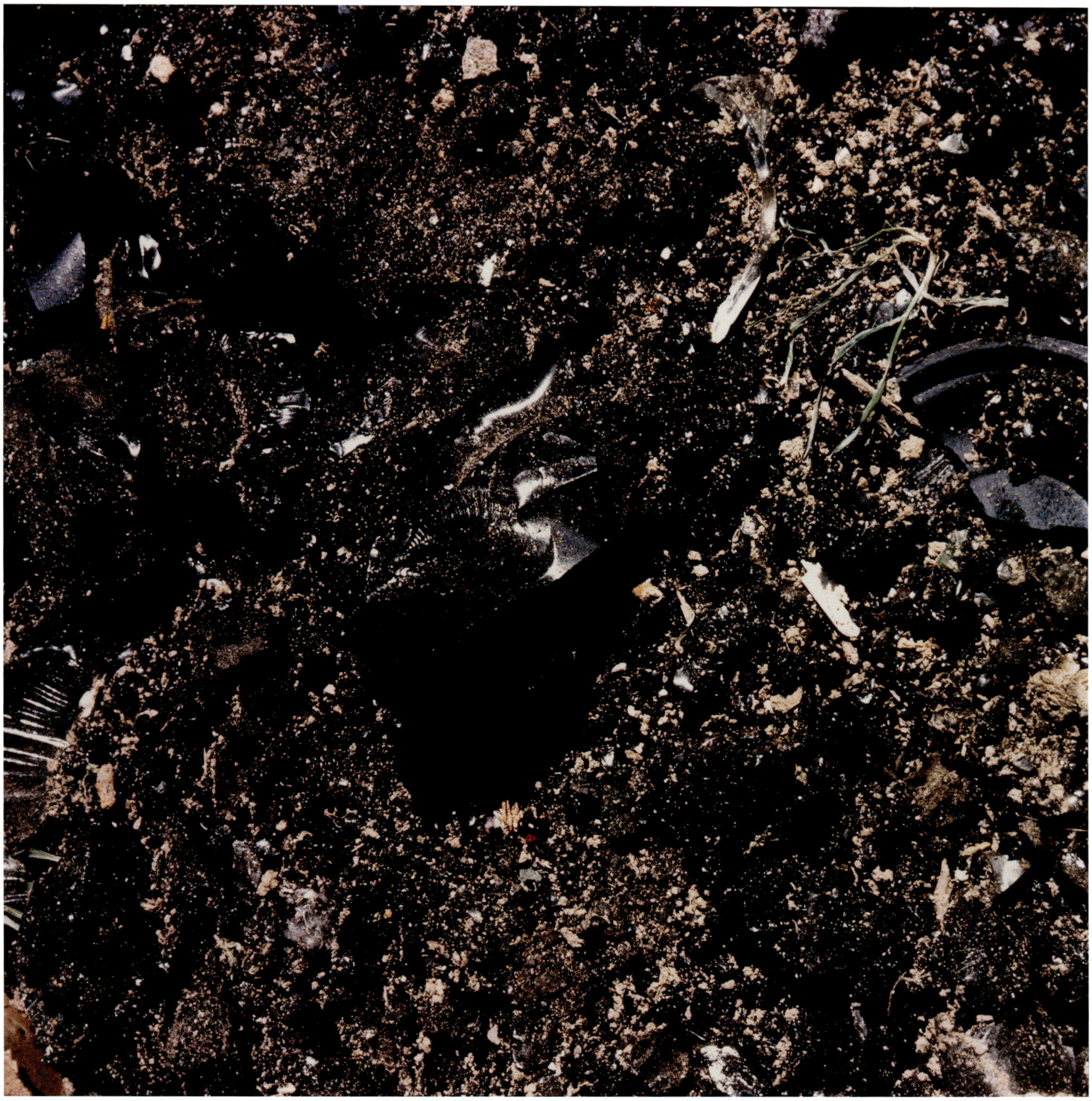

pl. 31 Anthony Hernandez, *Angeles National Forest*, 1987

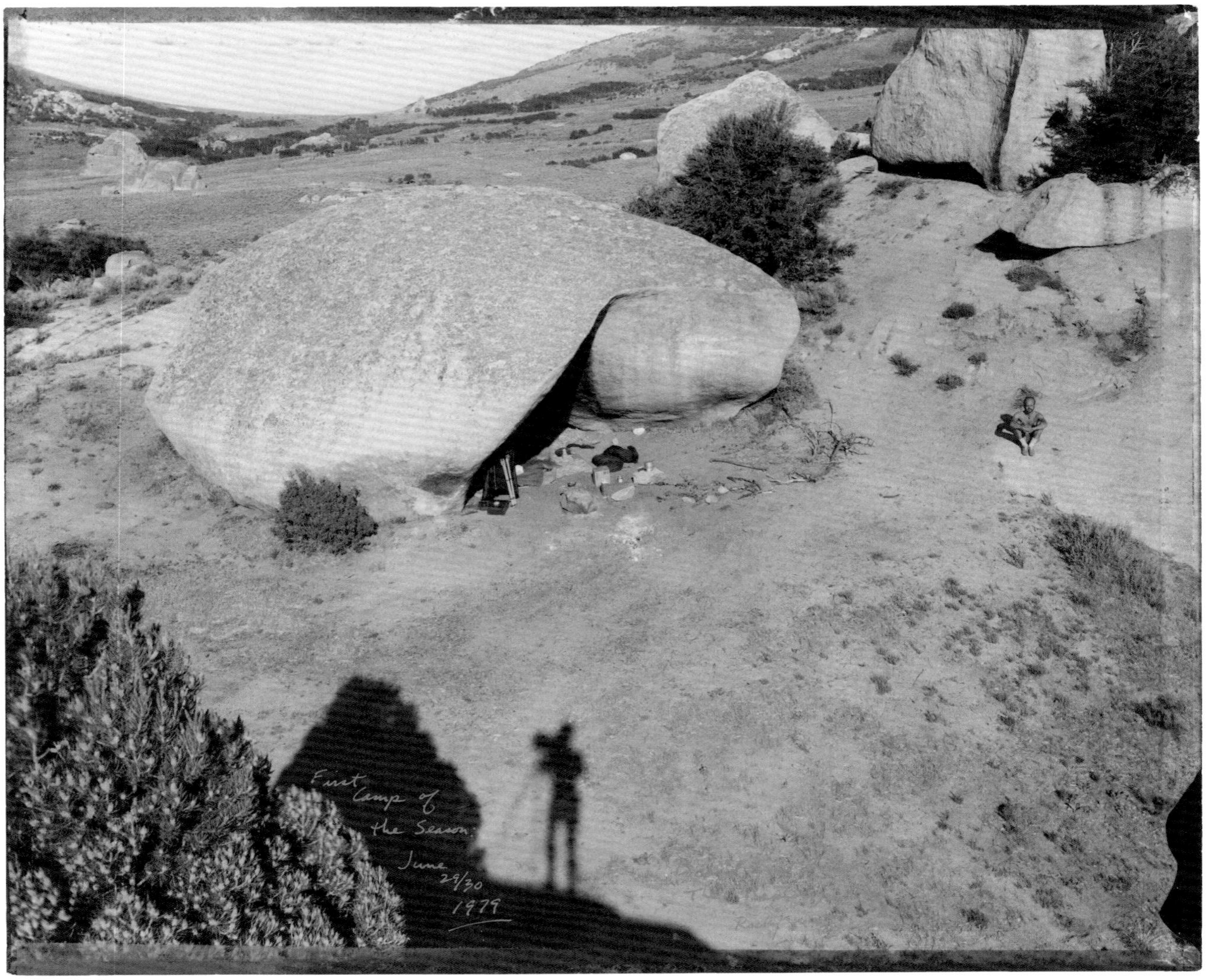

pl. 32 Mark Klett, *First Camp of the Season: June 29/30 1979, "Bread Loaf Rock" City of Rocks, Idaho, 1979*

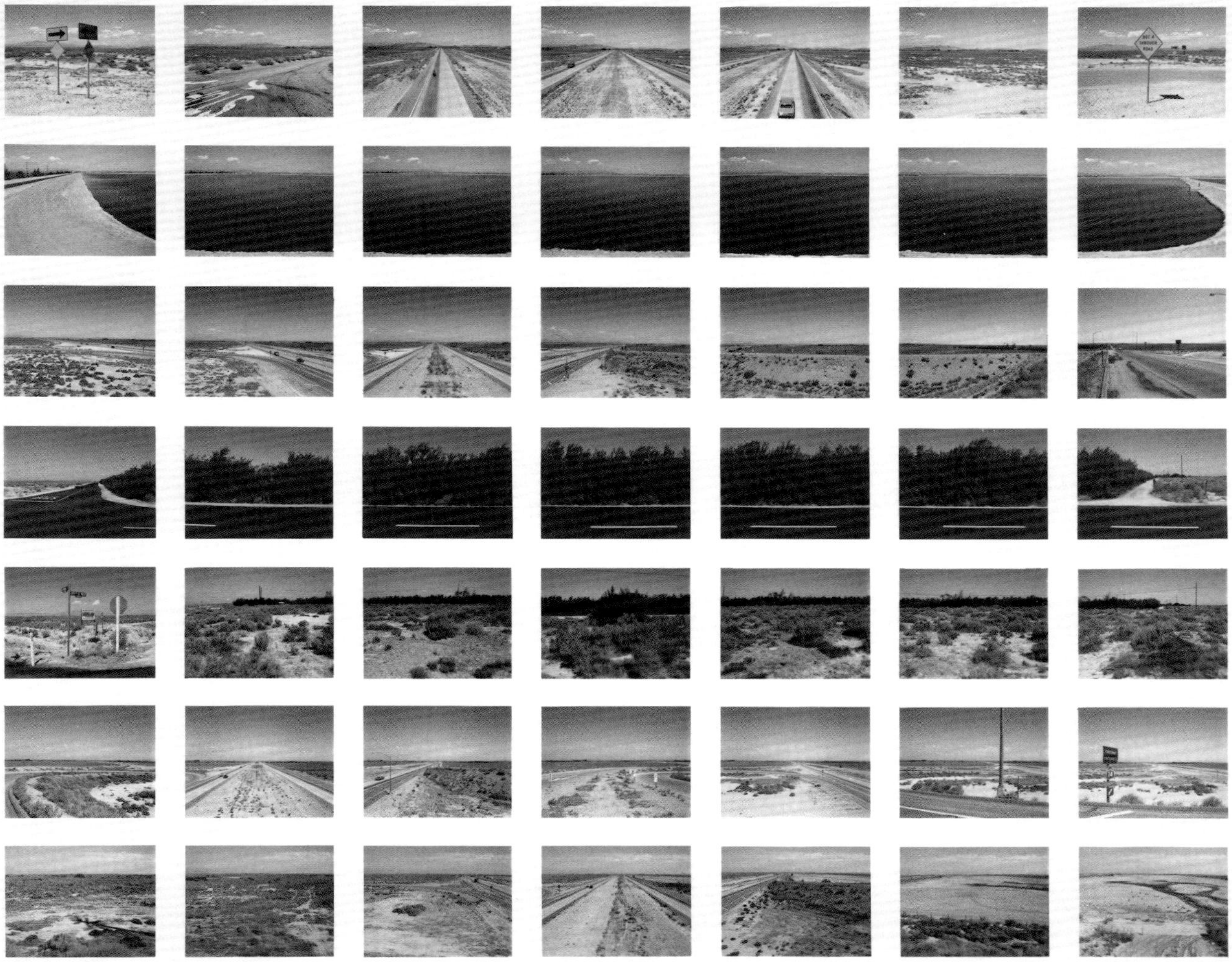

pl. 33 Robbert Flick, *SV 033/81, East of Lancaster, California*, 1981

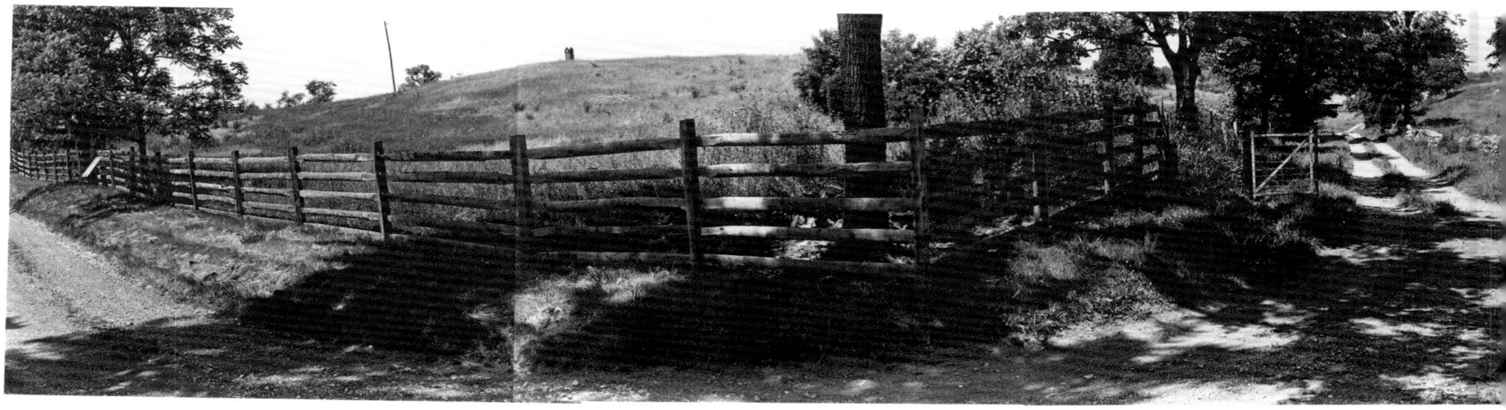

pl. 34 Deborah Bright, *Bloody Lane, The Battle of Antietam*, 1983

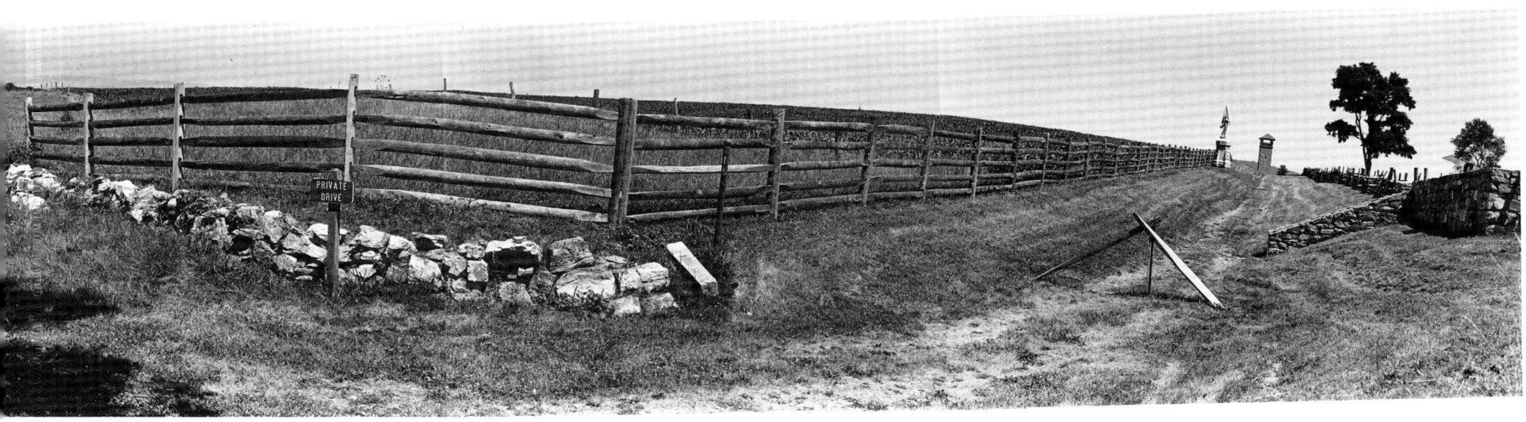

BLOODY LANE: Battle of Anteitam (Maryland).
September 17, 1862. Duration: one day.
Photographed June, 1983.

View of the length of sunken farm road called Bloody Lane, looking down the private drive to the Roulette Farm. Confederate troops entrenched along Bloody Lane held off repeated suicidal charges by Union forces from the hill opposite where a lone monument was erected (left background). Later outflanked at the point where the observation tower now stands (extreme right), the Southern ranks were caught in a lethal enfilade. At day's end, so many corpses clogged Bloody Lane that observers recalled unanimously that a person could walk its entire length without stepping on the ground. Still the United States' "bloodiest day," the total casualties at Antietam numbered about 41,000.

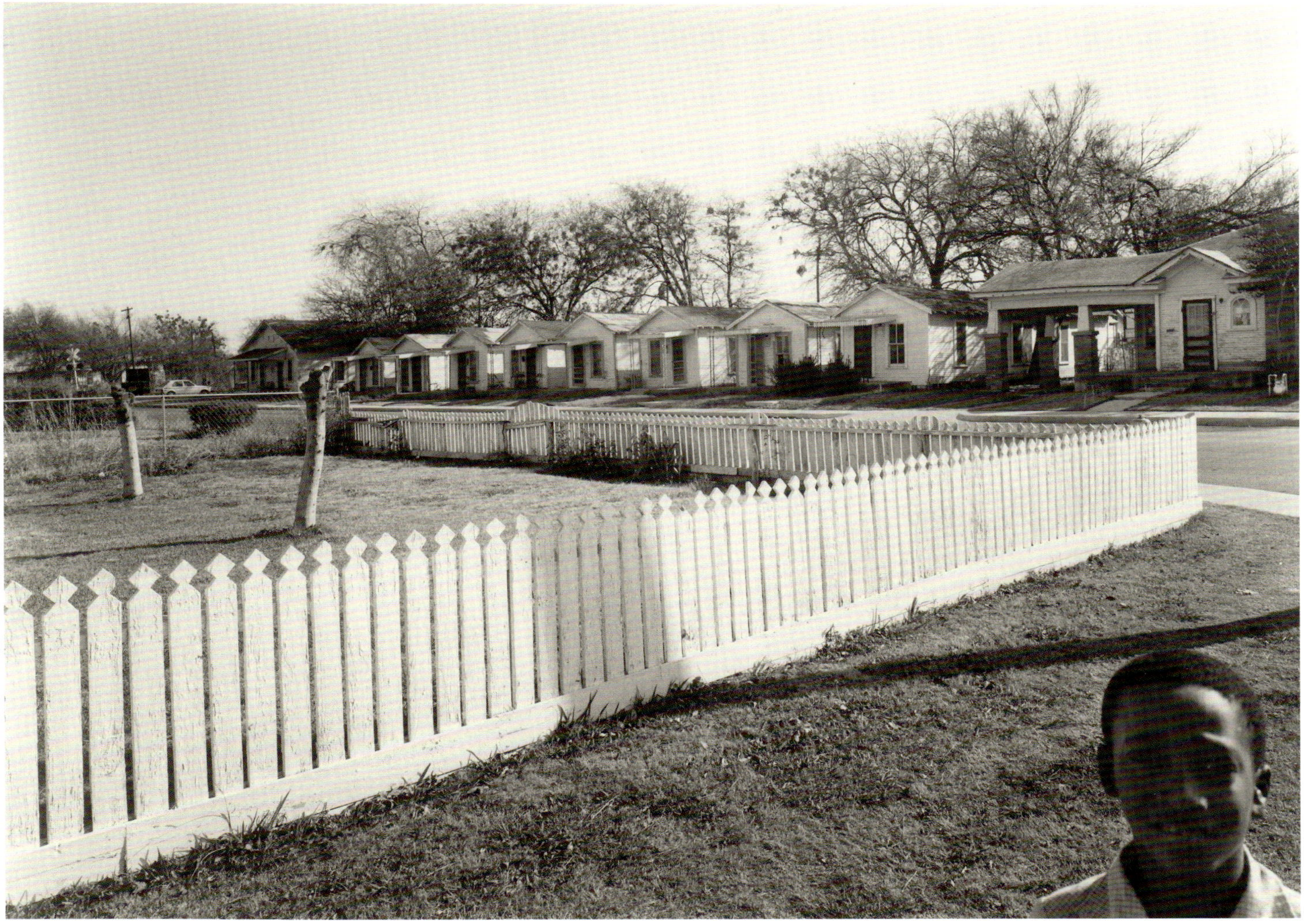

pl. 35 Peter Feresten, *E. Hattie Street, Fort Worth, TX*, 1983

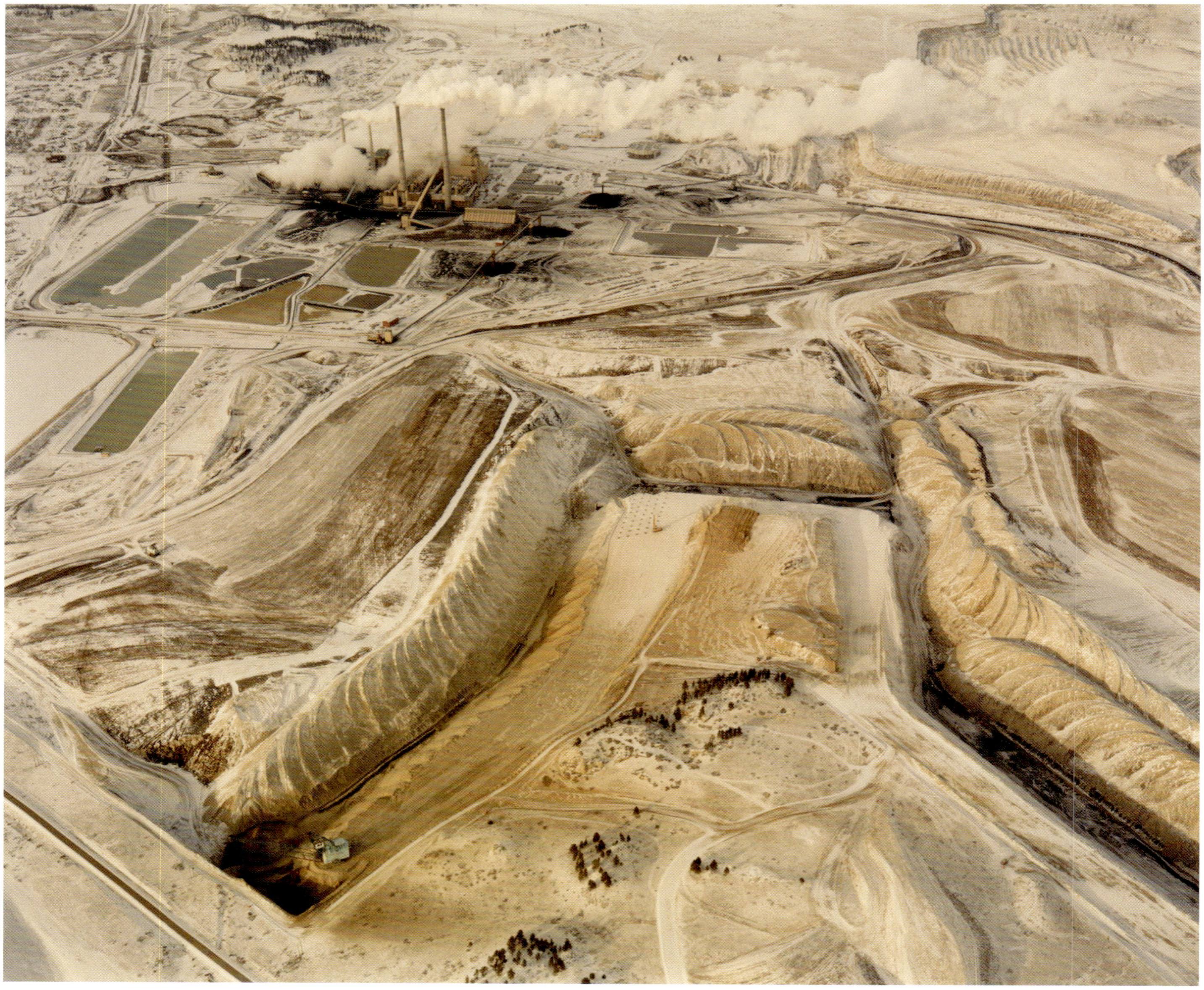

pl. 36 David T. Hanson, *Coal Strip Mine, Power Plant and Waste Ponds*, 1984

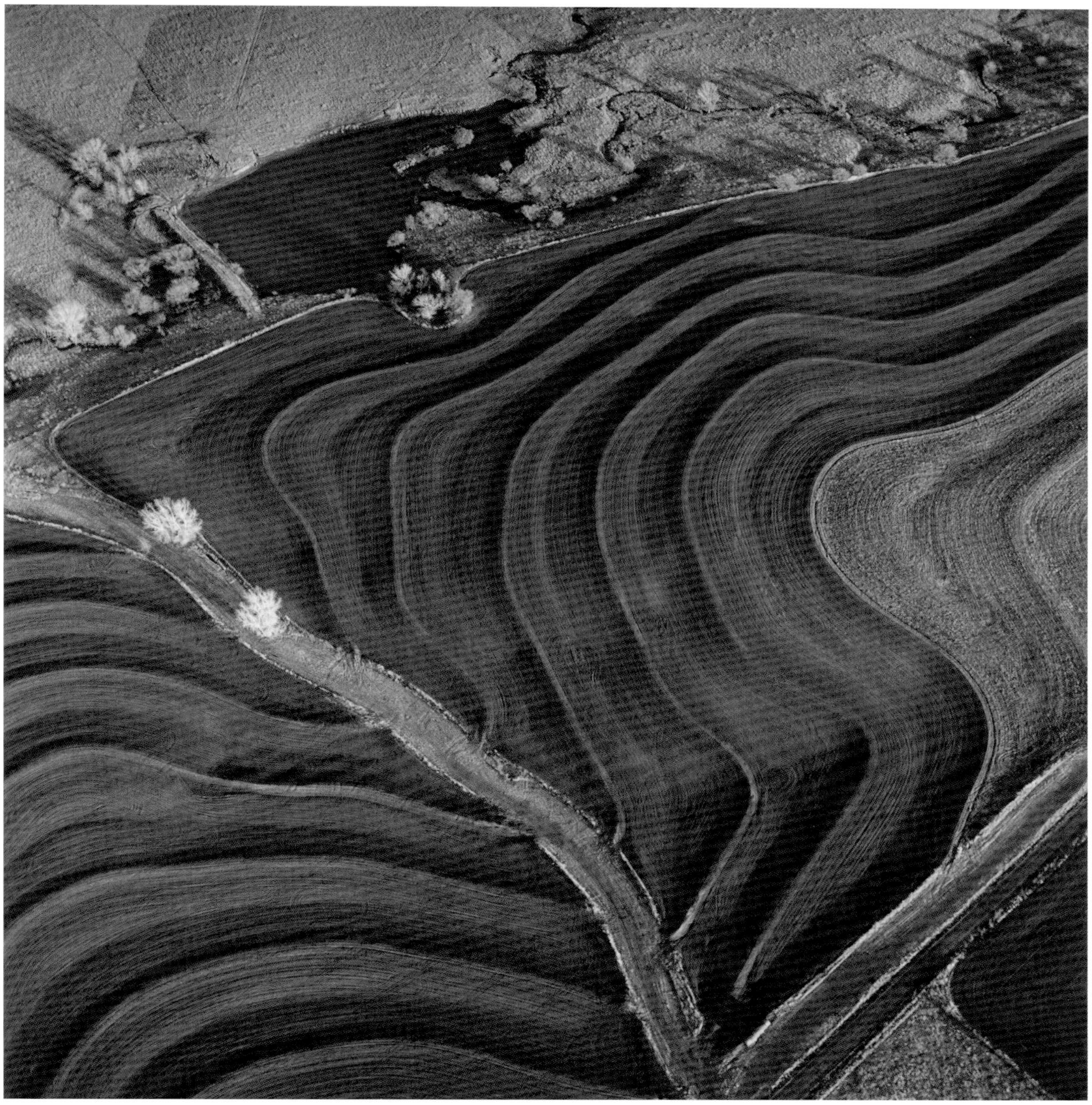

pl. 37 Terry Evans, *Terraced Plowing with a Grass Waterway*, 1991

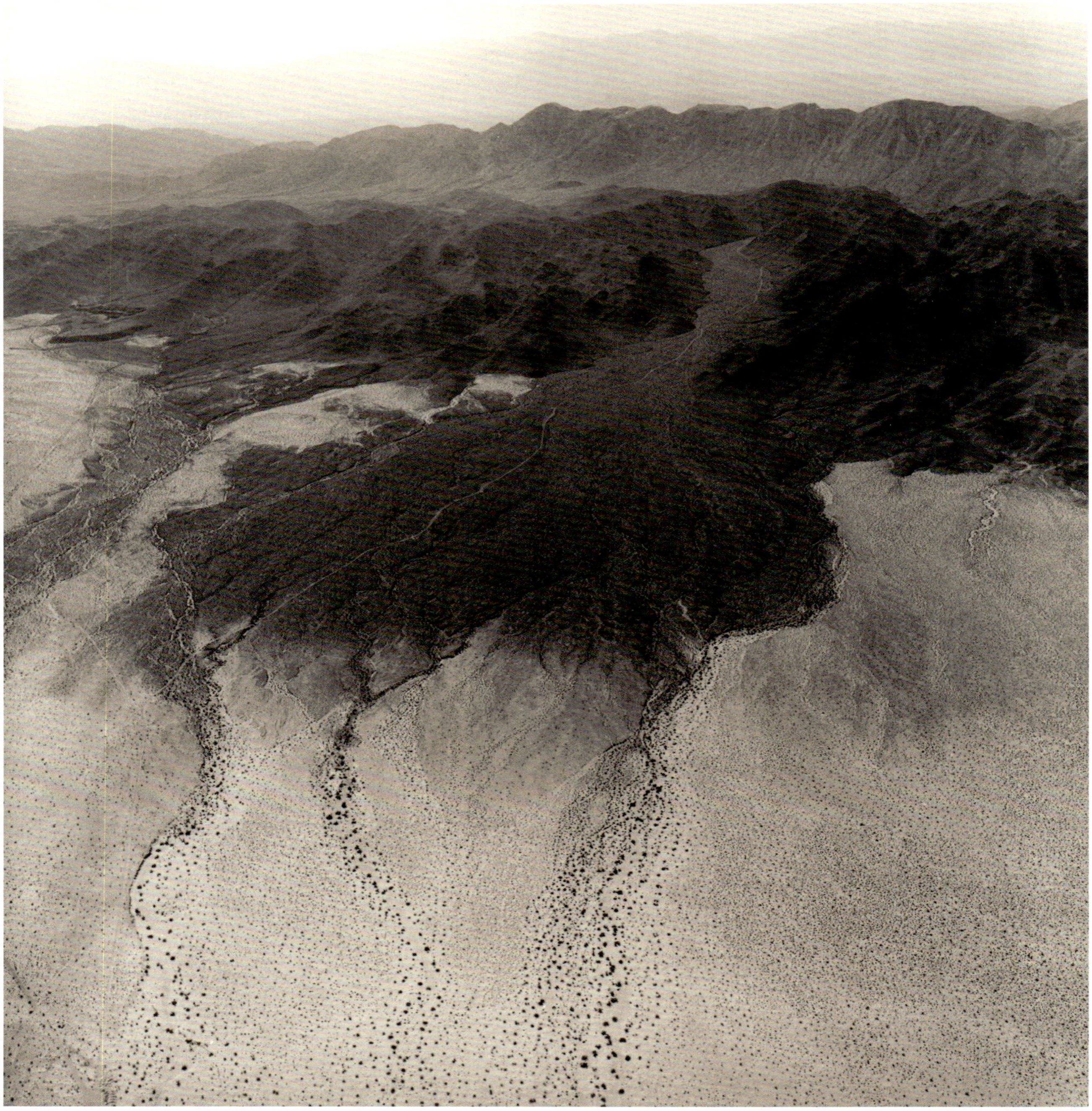

pl. 38 Emmet Gowin, *Alluvial Fan, Natural Drainage near Yuma Proving Ground and the California Arizona Border*, 1988

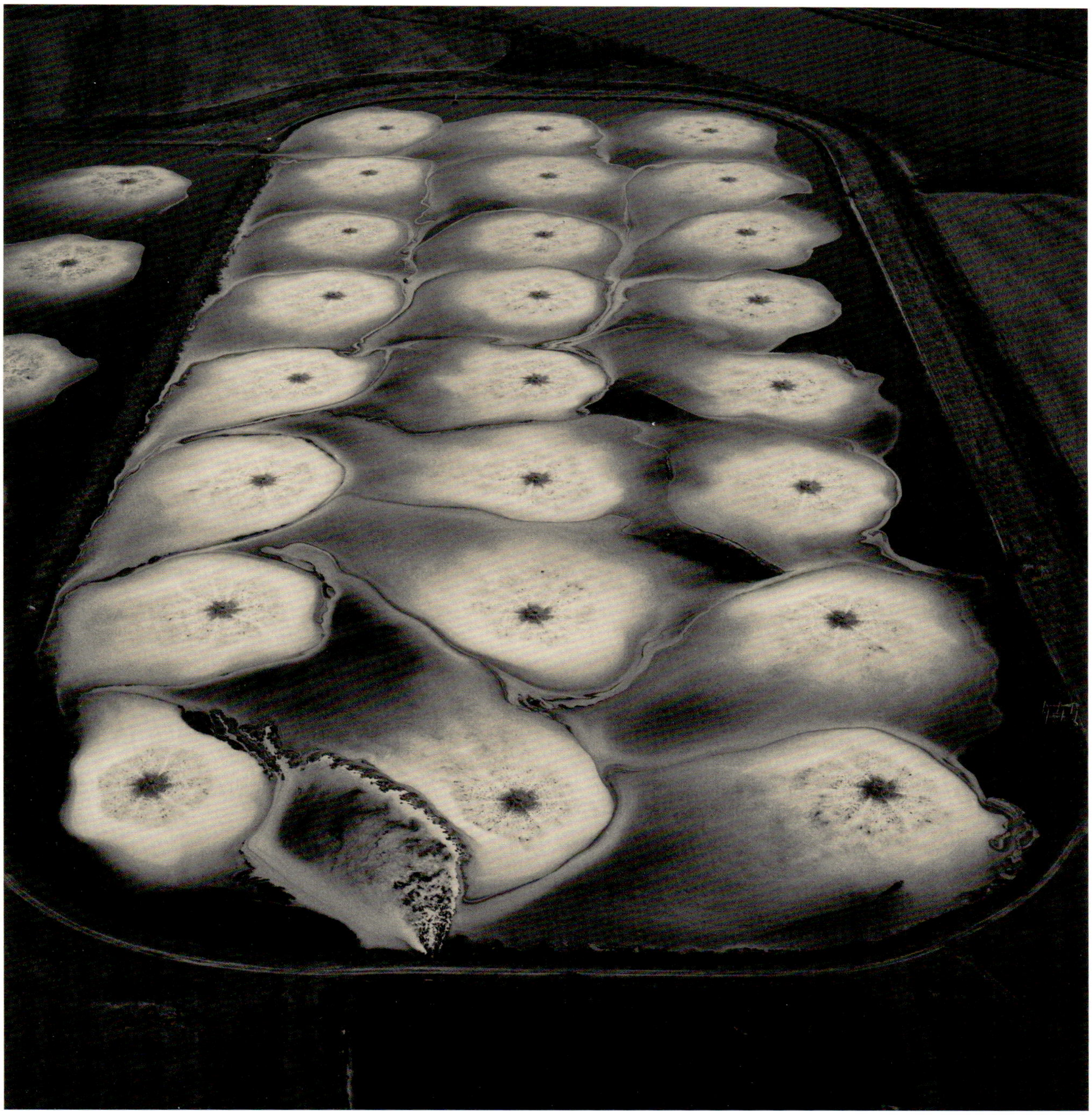

pl. 39 Emmet Gowin, *Aeration Pond, Toxic Water Treatment Facility, Pine Bluff, Arkansas*, 1989

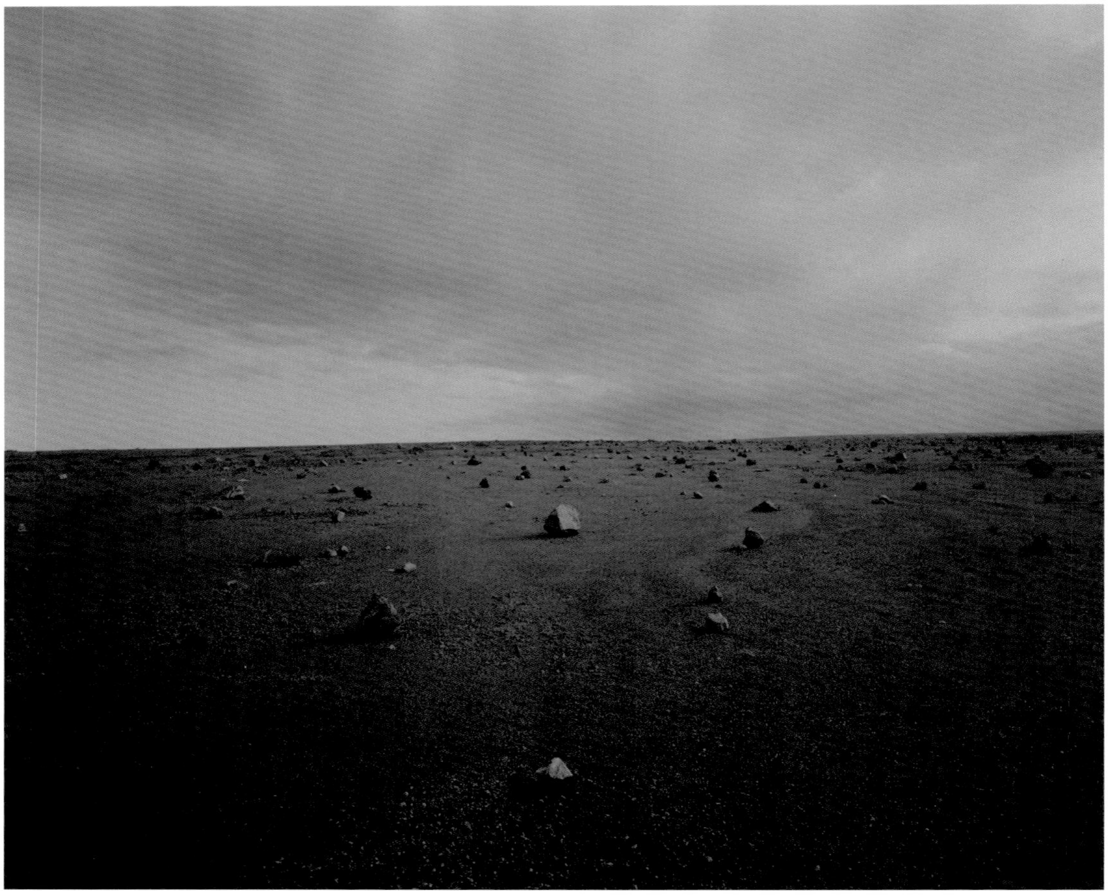

pl. 40 Linda Connor, *Stones, Kau Desert, Hawaii*, 1991

pl. 41 Sally Mann, *Untitled #27, Antietam*, 2001

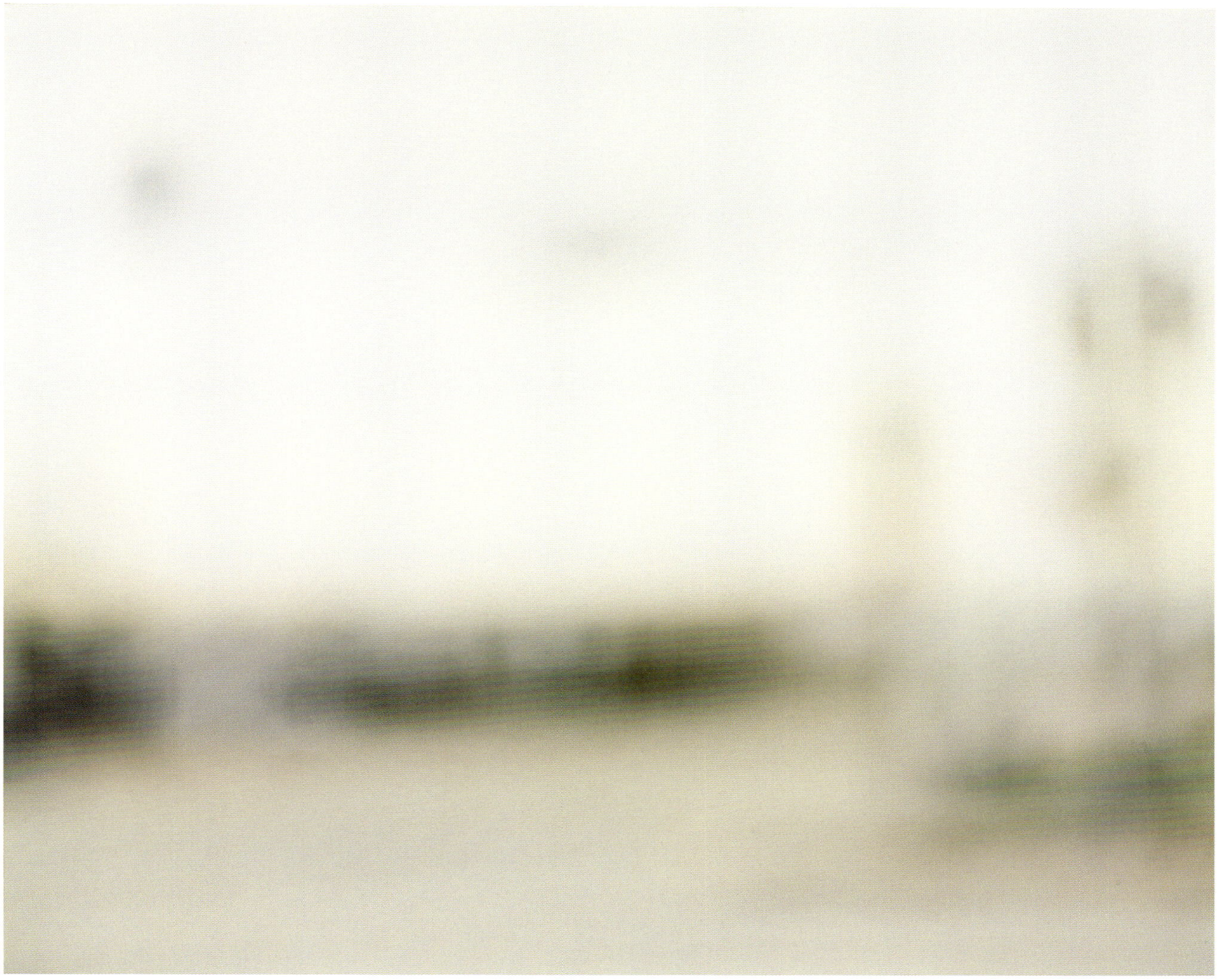

pl. 42 Uta Barth, *Field #14*, 1996

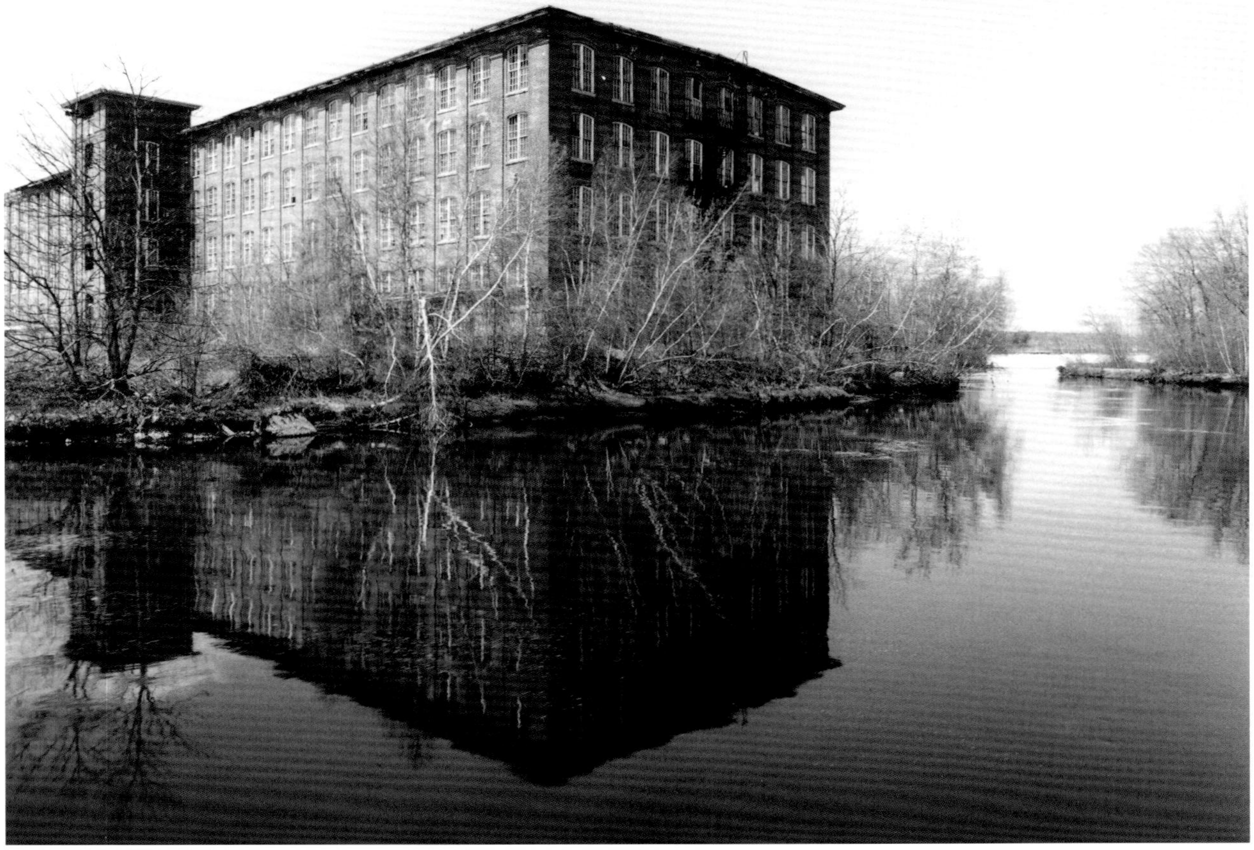

pl. 43 Salvatore Mancini, *Fisherville Mill, Grafton, Massachusetts*, 1994

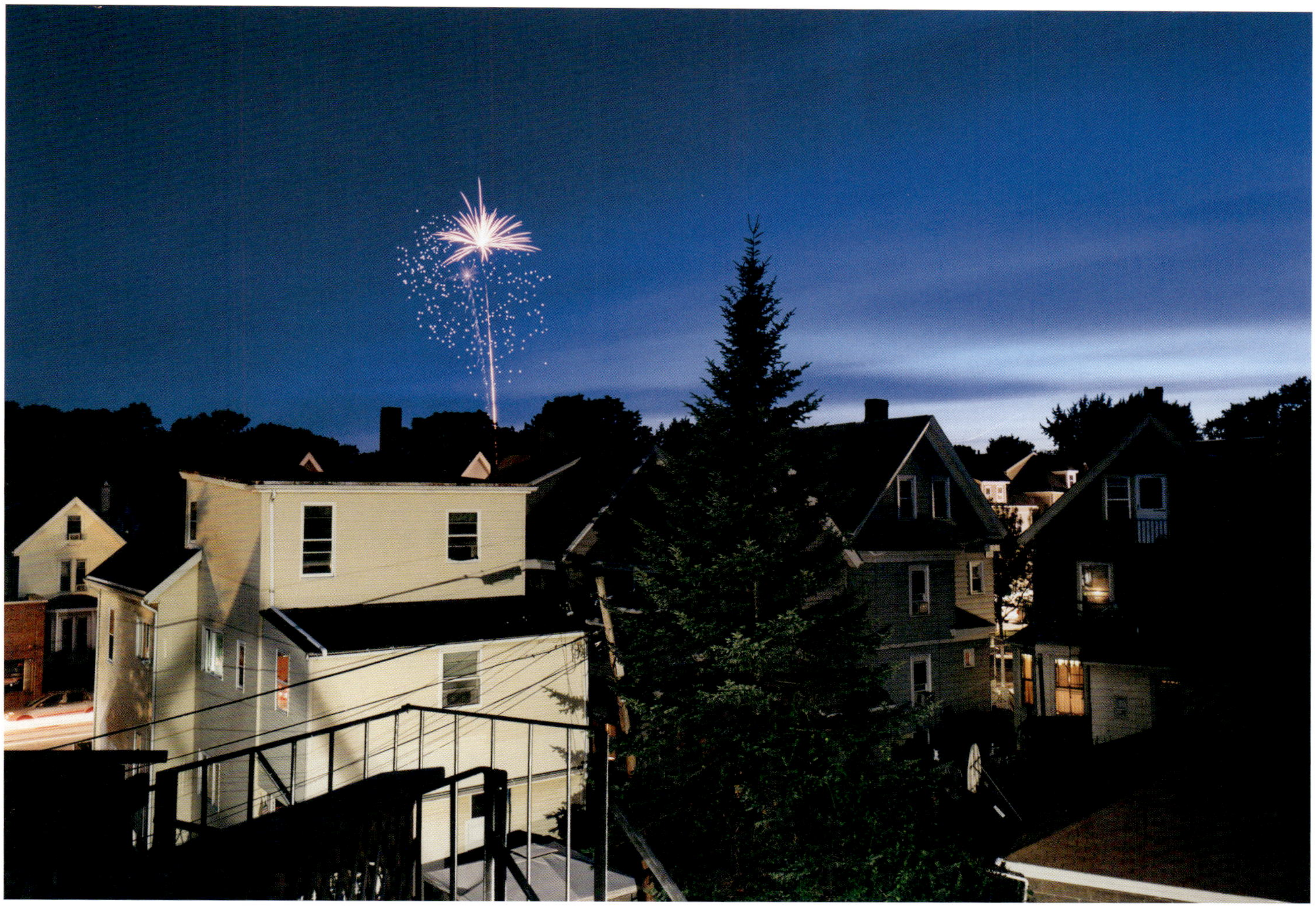

pl.44 Mary Kocol, *Unexpected Fireworks over Somerville, Massachusetts*, 2006

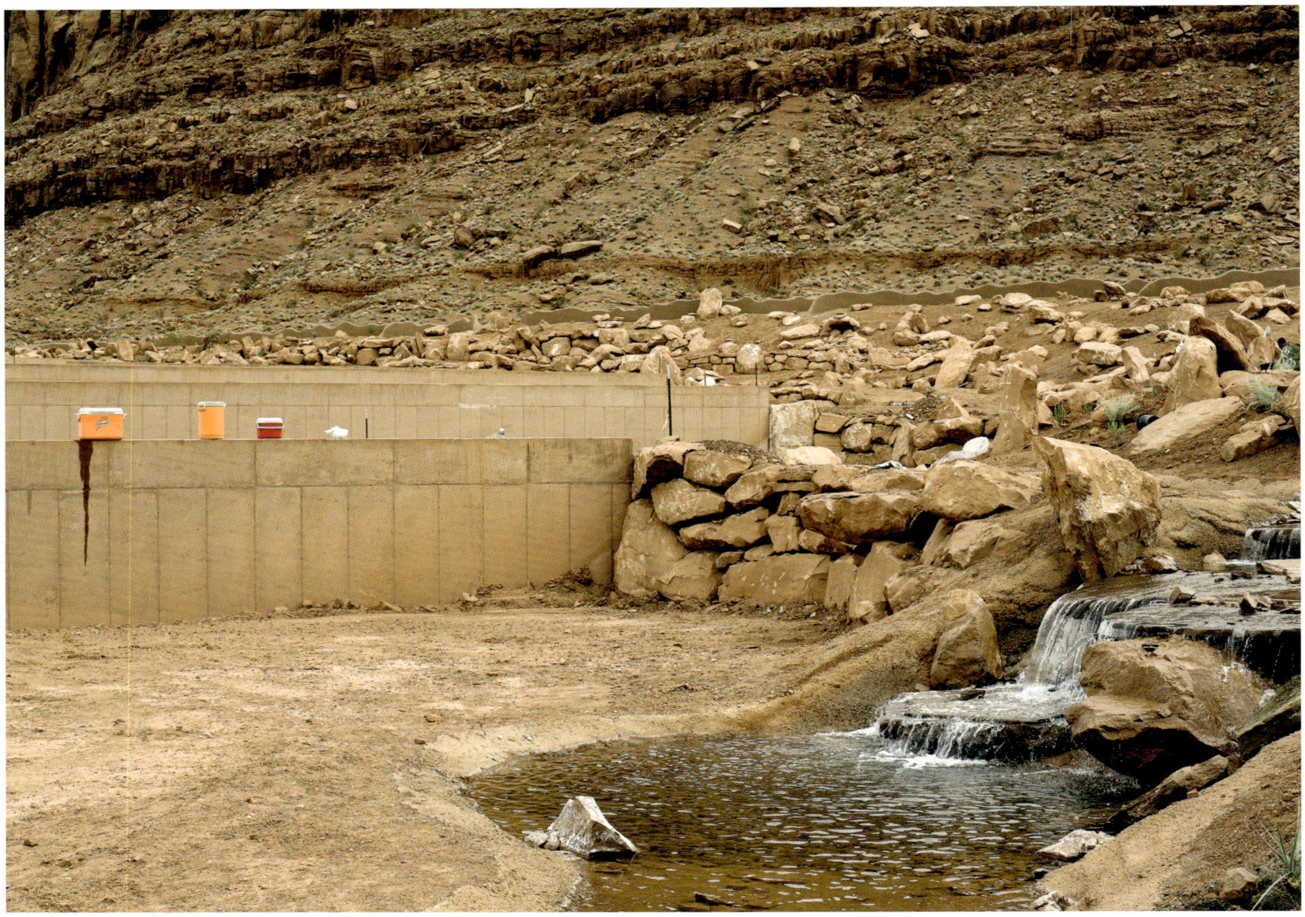

pl. 45 Steven B. Smith, *Coolers, Ivins, Utah*, 2007

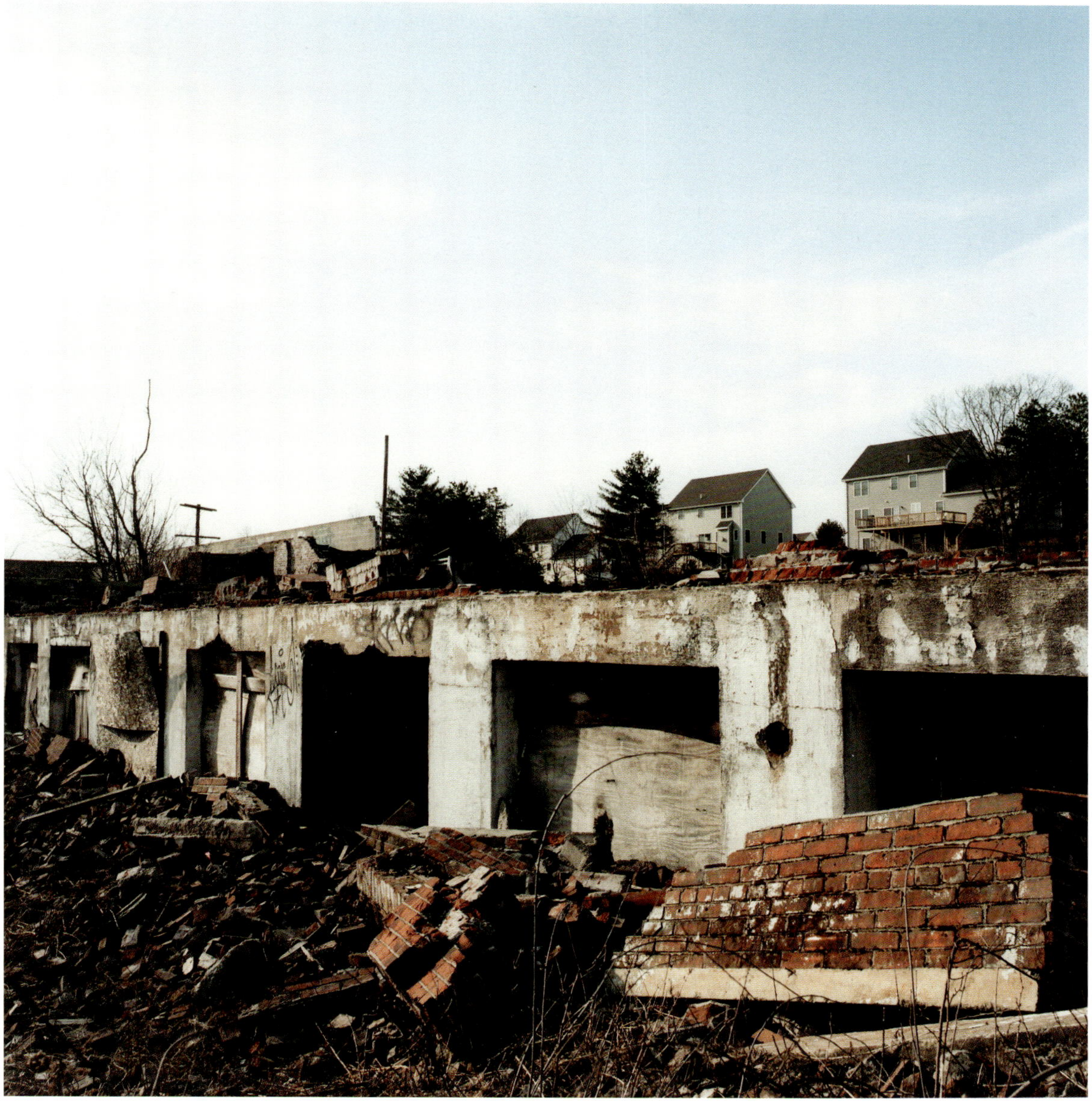

pl. 46 Michael Cevoli, *Cottage Street Mill with Houses, Franklin, MA*, 2008

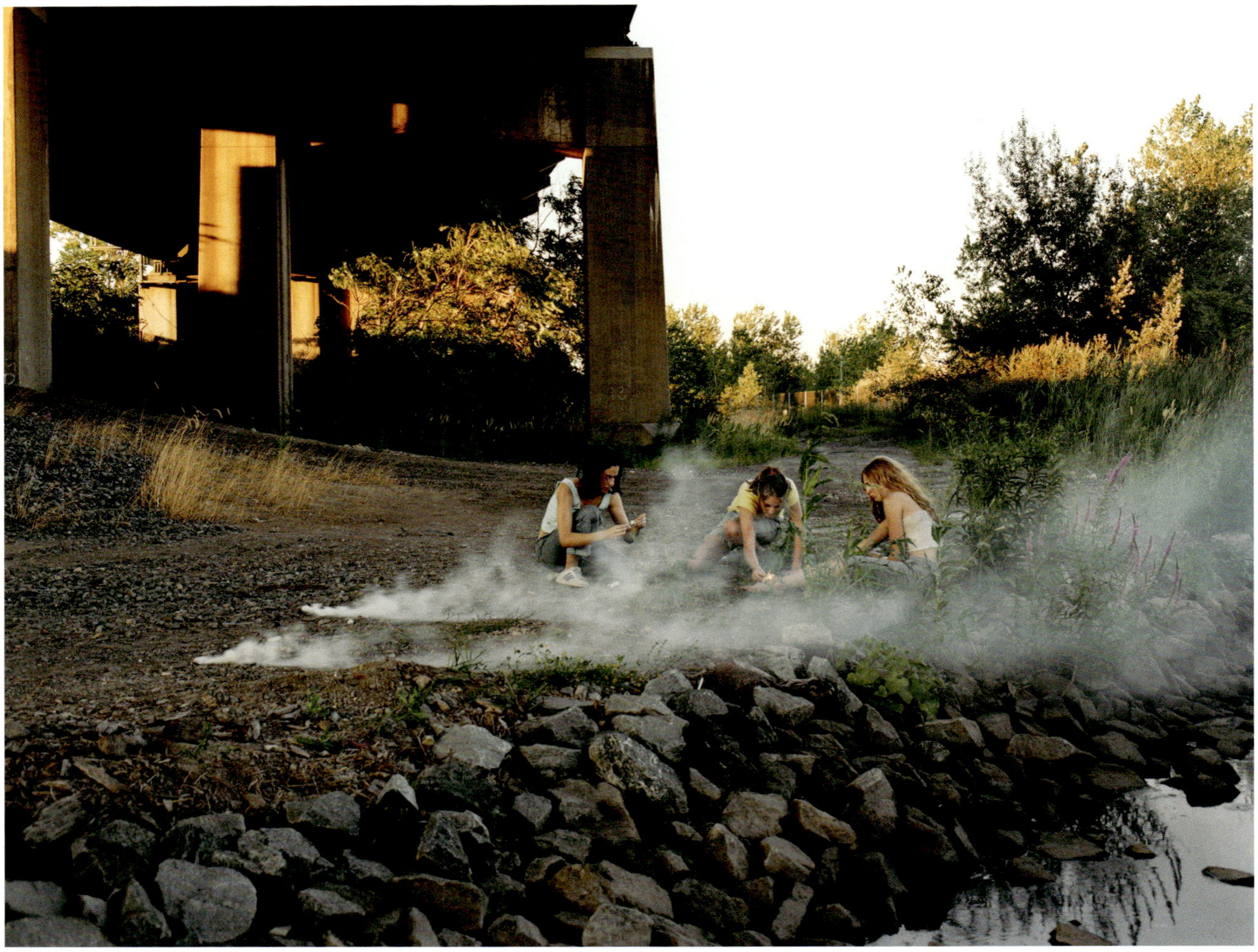

pl. 47 Justine Kurland, *Smoke Bombs*, 2000

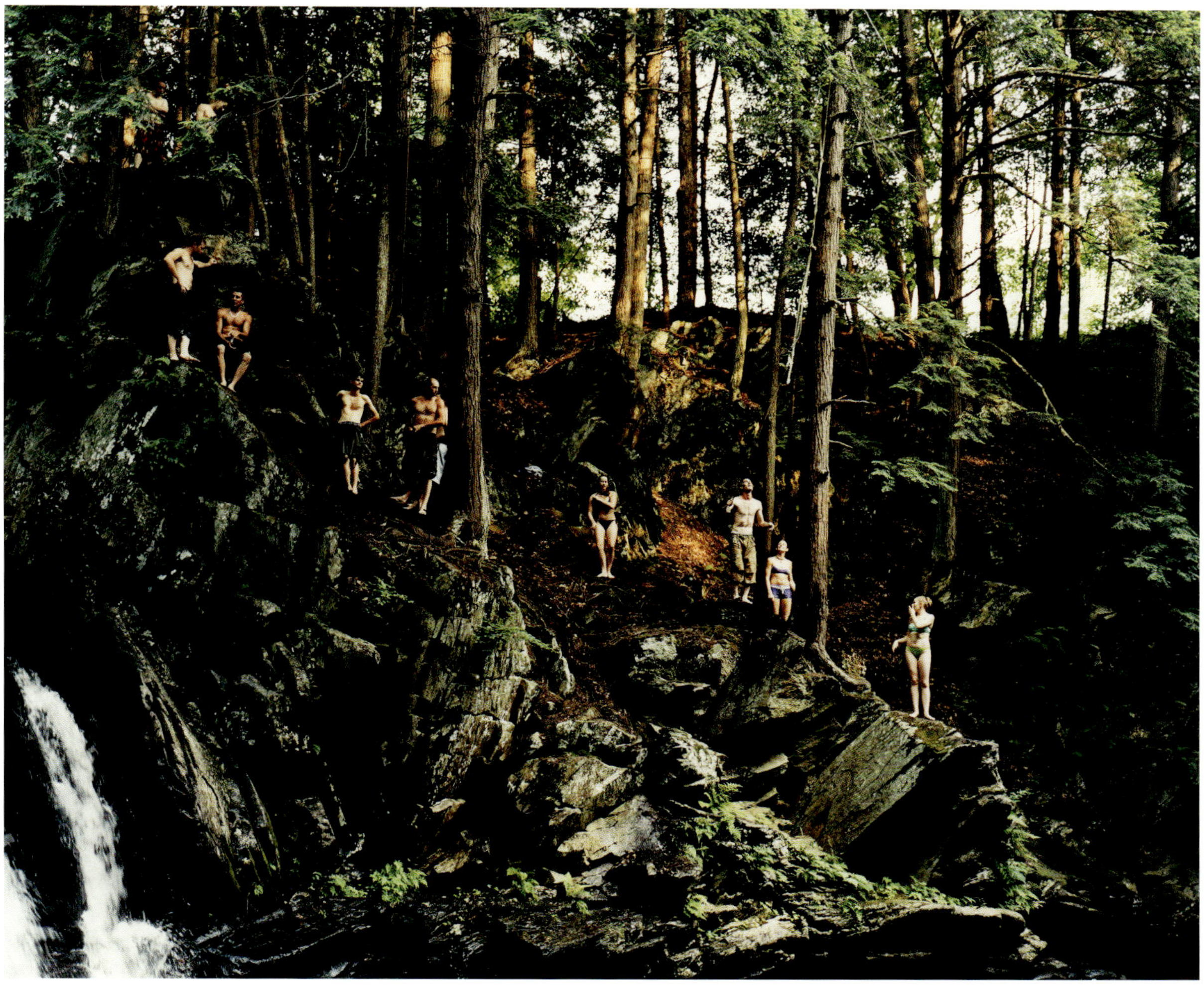

pl. 48 Justin Kimball, *Deep Hole, New Hampshire*, 2002

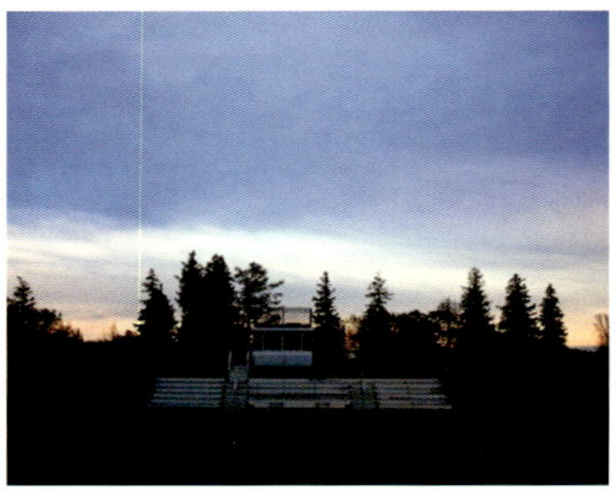

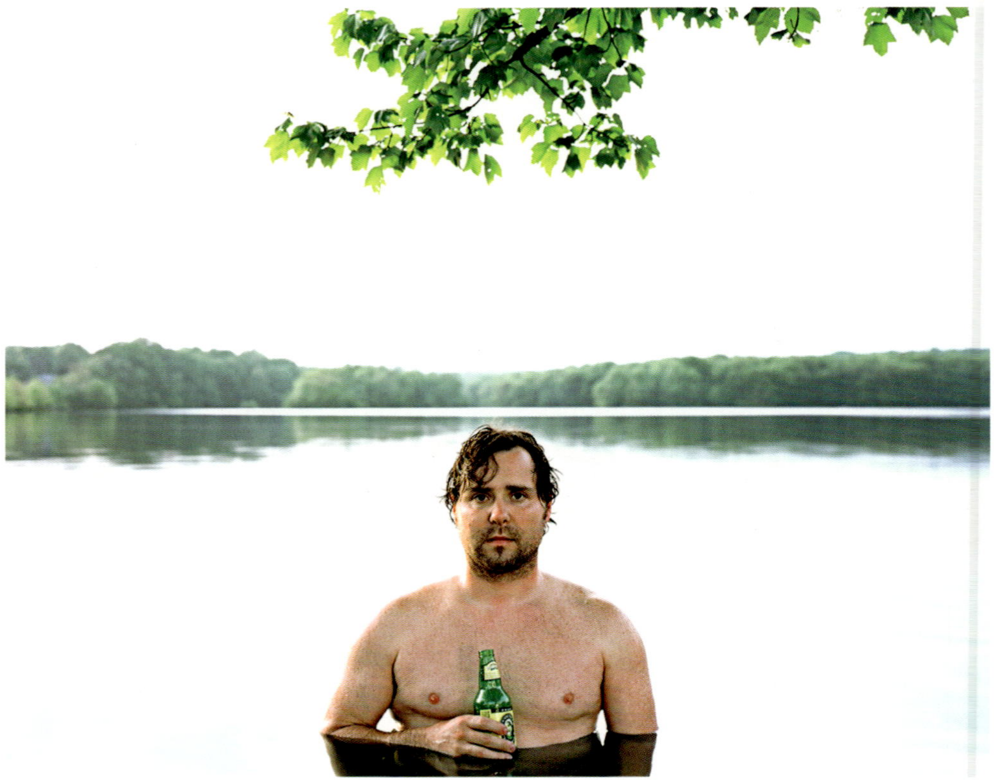

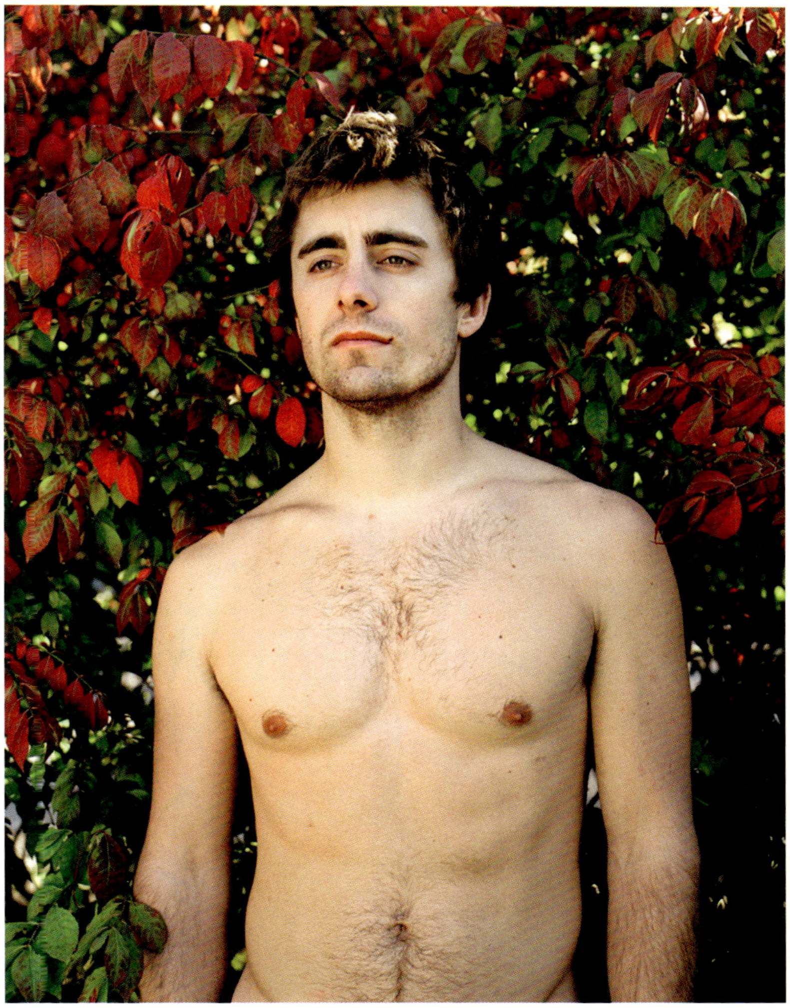

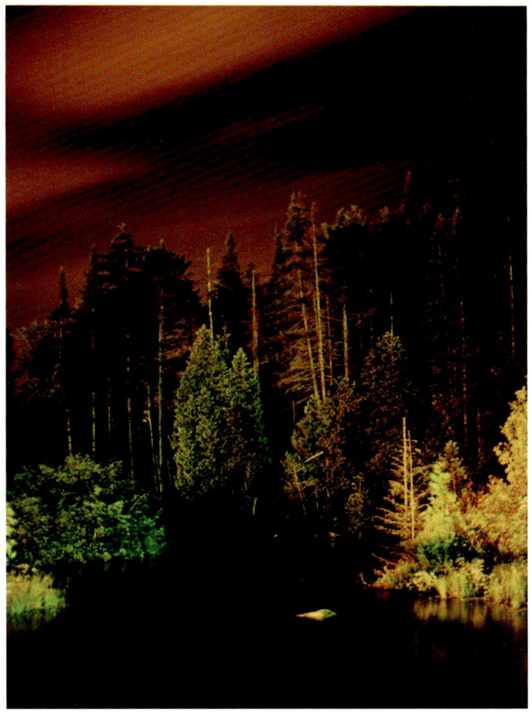

pl. 49 Jesse Burke, *Bleachers*, 2007, *Woodchuck*, 2005, *Spring Training, Nils*, 2000, *Upstate*, 2006

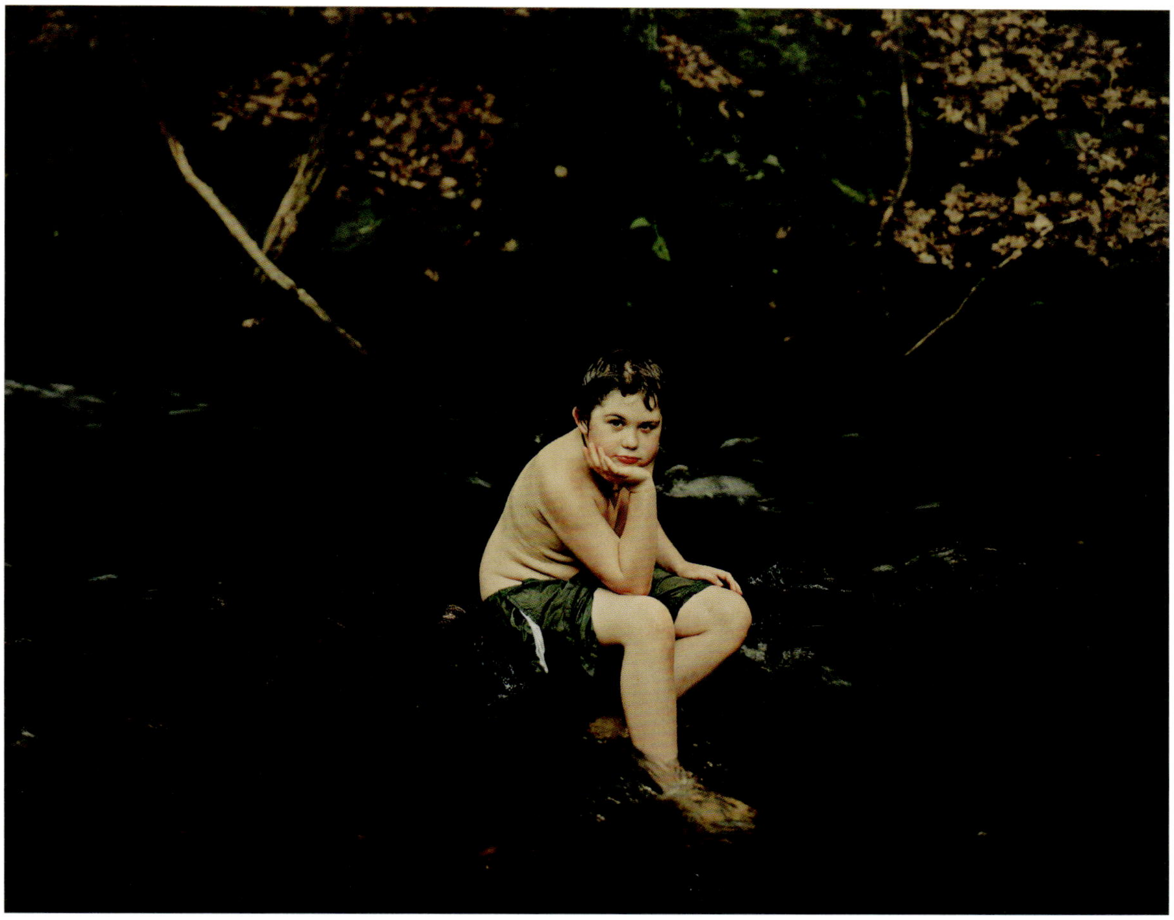

pl. 50 Josephine Sittenfeld, *Ethan, Puffer's Pond*, 2009

WORKS IN THE EXHIBITION

All dimensions are sheet size unless otherwise noted; height precedes width. Page numbers for illustrated works follow the artists' names.

Berenice Abbott
American, 1898–1991
New York at Night, 1932
Gelatin silver print, 13⅜ × 10½ in.
RISD Museum: Museum purchase with funds from the National Endowment for the Arts 73.167

Ansel Adams (p. 36)
American, 1902–1984
Half Dome, Blowing Snow, Yosemite National Park, California, ca. 1955
Gelatin silver print, 14⅛ × 18¾ in.
RISD Museum: Museum purchase with funds from the National Endowment for the Arts 75.097

Antelope House Ruin, Canyon de Chelly National Monument, Arizona, 1942
From *Portfolio VI*, 1974
Gelatin silver print, 19⅝ × 15⅜ in.
RISD Museum: Gift of Mrs. Barnet Fain 75.009

Robert Adams (p. 94)
American, b. 1937
Bulldozed Slash, Tillamook County, Oregon, 1976
Gelatin silver print, 7 × 9 in.
Private collection

Eleanor Antin
American, b. 1935
100 Boots Taking the Hill (1-5), Lomas Santa Fe, California, June 13, 1972
From the series "100 Boots"
Five offset photo lithograph postcards, 4½ × 7 in. each
RISD Museum: Walter H. Kimball Fund 2012.37.1-.5

Leander Baker
American, 1841–1925
View of Providence Storefronts, ca. 1895
From the series "Providence Views"
Albumen print stereograph, mount: 3⅜ × 6⅞ in.
RISD Museum: Gift of Alice K. Miles 1986.035.11

Lewis Baltz (pp. 29, 45)
American, b. 1945
Nevada, 1977
Portfolio of fifteen gelatin silver prints, 8 × 10 in. each
RISD Museum: Gift from the Collection of Joe Deal and Betsy Ruppa 2010.82.35.1–.15

George N. Barnard
American, 1819–1902
Nashville from the Capitol, 1864–1865
From the album *Photographic Views of Sherman's Campaign*, 1866
Albumen print, mount: 16 × 20 in.
RISD Museum: Walter H. Kimball Fund 77.059

Thomas Barrow (p. 87)
American, b. 1938
f/t/s Cancellations—Horizon Rib, 1974
f/t/s Cancellations (Brown)—Field Star, 1975
From the series "Cancellations"
Toned gelatin silver prints, 11 × 14 in. each
RISD Museum: Gift from the Collection of Joe Deal and Betsy Ruppa 2010.82.2-3

Uta Barth (p. 109)
German, b. 1958
Field #14, 1996
Color chromogenic print, 23 × 29 in.
RISD Museum: Gift of the Buddy Taub Foundation, Jill and Dennis Roach, Directors 2002.73

William H. Bell (p. 64)
American, 1830–1910
Perched Rock, Rocker Creek, Arizona, 1872
From the album *Explorations and Surveys West of the 100th Meridian*
Albumen print, mount: 20 × 16 in.
RISD Museum: Jesse Metcalf Fund 77.023

Cañon of Kanab Wash, Colorado River, Looking South, 1872
From the album *Explorations and Surveys West of the 100th Meridian*
Albumen print, mount: 20 × 16 in.
Courtesy John Hay Library, Brown University

Henry Hamilton Bennett (p. 34)
American, 1843–1908
In and about the Dells of the Wisconsin River, Cold Water Cañon above Whirlpool Chamber, No. 444
In and about the Dells of the Wisconsin River: To Circle Bend, from the Navy Yard, No. 451
In and about the Dells of Wisconsin: Crooked Pillar Near Sugar Bowl, No. 285
In and about the Dells of the Wisconsin River: Looking out of Boat Cave, No. 150
From the series "Wanderings Among the Wonders and Beauties of Wisconsin Scenery," ca. 1880–1900
Albumen print stereographs, mount: 3⅜ × 7 in. each
RISD Museum: Anonymous gift 84.028.7-9 and 81.050

Henry Bosse (p. 66)
American, 1844–1903
From Foot of Boulanger Slough Looking Downstream, 1891
From the series "Views on the Mississippi River"
Cyanotype, mount: 16 × 20 in.
RISD Museum: Helen M. Danforth Acquisition Fund 2012.38

Barbara Bosworth (p. 25)
American, b. 1953
Niagara Falls, 1986
Gelatin silver print, 8 × 10 in.
Private collection

possibly Julius T. Boysen
American, 1869–1939
Untitled, ca. 1903 (printed ca. 1930)
Toned gelatin silver print, 39 × 29 in.
RISD Museum: Gift of Mr. F. Steele Blackall III 82.064.4

Mathew B. Brady
American, 1823–1896
Flirtation Walk, ca. 1865
From the series "West Point Views"
Albumen print stereograph, mount: 3¼ × 6¾ in.
RISD Museum: Anonymous gift 83.166

Deborah Bright (pp. 98–99)
American, b. 1950 (RISD Faculty 1989–2012)
Bloody Lane, The Battle of Antietam, 1983
From the series "Battlefield Panoramas"
Six selenium-toned gelatin silver prints, 13 × 19 in. each
RISD Museum: Gift of the Artists' Development Fund of the Rhode Island Foundation 1991.065

Anne Brigman (p. 55)
American, 1869–1950
Soul of the Blasted Pine, 1908
from *Camera Work*, no. 25, January, 1909
Photogravure, 6⅛ × 8¼ in.
Collection Susan Ehrens

Jesse Burke (pp. 116–17)
American, b. 1972 (RISD MFA 2005)
Bleachers, 2007
Woodchuck, 2005
Spring Training, Nils, 2005
Upstate, 2006
From the series "Intertidal"
Digital color chromogenic prints, 11 × 14, 30 × 38, 38 × 30, and 27 × 20 in.
RISD Museum: Museum purchase: Gift of Dr. Joseph A. Chazan; *Upstate*, Collection Laura Stanton and Craig Hopkins

Edward Burtynsky (p. 47)
Canadian, b. 1955
OMYA #51, Calcium Carbonate Waste Area, Proctor, Vermont, 1991
Digital color chromogenic print, mount: 34 × 41 in.
Courtesy Howard Greenberg Gallery, New York

Harry Callahan (p. 76)
American, 1912–1999 (RISD Faculty 1961–1976)
Eleanor, Chicago, 1952
Gelatin silver print, 8 × 10 in.
RISD Museum: Gift of Wayne Miller 2009.121.1

Cape Cod, 1972
Gelatin silver print, 11 × 14 in.
RISD Museum: Gift of Mr. and Mrs. Gilman Angier 78.039

Michael Cevoli (p. 113)
American, b. 1982 (RISD BFA 2004, MFA 2009)
Cottage Street Mill with Houses, Franklin, MA, 2008
Color inkjet print, 17 × 15 in.
RISD Museum: Gift of the artist in honor of Joe Deal 2010.90

Linda Connor (p. 106)
American, b. 1944 (RISD BFA 1967)
Stones, Kau Desert, Hawaii, 1991
Gold-toned printing-out paper, 8 × 10 in.
RISD Museum: Gift of Douglas Nickel and Genoa Shepley 2009.51

Barbara Crane
American, b. 1928
Cloudscape, 1969
Gelatin silver print, 5 × 20 in.
RISD Museum: Gift of Aaron Siskind 1987.103.5

Ralston Crawford (p. 79)
American, 1906–1978
High Tension Lines, ca. 1950
Gelatin silver print, 8 × 10 in.
RISD Museum: Gift of Neelon Crawford 2007.129.5

Gregory Crewdson (p. 56)
American, b. 1962
Untitled (Cement Canal), 2007
Color inkjet print, 58½ × 89½ in.
Courtesy Gagosian Gallery, New York

Edward Curtis
American, 1868–1952
An Inland Waterway, 1914
From the portfolio *The North American Indian*, vol. 10
Photogravure, mount: 18 × 22¼ in.
RISD Museum: Gift of Mr. and Mrs. Erwin Strasmich 1992.130

Joe Deal (pp. 4, 12, 44, 54, 90, 91)
American, 1947–2010
(RISD Provost 1999–2005, Faculty 2005–2009)
The Fault Zone, 1981
Portfolio of 19 gold-toned gelatin silver prints, 15 × 15 in. each
RISD Museum: Museum purchase: Georgianna Sayles Aldrich Fund and Gift of James D. and Diane D. Burke 2003.76.1–.19

Kite, Chino Hills, California, 1984
From the series "Subdividing the Inland Basin"
Gelatin silver print, 14 × 17 in.
RISD Museum: Gift of the Artist 2003.104.2

John Divola (p. 86)
American, b. 1949
Zuma #8, 1977 (printed 2007)
Zuma #28, 1978 (printed 2006)
Color inkjet prints, 24 × 30 in. each
RISD Museum: Gift of the artist in honor of Joe Deal 2010.16.2 and .1

Arthur Wesley Dow
American, 1857–1922
Untitled, 1906
Gelatin silver print, 9 ½ × 12 ¾ in.
RISD Museum: Walter H. Kimball Fund 2010.12

John Dowell
American, b. 1941
Wacker Drive, 2005
Color inkjet print, 23¼ × 29¼ in.
RISD Museum: Mary B. Jackson Fund 2006.8

Terry Evans (p. 103)
American, b. 1944
Terraced Plowing with a Grass Waterway, 1991
From the series "Inhabited Prairie"
Gelatin silver print, 20 × 16 in.
RISD Museum: Gift of Jan Howard and Dennis Teepe in honor of Joe Deal 2009.125

Walker Evans (p. 70)
American, 1903–1975
View of Easton, Pennsylvania, 1936
From the portfolio *American Photographs II*
Gelatin silver print, 8 × 10 in.
RISD Museum: Gift of James Dow 71.043.40

Peter Feresten (p. 101)
American, 1945–2007 (RISD BFA 1972, MFA 1974)
E. Hattie Street, Fort Worth, TX, 1983
Gelatin silver print, 16 × 20 in.
RISD Museum: Gift of the artist's RISD colleagues, Kathy Florsheim, David Akiba, Henry Horenstein, Gus Kayafas, Susan Hacker Stang, Arno Minkkinen, Tom Tarnowski, Luther Smith, Mary Kay Simqu, Earl Iversen, and Alan Metnick in memory of the artist 2008.97.1

Robbert Flick (p. 97)
Canadian, b. 1939
SV 033/81, East of Lancaster, California, 1981
From the series "Sequential Views"
Gelatin silver print, 16 × 20 in.
RISD Museum: Gift of Robbert Flick and Susan Rankaitis in honor of Joe Deal 2009.126.1

Lucas Foglia
American, b. 1983
Greg and Zane after Horn Hunting, Wyoming, 2011
From the series "Frontcountry"
Digital color chromogenic print, 23½ × 30 in.
RISD Museum: Museum purchase: Gift of Dr. Joseph A. Chazan 2012.43

Lee Friedlander (p. 84)
American, b. 1934
Atlantic City, New Jersey, 1971
Gelatin silver print, 11 × 14 in.
RISD Museum: Museum purchase with funds from the National Endowment for the Arts 79.092

Mechanics' Monument, San Francisco, California, 1972
From the series "The American Monument"
Gelatin silver print, 11 × 14 in.
RISD Museum: Gift of Smith Glasson 2009.54

Oliver Gagliani (p. 74)
American, 1917–2002
Untitled, 1948
Untitled, 1962
Gelatin silver prints, 4 × 5 in. each
RISD Museum: Gift of Leland Rice 2008.116.6, .8

Untitled, 1958
From *Portfolio No. 1, Color*
Color chromogenic print, 5 × 4 in.
RISD Museum: Gift of Laurence Gagliani 2010.126.1

Untitled, 1966
Gelatin silver print, 7¾ × 7¾ in.
RISD Museum: Gift of Leland Rice 2003.152.2

Sally Gall
American, b. 1956 (RISD BFA 1978)
Monadnock, 1990
Gelatin silver print, 16 × 20 in.
Collection Smith Glasson

Laura Gilpin (frontispiece)
American, 1891–1979
Footprints in the Sand, 1931
Platinum print, 10 × 8 in.
RISD Museum: Museum purchase with funds from the National Endowment for the Arts 79.053

Frank Gohlke (pp. 92–93)
American, b. 1942
Edge of landslide—debris flow, below Coldwater Lake containment dam—8 miles NW of Mt. St. Helens, Washington, 1981
Aerial View: fir and hardwood forest outside of blast zone—vicinity of Mt. St. Helens, Washington, 1981
Aerial View: edge of eruption impact zone showing blown-down, standing dead and living trees. Salvage in progress. Approximately 14 miles NW of Mt. St. Helens, Washington, 1981
Salvaging dead timber on Spud Mountain—looking NE at Coldwater Lake from a point 7.5 miles NW of Mt. St. Helens, Washington, 1982
From the series "Mount St. Helens"
Gelatin silver prints, 16 × 20 in. each
RISD Museum: Gift from the Collection of Joe Deal and Betsy Ruppa 2010.82.11, .12, .15, .14

Near Crowley, Texas, 1978
Gelatin silver print, 16 × 20 in.
RISD Museum: Gift from the Collection of Joe Deal and Betsy Ruppa 2010.82.13

Emmet Gowin (pp. 104–105)
American, b. 1941 (RISD MFA 1967)
Old Hanford City Sites and the Columbia River, Hanford Nuclear Reservation near Richland, Washington, 1986
Alluvial Fan, Natural Drainage near Yuma Proving Ground and the California Arizona Border, 1988
Toned gelatin silver prints, 11 × 14 in. each
Promised gift of Dr. and Mrs. William G. Tsiaras

Aeration Pond, Toxic Water Treatment Facility, Pine Bluff, Arkansas, 1989
Erosion in a Dark Field, Pivot Agriculture Near the Grand Coulee Dam, Washington, 1991
Toned gelatin silver prints, 11 × 14 in. each
RISD Museum: Mary B. Jackson Fund 2009.108.2, .4

David T. Hanson (p. 102)
American, b. 1948 (RISD MFA 1983)
Coal Strip Mine, Power Plant and Waste Ponds, 1984
From the series "Colstrip, Montana"
Color chromogenic print, 16 × 20 in.
RISD Museum: Museum purchase: Gift of the Artists' Development Fund of the Rhode Island Foundation 1988.015

Frank Jay Haynes
American, 1853–1921
Geyser Hill, Upper Basin, 1886
From the series "Scenery of the Yellowstone National Park"
Albumen print, mount: 10 × 12¼ in.
RISD Museum: Mr. and Mrs. Julius Bloom Photography Fund 77.031

Anthony Hernandez (p. 95)
American, b. 1947
Angeles National Forest, 1987
Silver-dye-bleach print (Cibachrome), 29⅜ × 29½ in.
RISD Museum: Gift from the Collection of Joe Deal and Betsy Ruppa 2010.82.24

James Douglas Hope
American, 1846–1929
Piuio Falls, Watkins Glen, New York, ca. 1875–1899
Albumen print, mount: 10⅞ × 8⅞ in.
RISD Museum: Transfer from the RISD Library 84.054.1

William Henry Jackson (p. 35)
American, 1843–1942
Fountain Geyser Crater (Yellowstone National Park), 1871
From the "U.S. Geological Survey of the Territories"
Albumen print stereograph, mount: 3⅞ × 6⅞ in.
RISD Museum: Mr. and Mrs. Julius Bloom Photography Fund 77.030

Camp on Stinking Water, 1871
Gardiners River Hot Springs, Diana's Baths, 1871
Ogden Cañon, Utah, 1872
From the "U.S. Geological Survey of the Territories"
Albumen prints, 5⅝ × 8⅝ in., 6⅛ × 8 in., 8½ × 6¾ in.
RISD Museum: Jesse Metcalf Fund 76.098, .100, .099

Pike's Peak from the Garden of the Gods, ca. 1880
From the "Colorado Midland Series"
Albumen print, 20⅞ × 16¾ in.
RISD Museum: Jesse Metcalf Fund 81.074

Philip Jameson
American, b. 1930
Beavertail, Jamestown, RI, 1999
Gelatin silver print, 16 × 20 in.
RISD Museum: Gift of Dr. and Mrs. John Jameson 2002.84.1

Harold Jones (p. 89)
American, b. 1940
Storm, 1977
Baptism, Sabino Canyon, 1978
Back Porch, 5:30 p.m., 1978
With Emmet, 1978
From the *Tucson Portfolio*, 1986
Selenium-toned gelatin silver prints, 20 × 16 in. each
RISD Museum: Gift of the artist in honor of Joe Deal 2010.51.1, .5, .9, .10

Gertrude Käsebier
American, 1852–1934
Baron De Meyer with Cat, 1903
Platinum print, 6¼ × 6⅛ in.
RISD Museum: Florence Koehler Collection 49.017.1

Justin Kimball (p. 115)
American, b. 1961 (RISD BFA 1985)
Greenfield, Massachusetts, 1996
Color chromogenic print, 20 × 24 in.
RISD Museum: Phil Seibert Alumni Acquisition Fund 2010.41.1

Deep Hole, New Hampshire, 2002
Color chromogenic print, 20 × 24 in.
RISD Museum: Gift of the artist in honor of Joe Deal 2010.41.2

Mark Klett (p. 96)
American, b. 1952
First Camp of the Season: June 29/30 1979, "Bread Loaf Rock" City of Rocks, Idaho, 1979
From "The Rephotographic Survey Project"
Gelatin silver print from dye diffusion negative (Polaroid), 16 × 20 in.
RISD Museum: Gift from the Collection of Joe Deal and Betsy Ruppa 2010.82.30

Mary Kocol (p. 111)
American, b. 1962 (RISD MFA 1987)
Unexpected Fireworks over Somerville, Massachusetts, 2006
Color chromogenic print, 42 × 30 in.
RISD Museum: Gift of the artist in memory of Professor William E. Parker 2010.50

Koichiro Kurita
Japanese, b. 1943
Weeping Beech V, Southold Long Island, NY, 2008
Platinum print on gampi paper, 34 × 26 ½ in.
Courtesy of the Artist

Justine Kurland (p. 114)
American, b. 1969
Smoke Bombs, 2000
From the series "Runaway Girls"
Color chromogenic print, 30 × 40 in.
RISD Museum: Mary B. Jackson Fund 2012.40

Christopher Grant La Farge (p. 67)
American, 1862–1938
Wesquage Beach Inlet, ca. 1900
Fields, South County, ca. 1900
Orchard, South County, ca. 1900
Bay at Sunset, ca. 1900
Platinum prints, 4½ × 6¼ in. each
RISD Museum: Gift of Mrs. Muriel A. La Farge 2002.98.24, .28, .30, .43

Untitled, ca. 1910
Autochrome, 5 × 7 in.
RISD Museum: Gift of Mrs. Muriel A. La Farge 2002.98.54

William Lamson
American, b. 1977
Action for the Paiva, 2010
HD video, dimensions variable
Courtesy the Artist and Pierogi, Brooklyn, NY

Annie Langan
American, b. 1979 (RISD MFA 2008)
Growth, 2008
From the series "Connections in Solitude"
Color inkjet print in three sheets, 15 × 16¾, 15 × 24¼, 15 × 16¾ in.
RISD Museum: Gift of the artist in honor of Joe Deal 2011.99

Scott Lapham (p. 46)
American, b. 1968 (RISD BFA 1990)
Providence Cold Storage #1, Demolished 1999, 1999
Gelatin silver print, 16 × 20 in.
RISD Museum: Gift from the Collection of Dr. and Mrs. Joseph A. Chazan 2005.132.5

An-My Lê (p. 61)
American, b. Vietnam 1960
29 Palms: Captain Folsom, 2003–2004
Gelatin silver print, 26 × 37½ in.
RISD Museum: Helen M. Danforth Acquisition Fund 2007.7.2

Russell Lee
American, 1903–1986
Box Elder County, Utah, 1940
Gelatin silver print, 9⅝ × 12½ in.
RISD Museum: Museum purchase with funds from the National Endowment for the Arts 79.055

Sol LeWitt
American, 1928–2007
The Area of Manhattan Between the Places Where Sol LeWitt Has Lived! 115 E 34th St., 185 Ave. C, 42 Montogomery St., and 117 Vester St., ca. 1980
Gelatin silver print, 8¾ × 2⅝ in. (irregular)
RISD Museum: Gift of Glenn Gissler 2011.110.39

Danny Lyon
American, b. 1942
Truck in the Desert Near Yuma, Arizona, 1962
From the portfolio *Danny Lyon*, 1979
Gelatin silver print, 11 × 14 in.
RISD Museum: Anonymous gift 81.256.1

Salvatore Mancini (p. 110)
American, b. 1947
Fisherville Mill, Grafton, Massachusetts, 1994
From the series "Nature to Profit: The Transformation of the Blackstone Valley"
Gelatin silver print, 14 × 17 in.
RISD Museum: Gift of Dr. and Mrs. Joseph A. Chazan 2001.39.33

Sally Mann (p. 107)
American, b. 1951
Untitled #27, Antietam, 2001
Gelatin silver print, 38 × 48 in.
Courtesy Gagosian Gallery, New York

Laura McPhee (p. 58)
American, b. 1958 (RISD MFA 1986)
Judy Tracking Radio-Collared Wolves From Her Yard, Summer Range, H-Hook Ranch, Custer County, Idaho, 2004
Smoke from a Wildfire Ignited by Sparks from a Burn Barrell, Champion Creek, Custer County, Idaho, 2005
From the series "River of No Return"
Color chromogenic prints, 30 × 40 in. each
RISD Museum: Purchased with funds donated by Donald Stanton and Helen M. Danforth Acquisition Fund 2008.54 and Gift of the artist and Carroll and Sons (Boston, MA) in honor of Joe Deal 2010.54

Ana Mendieta
American, b. Cuba, 1948–1985
Furrows, 1984
Gelatin silver print, 7 × 9½ in.
RISD Museum: Mary B. Jackson Fund 1998.4.3

Gary Metz (p. 83)
American, 1941–2010 (RISD Faculty 1984–2007)
Untitled, 1973
From the series "Quaking Aspen (populus tremuloides)"
From the *Silver Bullet Gallery Portfolio*, 1983
Gelatin silver print, 11 × 14 in.
RISD Museum: Museum purchase: gift of Mr. and Mrs. Julius Bloom Photographic Fund and bequest of Lyra Brown Nickerson, by exchange 84.152.10

Roger Minick
American, b. 1944
Untitled, 1977
From the portfolio *New California Views*, 1979
Toned gelatin silver print, 9 × 13 ½ in.
RISD Museum: Walter H. Kimball Fund 79.134

Richard Misrach
American, b. 1949
Battleground Point #20, 1999
Color chromogenic print, 58 × 70 in.
Collection Mr. and Mrs. J. Geddes Parsons

Denny Moers
American, b. 1953
Birds Over Riverbed, 1993
Toned gelatin silver print, 15¾ × 22½ in.
RISD Museum: Gift of Dr. and Mrs. Joseph A. Chazan 1998.99.3

Catherine Opie (p. 61)
American b. 1961
Football Landscape #12 (Alice vs. W. B. Ray, Corpus Christi, TX), 2008
Color chromogenic print, 48 × 64 in.
Courtesy of the Artist and Mitchell-Innes & Nash, New York

Timothy O'Sullivan (pp. 26, 65)
American, b. Ireland, 1840–1882
Rock Carved by Drifting Sand Below Fortification Rock, Arizona, 1871
Black Cañon, Colorado River, Looking Above from Camp, 1871
Snow Peaks, Bull Run Mining District, Nevada, 1871
Ancient Ruins in the Cañon de Chelle, NM, 1873
View on Apache Lake, Sierra Blanca Range, Arizona, 1873
From the album *Explorations and Surveys West of the 100th Meridian*
Albumen prints, mount: 16 × 20 in. each
Courtesy John Hay Library, Brown University

Water Rhyolites, Near Logan Springs, Nevada, 1871
From the album *Explorations and Surveys West of the 100th Meridian*
Albumen print, mount: 16 × 20 in.
RISD Museum: Jesse Metcalf Fund 77.022

John Pfahl
American, b. 1939
Red Setters in Red Field, Charlotte, North Carolina, 1976
Color chromogenic print, 8 × 10 in.
RISD Museum: Gift of Ellen Carey 2011.10.6

Neal Rantoul (p. 6)
American, b. 1946
Near Pullman, Washington, 2009
From the series "Wheat"
Color inkjet print in two sheets, 17 × 25 in. each
RISD Museum: Gift of the artist in honor of Joe Deal 2010.47

Doug Rickard (p. 51)
American, b. 1968
#82.948842, Detroit, MI, 2009, 2010
From the series "A New American Picture"
Color inkjet print, 26 × 41½ in.
RISD Museum: Mary B. Jackson Fund 2012.41

Arthur Rothstein (p. 38)
American, 1915–1985
Father and Sons Walking in the Face of a Dust Storm, Cimarron County, Oklahoma, 1936
Gelatin silver print, 9⅞ × 12¾ in.
RISD Museum: Gift of Mr. and Mrs. Gilman Angier 80.088

Ed Ruscha
American, b. 1937
Every Building on the Sunset Strip, 1966
Artist book, 7⅛ × 5⅝ in. closed
Courtesy Fleet Library at RISD, Special Collections

A. J. Russell (p. 63)
American, 1830–1902
The Great West Illustrated in a Series of Photographic Views Across the Continent; Taken along the Line of the Union Pacific Railroad, West from Omaha, Nebraska, 1869
Bound album of albumen prints, 13 × 18 × 2 in.
Courtesy John Hay Library, Brown University

Stephen Shore (p. 85)
American, b. 1947
U.S. 10, Post Falls, Idaho, 1974
Color chromogenic print, 16 × 20 in.
RISD Museum: Museum purchase with the aid of funds from the National Endowment for the Arts 79.089

Untitled, 1975
From the portfolio *New California Views*, 1979
Color chromogenic print, 8 × 10 in.
RISD Museum: Walter H. Kimball Fund 79.138

Art Sinsabaugh (pp. 80–81)
American, 1924–1983
Chicago Landscape, #24, 1964
Gelatin silver print, 14¾ × 22¼ in.
RISD Museum: Gift of Aaron Siskind 1987.103.13

Aaron Siskind (p. 77)
American, 1903–1991 (RISD Faculty 1971–1976)
Martha's Vineyard 114B, 1954
Gelatin silver print, 14 × 17 in.
RISD Museum: Gift of Mr. Robert B. Menschel 77.145.21

Josephine Sittenfeld (p. 119)
American, b. 1980 (RISD MFA 2008)
Ethan, Puffer's Pond, 2010
Color inkjet print, 17 × 22 in.
RISD Museum: Gift of the artist in honor of Joe Deal 2010.87

Steven B. Smith (p. 112)
American, b. 1963 (RISD Faculty 1996 to present)
Coolers, Ivins, Utah, 2007.
From the series "Irrational Exuberance"
Color inkjet print, 17 × 22 in.
RISD Museum: Gift of Heather Smith in honor of Joe Deal 2010.86

Sage Sohier
American, b. 1954
British Red Coat Re-enactor, Battle of Concord and Lexington, Lexington, MA, 2002
From the series "Perfectible Worlds"
From *The PRC Portfolio*, 2008
Color inkjet print, 17 × 21 in.
RISD Museum: Helen M. Danforth Acquisition Fund 2009.47.16

Frederick Sommer (p. 72)
American, 1905–1999
Arizona Landscape, 1943
Gelatin silver print, 7½ × 9½
Promised gift from the collection of Marc Harrison

Alec Soth (cover and p. 58)
American, b. 1969
2008_08zl0031, 2008
From the series "Broken Manual"
Color inkjet print, 32 × 40 in.
RISD Museum: Mary Ann Lippitt Acquisition Fund 2012.39

Alfred Stieglitz
American, 1864–1946
Ploughing, 1904
From *Camera Work*, no. 12, October, 1905
Photogravure, 8⅛ × 11¼ in.
RISD Museum: Gift of Alfred Morris 2010.119

Seneca Ray Stoddard (p. 24)
American, 1843–1917
The Adirondacks, Upper Au Sable Lake from Boreas Bay, 1887
Albumen print, mount: 16 × 20 in.
RISD Museum: Gift of Professor Barton St. Armand 1988.077

Paul Strand
American, 1890–1976
Truckman's House, New York, 1920 (printed 1976)
From *Paul Strand: Portfolio Three*, 1981
Toned gelatin silver print, 10 × 8 in.
RISD Museum: Gift of Peter C. Jones RISD 1974 1987.107.3

Thomas Struth (p. 49)
German, b. 1954
Paradise, 2004
Portfolio of six color inkjet prints, 13 × 19 in. each
RISD Museum: Mary B. Jackson Fund 2006.11

Millee Tibbs
American, b. 1976 (RISD MFA 2007)
Self-Portrait in the Fog, 2009
From the series "Self-Portraits"
Color inkjet print, 20 × 24 in.
RISD Museum: Gift of the artist in honor of Joe Deal 2010.46.2

Jerry Uelsmann
American, b. 1934
Apocalypse II, 1967
Gelatin silver print, 11 × 14 in.
RISD Museum: Gift of Aaron Siskind 1987.103.15

Unknown artist
American, published by H. C. White Co. (1899–1915)
The American Falls from the Steamer "Maid of the Mist," Niagara Falls, U.S.A., ca. 1903
Albumen print stereograph, mount: 3½ × 7 in.
RISD Museum: Anonymous gift 1987.074.2

Unknown artist
Untitled (Rochester Falls), ca. 1900
Untitled (Rochester Falls), ca. 1900
Cyanotypes, 5 × 7 in. each
RISD Museum: Gift of Professor Barton St. Armand 1994.098.3, .6

Unknown artist
American
Untitled (Providence), ca. 1940
Gelatin silver print, 16 × 20 in.
RISD Museum: Gift of Professor Barton St. Armand 1994.098.21

Unknown artist
American
Providence Panorama from Grosvenor or Banigan Building, ca. 1900
Six cyanotype prints, 7⅝ × 9½ in. each
RISD Museum: Mary B. Jackson Fund 2005.35

Unknown artist
American
Westminster Street, from Market Square, Providence, RI, 1874
Albumen print, mount: 13⅛ × 9½ in.
RISD Museum: Gift of Paula and Mack Lee 2010.94

John Vachon
American, 1914–1975
Surrey, North Dakota, 1940
Gelatin silver print, 9¾ × 13⅛ in.
RISD Museum: Mary B. Jackson Fund 79.054

Willard Van Dyke (p. 69)
American, 1906–1986
Death Valley Dunes, 1930 (printed 1932)
Gelatin silver print, 7½ × 9 ½in.
RISD Museum: Mary B. Jackson Fund 2012.8

Carleton Watkins (p. 33)
American, 1829–1916
Cape Horn, Columbia River, 1867
Albumen print, 20¾ × 16⅛ in.
RISD Museum: Helen M. Danforth Acquisition Fund 1987.010

Tooth Bridge and Eagle Creek Crossing, Cascades, ca. 1882
From "Watkins' New Series, Columbia River Scenery"
Albumen print, 7 ¾ × 12 ⅛ in.
RISD Museum: Gift of Douglas R. Nickel 2012.47

Jack Warren Welpott
American, b. 1923
White Sands, 1977
Gelatin silver print, 11 × 14 in.
RISD Museum: Gift of Aaron Siskind 84.186.34

Henry Wessel (p. 88)
American, b. 1942
Night Walk, Los Angeles, No. 28, 1995
From the series "Night Walk: LA"
Gelatin silver print, 15 × 22¼ in.
RISD Museum: Gift of Mark Pollack 2012.52

Brett Weston (pp. 71, 75)
American, 1911–1993
Untitled (Brooklyn Bridge), 1943
Pond, 1950
Gelatin silver prints, 7⅝ × 9⅝ in. each
RISD Museum: Gift of Dan Miller 2008.112.1, .5

Edward Weston (p. 73)
American, 1886–1958
Hill and Telephone Poles, 1937
Cliff with Seagull, Point Lobos, 1946
Gelatin silver prints, printed ca. 1970 by Cole Weston, 7½ × 9½ in. each
RISD Museum: Museum Works of Art Fund 71.117.4, .5

Minor White
American, 1908–1976
Driftwood and Eye, 1951
From *The First Apeiron Portfolio*, 1973
Gelatin silver print, 8 × 10 in.
RISD Museum: Gift of Dr. and Mrs. Marshall N. Fulton 74.097.18

Clarence H. White (p. 37)
American, 1871–1925
Morning, 1905
From *Camera Work*, no. 23, July 1908
Photogravure, 8 × 6 in.
RISD Museum: Walter H. Kimball Fund 76.093

J. N. (Jerome Nelson) Wilson
American, 1827–1897
Untitled (Bonaventure Cemetery, Savannah, Georgia), ca. 1880
Albumen print stereograph, mount: 3½ × 6¾ in.
RISD Museum: Anonymous gift 84.028.11

Garry Winogrand (p. 82)
American, 1928–1984
Utah, 1964
Castle Rock, Colorado, 1960
From the portfolio *Garry Winogrand*, 1978
Gelatin silver prints, 11 × 14 in. each
RISD Museum: Gift of Mr. Frederick J. Myerson 82.303.3, .14

This catalogue is published to accompany the exhibition *America in View: Landscape Photography 1865 to Now*, Museum of Art, Rhode Island School of Design, Providence, Rhode Island, September 21, 2012 – January 13, 2013.

Support for *America in View* is provided by Dr. Joseph A. Chazan, Robert Lehman Foundation, and Dr. and Mrs. William G. Tsiaras. Additional support from Mrs. Houghton P. Metcalf, Jr., Mary Kate Rittman, Betsy Ruppa, John W. Smith and Rocky Caldararo, and Mr. and Mrs. William A. Viall II.

MUSEUM OF ART, RHODE ISLAND SCHOOL OF DESIGN
224 Benefit Street
Providence, Rhode Island 02903
401.454.6500
www.risdmuseum.org

ISBN 978-0-985-61890-2
Library of Congress Control Number: 2012939698

Cover: Alec Soth, *2008_08zl0031*, 2008
Frontispiece: Laura Gilpin, *Footprints in the Sand*, 1931

Jennifer Liese, editor
Lucinda Hitchcock, designer
Erik Gould, photographer
Printed by: Meridian Printing, East Greenwich, RI
Typefaces: Din Next, National, and Sentinel
Paper: PhoenixMotion Xantur

Photo Credits

Every effort has been made to identify and locate all copyright holders. Any omissions or errors will be corrected in subsequent editions. p. 2: © 1979 Amon Carter Museum of American Art, Fort Worth, TX; pp. 4, 12, 44, 54, 90, 91: Joe Deal © The Estate of Joe Deal, courtesy Robert Mann Gallery; p. 6: © Neal Rantoul, *Near Pullman, Washington*, photograph courtesy Panopticon Gallery, Boston, MA; p. 18: Image © The Metropolitan Museum of Art; p. 20: © The National Gallery, London; p. 25: © Barbara Bosworth; pp. 29, 45: © Lewis Baltz; p. 36: Collection Center for Creative Photography, University of Arizona © 2012 The Ansel Adams Publishing Rights Trust; p. 37: © Aperture Foundation, Inc., Paul Strand Archive; p. 38: Library of Congress, Prints & Photographs Division, FSA/OWI Collection, LC-USF34-9058-C; pp. 39, 70: Library of Congress, Prints & Photographs Division, FSA/OWI Collection, LC-USF34-9058-C, LC-USF342-T01-001162-A; p. 41: Robert Frank © Robert Frank, from *The Americans*; courtesy Pace/MacGill Gallery, New York; p. 42: © Ed Ruscha; p. 46: © Scott Lapham; p. 47: © Edward Burtynsky, courtesy Nicholas Metivier, Toronto / Howard Greenberg & Bryce Wolkowitz, New York; p. 49: © Thomas Struth; p. 51: © Doug Rickard, courtesy Yossi Milo Gallery, New York; p. 56: © Gregory Crewdson, courtesy Gagosian Gallery; cover and p. 58: © Alec Soth; p. 58: © Laura McPhee; p. 61: Courtesy of the artist and Mitchell-Innes & Nash; p. 61: © An-My Lê; p. 69: © Willard Van Dyke; pp. 71, 75: © The Brett Weston Archive; p. 72: © Frederick & Frances Sommer Foundation; p. 73: © 1981 Center for Creative Photography, Arizona Board of Regents; p. 74: Oliver Gagliani, © Estate of Oliver Gagliani; p. 76: © The Estate of Harry Callahan, Courtesy Pace/MacGill Gallery, New York; p. 77: Courtesy Aaron Siskind Foundation; p. 79: Reproduced with permission from the Ralston Crawford Estate; p. 80: © Katherine Anne Sinsabaugh & Elisabeth Sinsabaugh de la Cova; p. 82: © The Estate of Garry Winogrand, courtesy Fraenkel Gallery, San Francisco; p. 83: © Gary Metz Estate; p. 84: © Lee Friedlander, courtesy Fraenkel Gallery, San Francisco; p. 85: Courtesy 303 Gallery, New York; p. 86: © John Divola; p. 87: © Thomas Barrow; p. 88: © Henry Wessel. *Night Walk #28*, 1995; p. 89: © 1986 Harold Jones; pp. 92, 93: © Frank Gohlke 1982, 1981; p. 94: © Robert Adams, courtesy Fraenkel Gallery, San Francisco, and Matthew Marks Gallery, New York; p. 95: Courtesy of the artist; p. 96: © Mark Klett; p. 97: © Robbert Flick, courtesy Robert Mann Gallery; p. 98: © 1983 Deborah Bright; p. 101: Courtesy Afterimage Gallery, Dallas; p. 102: © 1984 David T. Hanson, from the book *Colstrip, Montana* by David T. Hanson (Taverner Press, 2010); p. 103: © Terry Evans; pp. 104, 105: © Emmet and Edith Gowin, Courtesy Pace/MacGill Gallery, New York; p. 106: © Linda Connor; p. 107: © Sally Mann, courtesy Gagosian Gallery; p. 109: Courtesy the artist and Tanya Bonakdar Gallery, New York; p. 110: © Salvatore Mancini; p. 111: Image © 2006 Mary Kocol, courtesy of the artist and Gallery NAGA, Boston; p. 112: © Steven B. Smith 2011; p. 113: Photo: Michael Cevoli; p. 114: © Justine Kurland, courtesy Mitchell-Innes & Nash; p. 115: Photograph by Justin Kimball, from the series "Where We Find Ourselves"; p. 116: © Jesse Burke; p. 119: © Josephine Sittenfeld.